Bring Out the Po

"Whether it's love and gratitude you're [...] *vant to help you share these things with God* [...] *d that listening presence, a presence that listen* [...] *r, your closest friend, your therapist…. The goal here is not merely to perform the act of prayer. The goal is to allow the natural unfolding of our souls, like a flower opening itself to the morning sun."*

—FROM THE INTRODUCTION

E ven Jews who pray regularly know how challenging prayer can be. Some are uneasy with the idea of God, of talking to God as an "Other," of petitioning for their needs. Some have trouble with the Hebrew or remain unmoved by the prayer book's kingly metaphors. Others are impatient with the shortcomings they perceive in their synagogues. They don't understand why prayer is relevant to their lives. They want access to prayer they can truly mean rather than just recite.

Reb Zalman offers a way around these problems through Hasidic spirituality and kabbalah. His solution is not to see prayer as obligation but as invitation—for song and silence; for connection and remembrance; to unburden and to trust. Through practical exercises, meditations and reflections, Reb Zalman will help you see communicating directly with God not as a duty but as engaging with a cherished friend.

"[This]is Reb Zalman at his deeply inspiring and spiritual best! [This book] will transform you, inviting you—no, compelling you—to go deeper and deeper into the very heart and soul of life!"
—RABBI IRWIN KULA, co-editor, *The Book of Jewish Sacred Practices: CLAL's Guide to Everyday & Holiday Rituals & Blessings*;
president, CLAL—The National Jewish Center for Learning and Leadership

"This marvelous book is like having Reb Zalman say, 'Sit with me a while and I'll tell you a few stories. You'll transform your prayers into lovers' trysts with God.' Who *wouldn't* want that?"
—SYLVIA BOORSTEIN, author, *That's Funny, You Don't Look Buddhist: On Being a Faithful Jew and a Passionate Buddhist*

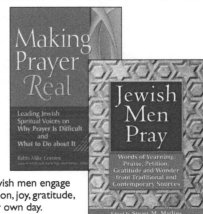

RABBI ZALMAN M. SCHACHTER-SHALOMI, the inspiration of the Jewish Renewal movement, is widely recognized as one of the most important Jewish spiritual teachers of our time. Professor emeritus at Temple University, he is the author of *First Steps to a New Jewish Spirit: Reb Zalman's Guide to Recapturing Intimacy & Ecstasy in Your Relationship with God* (Jewish Lights), *From Age-ing to Sage-ing* and *Wrapped in Holy Flame*, among other books.

JOEL SEGEL, editor of many books on spirituality, is coauthor (with Reb Zalman) of *Jewish with Feeling: A Guide to Meaningful Jewish Practice*.

RABBI LAWRENCE KUSHNER, author, lecturer and spiritual leader, is author of *Honey from the Rock: An Easy Introduction to Jewish Mysticism*, *Invisible Lines of Connection: Sacred Stories of the Ordinary*; and many other acclaimed books.

"Opens the gates of prayer. Through every word of this wise, loving and playful book, you will be blessed by Reb Zalman's integrity, humility and unbounded joy. By graciously embracing the totality of body, heart, mind and soul, and by being so very *real*, he sends us each to our own encounter."
—**RABBI SHEFA GOLD**, author, *The Magic of Hebrew Chant: Healing the Spirit, Transforming the Mind, Deepening Love*

"An adventure of heart, mind and soul ... let the Grand Master of the High Art of Davenology guide you through the inner landscapes of Jewish prayer. Whether you are a skilled davener or new to this path, you will find insight and wisdom beyond anything you have yet encountered!"
—**RABBI MARCIA PRAGER**, author, *The Path of Blessing: Experiencing the Energy and Abundance of the Divine*

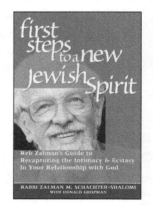
For People of All Faiths, All Backgrounds
JEWISH LIGHTS Publishing

www.jewishlights.com
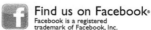 Find us on Facebook®
Facebook is a registered trademark of Facebook, Inc.

Praise for *Davening: A Guide to Meaningful Jewish Prayer* and Rabbi Zalman Schachter-Shalomi's Other Work

"It is an extraordinary and rare gift to receive the wisdom of a master of prayer, a *gadol hador*, who shares his deep practical insights, gathered during a lifetime of learning, practice, daring experimentation and concern for the spiritual relevance of the Jewish spiritual tradition for our generation. This soulful book is precious for those of us who seek to ever deepen our connection with God."
—**Rabbi J. Rolando Matalon,** Congregation B'nai Jeshurun

"A treasure trove of beautiful, wise, useful and generous spiritual teachings from a great and beloved master of Jewish learning and prayer. The stories of Reb Zalman's long and blessed life, too, are a useful and beautiful resource."
—**Rabbi Sheila Peltz Weinberg**, Institute for Jewish Spirituality

"Rabbi Zalman has blended mysticism, scholarship and *sechel* into a unique and down-to-earth book for those who want to make Judaism their personal spiritual path. A book for anyone who wants to practice Judaism as a living religion."
—**Rachel Naomi Remen, MD**, author, *Kitchen Table Wisdom*

"[An] enlightening mystical masterpiece. An inspiring and expansive vision of Judaism that is informed by mysticism, Hasidism, everyday spirituality, creative use of ritual and an intriguing understanding of meaningful Jewish practice."
—**SpiritualityHealth.com**

"Zalman's teachings have inspired a generation of Jews, encouraging an open-hearted, open-minded Judaism. I count myself as one of his students, and commend [his work] to seekers of meaning and joy."
—**Anita Diamant**, author, *The Red Tent*

"Whether by birth, by marriage or by choice, whether practicing or not, virtually anyone remotely affiliated with Judaism should read this book."
                                                    —*Publishers Weekly*

"This is a book of courage. Zalman understands the heart of his reader."
              —**Rabbi Harold M. Schulweis**, author, *Conscience: The Duty to Obey and the Duty to Disobey* and other books

"What he has to say about work, marriage, divorce, the pace of life in our modern world, and how to cope with a myriad of problems we human beings face addresses all of humankind."
                                                  —**Joshu Sasaki Roshi**

Davening

A GUIDE TO
Meaningful
Jewish Prayer

Rabbi Zalman Schachter-Shalomi
with Joel Segel

Foreword by Rabbi Lawrence Kushner

For People of All Faiths, All Backgrounds

JEWISH LIGHTS Publishing

Davening:
A Guide to Meaningful Jewish Prayer

2014 Quality Paperback Edition, Second Printing

Library of Congress Cataloging-in-Publication Data
Schachter-Shalomi, Zalman, 1924–
  Davening : a guide to meaningful Jewish prayer / Zalman Schachter-Shalomi with Joel Segel ; foreword by Lawrence Kushner.
      p. cm.
  Includes bibliographical references.
  ISBN 978-1-58023-627-0 (Pbk.)
  ISBN 978-1-68336-022-3 (Hardcover)

  1. Prayer—Judaism. I. Segel, Joel. II. Title.
  BM669.S25 2012
  296.4'5—dc23

                                                              2012027503
  ISBN 978-1-58023-683-6 (eBook)

Cover design: Heather Pelham
Cover art: Tallit designed by Reeva Shaffer of Reeva's 'riting with *ruach*; www.reevas.com; (703) 218-3669

Published by Jewish Lights Publishing
www.jewishlights.com

To the memories of Reb Avrohom Pariz, Reb Yisroel Jacobson, and the Reverend Howard Thurman.

    —Z. S. S.

To Mum, who first taught me to daven,
and to Zaida, who never davened in a hurry.

    —J. J. S.

Contents

THE DOCTOR OF PRAYER

BY RABBI LAWRENCE KUSHNER

A newly ordained colleague recently asked me if she should make the trip to Boulder, Colorado, and pay a visit to Reb Zalman, who is now in his late 80s. "If you were alive during the time of the Baal Shem Tov," I asked, "would you want to meet him?"

There aren't so many people who have the distinction of living to see the movement they planted shape the course of Judaism. And, while it must be for future historians and sociologists to determine their importance, we can safely say, even now, that Zalman's teaching and the Renewal movement have had a profound impact on contemporary American Judaism, especially on the way we pray. Permit me a few examples:

> ***Sing-song***. When he realized that many American Jews were unlikely to master enough Hebrew to pray in the holy language, Zalman taught us how to mumble—daven—in English. Zalman also began calling out page numbers and other dramaturgical instructions in sing-song English, so as not to interrupt the flow of prayers. Then he reminded us that cacophony (even in English) is authentically Jewish.

> ***Bodies***. Back in the 70s, Zalman realized that, under a strobe light, all actions appear jerky. And, if everyone appears jerky, then pretty soon no one worries about how he or she looks. So

when I invited Zalman to lead our congregation in prayer for
the weekend, he had us rent an industrial strobe light. "If everyone moves like a chicken, then people won't be so self-conscious
about how they look and then they'll start moving more," he
said. "We need to bring our bodies with us when we pray."

Names. Zalman reminded us that in matters of political lineage, by which we are called to the Torah or otherwise identified as Kohen, Levi, or Israelite, we give our names as the son
or daughter of our fathers. But, in matters of spiritual descent,
by which we are traditionally reckoned as a Jew or in matters of
personal prayer, we give our names, instead, as son or daughter
of our mothers. When we begin to speak with God, Zalman
suggested that we identify ourselves as the children of our mothers, "like a radio station announcing its call letters as it goes on
the air."

Days. Zalman initiated the pre-Shabbos *kavanah* of reflecting,
one by one, on the days of the week just gone by, as a spiritual
preparation for Kabbalat Shabbat. "Find something in each
day," he counseled, "that you're glad to leave behind in the
last week, as well as something you'd like to bring with you into
Shabbos."

It is a very, very long list. Whether borrowing from the Catholics the
idea of going away for a weekend retreat; using words or phrases in
the siddur as meditational mantras, like the Buddhists; or, of course,
re-appropriating the wearing of a big tallis from the Orthodox and
then adding the colors of the rainbow to it, Zalman Schachter-
Shalomi's fecund and seminal "Torah" is the mother-lode of a syner-
gistic Judaism for the twenty-first century. Indeed, it would be hard
today to find a community where prayer is alive that has not been
influenced and inspired by Zalman.

You are about to read a "prescription" written by the "Doctor of
Prayer."

INTRODUCTION

If you have ever tasted an apple plucked right off a New England tree, you will know the difference between a supermarket apple and a real apple. A supermarket apple has been washed, waxed, refrigerated. Vital parts of its chemistry have ebbed away. But an apple plucked from the mother tree? A *mechayeh.* Tastes like a living apple.

Prayer is the same. Many who live their lives as Jews, even many who pray every day, live on a wrapped and refrigerated version of prayer. We go to synagogue dutifully enough. We rise when we should rise, sit when we should sit. We read and sing along with the cantor and answer "Amen" in all the right places. We may even rattle through the prayers with ease. We sacrifice vitality for shelf-life, and the *neshomeh,* the Jewish soul, can taste the difference.

True prayer is a bursting forth of the soul to God. What can be more natural and more human than turning to God's listening presence with our thanks and our burdens? Prayer is one of the simplest and easiest of practices. It's always right there. The act of speaking directly to God, of opening our hearts to God's response, is one of the ultimate mystical experiences. Like great art and great music, prayer brings out the poetry of soul. Some of our most beautiful writings can be found in the pages of prayer.

Without true prayer, on the other hand, a very deep yearning that we have goes unanswered. We try to satisfy that hunger for God in other ways. We mistake the yearnings of soul for the cravings of body. We feed them with food and drink, drugs and sex, money and power, but these things just inflame our appetites further. We might seek higher things, intellectual pursuits or artistic accomplishments. Even these do not touch us in that loneliest of places, the place that longs to be filled with God. That's why prayer, to me, is not a luxury but a necessity, a safeguard for our survival and our sanity.

Yet few Jewish practices have proved harder for us, as a people. How many have stood at the gates of prayer, unable to enter? The very idea of God makes the modern mind uncomfortable. Talking to God as an Other is theologically problematic. "Petitionary prayer," asking God for our needs, is yet another level of difficulty. The Hebrew is hard, and the translation doesn't read well. We are impatient with all our synagogue's shortcomings. Maybe we just don't understand how prayer is relevant to our lives.

The difficulty of prayer affects even those who are intimate with the religious life and mind. I have been lucky to meet and talk with many great theologians and philosophers of religion. These are people who are in touch with the spirit of the times. They have turned away from triumphalism (the idea that one belief system is right and all the others wrong) and toward an organic perspective, which sees every true religion as an organ of a living planet. Their conversation draws easily upon a lexicon of terms like *zikr*, karma, chakras, bardos, revelation, redemption, submission, confession. They embrace worldviews that see creation evolving from inert matter to living beings, from life to consciousness, and finally to full knowledge and awareness of God. And yet, for all their holistic thinking, they cannot make sense of prayer.

This struck me as strange. As long as we remain in intellectual realms, we are in great harmony. But when it comes to the prayer of petition, the prayer of devotion, the yearning of the heart for the divine Other, they shy away from it. They look at me as if I had reverted to an old anthropomorphism, as if I were stuck in the superstitious and magical past. That is when I understood: the more conceptually abstract and theologically correct our notion of God, the harder it is for us to pray.

Theology is not prayer. Thomas Aquinas was one of the greatest theologians in the history of the church. Three months before he died, he experienced a revelation of God that caused him to dismiss everything he had written over a lifetime of scholarship as empty straw. He wrote no more after that. In that moment of revelation, Aquinas realized: a belief system that tries to make sense of God ideas without the experiential basis is like a card house built from concepts. As the American scholar Will Herberg pointed out, there is a great deal of difference between the living God and even the best God ideas.[1] We cannot make a covenant with a God idea. We cannot pray to a God idea. God ideas can only express themselves in words. Such words, the kabbalist Rabbi Isaac Luria warned, are simply an allegory for a reality that lies beyond anything words can say. This does not mean that God ideas have no place, but confusing them with prayer would be like writing a piece for violin and asking the timpanist to play it.

Experiences of God are not that hard to come by: all that's required is a little yearning, a little searching, a welcoming of God within. *Ve-asu li mikdash ve-shakhanti be-tokham,* says the book of Exodus (25:8): Only set aside a place, and I will come.

A long time ago, in 1939, when I was in Antwerp as a young refugee, I had a sacred moment, a glimpse beyond the everyday. It was a Shabbos afternoon, and I was out with my *chaverim,* friends with whom I used to study and daven and sing. We were in a park, sitting on a promontory overlooking the harbor in Antwerp. The grass was green, and the view was beautiful, but suddenly I felt that I had to get away and be by myself.

I was a teenager at this point, becoming independent of my parents. I had my own job, I was bringing money home. But I was also in the process of finding my own relationship with God. Of course, my parents raised me to live a Jewish life, to perform the commandments and daven three times a day as devout Jews have always done. But this was not enough for me. In the Song of the Sea, Torah tells us, the Israelites sang, "This is my God, and I will glorify Him; the God of my father, and I will exalt Him" (Exodus 15:2). An oft-quoted commentary by the Baal Shem Tov points out the order: first "my God," then "the God of my father." I will exalt the God of my father, but having my own connection is higher than this.

So I left my friends behind and took a little walk. And it was as if, for one timeless moment—how can I put it? The heavens opened.[2] I felt the *Elokus*, the godliness inside and around me, and everything was all one. I felt like the simple handmaiden who, midrash tells us, "saw at the Sea what the prophets never saw."[3]

At the same time came the knowledge that God has to remain *be-he'alem ve-hester*, as the *Tanya* says: concealed and in hiding.[4] Why? Because this is the only way that we can have freedom of choice. I understood why it has to be that way, and I experienced that knowledge and that freedom as God's compassionate gift. And then I prayed, asking that please, may the faith and certainty of that moment always be with me.

Over the years I would come to know the reality of prayer as a palpable thing. Many days I knew beyond doubt that I had been seen and heard, that my prayers would in some way be answered. At the same time, I was always glad for the smidgen of skepticism that lurks on the side, checking for integrity and sincerity. We need that skepticism for quality assurance, because fooling oneself is easy. This is why I so love the statement in Psalm 34:9, "Taste and see that God is good." Don't take my word for it, the psalmist is saying. Taste and see! Only your own experience will ultimately convince you. But don't argue with me if you did not taste with a real openness to experience!

The psalmist had tasted and he knew. "As for me," he said, "nearness to God is good" (Psalm 73:28). I have tried this in my own life and found it true. The closer I am to God, the more truly and deeply happy I am. The more I aspire to align myself with the highest and holiest, the better a Zalman I can be. For who am I if not God's willingness to play the role of Zalman for yet another day?

The one thread running through my life from that sublime moment in Antwerp has been my witness to the reality of prayer. Whenever and wherever I could teach, it was about what I called, for want of a better word, *davenology*: the search to share the reality that I myself have known. Davening, for me (or *davenen*, as we said it then), is not an intellectual exercise, nor does it belong in that realm.

It is chiefly a heart encounter, a lover's tryst with something alive, immediate, and true.

Daven is a Yiddish word. It is still used in many communities and has all but died out in others. I want to bring it back, because *davening* best describes the kind of prayer I want to talk about here. True, many who daven pray by rote. So let us give that word the highest *kavanah,* the highest aspiration that we can.

The Baal Shem Tov, founder of the Hasidic movement, had a beautiful teaching on a famous verse from the story of Noah's ark. "Make yourself an ark," God tells Noah (Genesis 6:14). Make it from gopher wood, cover it with pitch; make it so high, so wide, so long. And "*tzohar ta'aseh la-teivah,* make an opening for daylight in the ark" (Genesis 6:16). The Baal Shem Tov, reading with the eyes of a mystic, saw a more esoteric meaning here. Yes, *teivah* means *ark,* he said. But it also means *word.* Give each word light, the Baal Shem said, "for every letter contains worlds and souls and godliness."[5]

Let davening mean that for us. Let us aim our davening as high as we can, hearing and uttering our prayers in a holy light. If we as Jews can use the word *davening* as a shorthand for praying on that level, where every letter contains worlds and souls and godliness— that would be a vocabulary word worth having.

If you've never found yourself able to pray, I hope this book will help make prayer possible for you. If you are a person who prays, I would like to open up new ways to pray, new channels of communication. Whether it's love and gratitude you're feeling or doubt and dread, I want to help you share these things with God. Sooner or later you may need that listening presence, a presence that listens to you better than your partner, your closest friend, your therapist. You may feel more thanks than you can express. You may have more love than you have vessels to receive it. Think of all the feelings that we can only imperfectly express to those around us but might be able to share with God! The goal here is not merely to perform the act of prayer. The goal is to allow the natural unfolding of our souls, like a flower opening itself to the morning sun.

I recently got a call from a student of mine. He and two friends had started studying *Tanya*, the foundational document of Chabad Hasidism, and he wanted to know if I had any advice. Like every other young Lubavitcher, I had spent many years studying *Tanya*. My suggestion to him was simple: Daven it in. The *Tanya* is rich and far from easy. You'll meet with your friends, you'll be reading, discussing. So many ideas to unpack! I'm sure many wonderful insights will come to you. But whatever you glean from your session that day, make sure you daven it in together afterward, like a farmer who plants a seed, turns the soil over it, waters it in. That way whatever insights come to you will be not just theoretical ideas but will take root in the soil of your lives.

This is my wish and my prayer for you. Read this book; if an insight emerges for you, take a few quiet moments to daven it in. And may you, too, as so many holy ones have before, experience the vision of prayer in your mind's eye, the living taste of prayer in your heart, and the deep and gentle glow of prayer in your soul.

WHISPER LANGUAGE

A story is told of a certain Rabbi Shimon, who comes to Rabbi Shmuel bar Nachman with a question. "I have heard that you are a master of *aggadah*," he begins.

Aggadah is not an easy word to translate. Sometimes *aggadah* simply means storytelling. More broadly, it can refer to any form of Rabbinic discussion that is outside the subject of *halakhah*, Jewish law. It tells us that whatever troubles Rabbi Shimon, it is not something about which he expects a "straight" answer. He comes seeking a different level of discourse: not *peshat*, the simple meaning of the text, but something deeper. He is looking for meanings that are encoded, hinted at. Secret.

Then Rabbi Shimon asks his question: "From what was the light of the First Day created?"

Other rabbis have wondered about the light of the First Day. God said, "'Let there be light,' and there was light" (Genesis 1:3). But the sun, the moon, the stars—the *me'orot* or luminous bodies—were not created until the Fourth Day. Where then did the light of the First Day come from? What was its source? What sort of special Light was this, that did not emanate from any of the luminary bodies we know? This is what Rabbi Shimon is asking.

Rabbi Shmuel bar Nachman was indeed a master of *aggadah*, a teacher to whom the Rabbis turn again and again, in dozens of passages throughout the midrashic sources, to explain passages of Torah. To answer Rabbi Shimon, the midrash tells us, he lowers his voice to a whisper. "It teaches us," Rabbi Shmuel whispers, "that the Holy One, blessed be God, wrapped himself in it like a garment—and the

1

luster of God's divine majesty illuminated the entire universe, from one end to the other!"

If a mysterious and many-layered answer was what Rabbi Shimon was looking for, he had come to the right person. At first glance, Rabbi Shmuel does not even appear to answer the question; he merely reflects it back in different language. What does his answer mean? Where exactly did this light come from? And what does the image of God enrobing Godself with a garment come to teach us?

With *aggadah* we have no choice: we have to slow down. We have to "turn it and turn it," as the Rabbis say, meditating on the meanings that emerge.

A more commonplace source of light may help us begin to understand. Think of fluorescent bulbs. A fluorescent bulb is a glass tube with electrodes at either end. When electricity flows through the electrodes, it produces a charge: electrons that collide with atoms of gas inside the tube, releasing ultraviolet light. But our eyes cannot see ultraviolet light! For that reason, the inside of fluorescent bulbs is covered with a phosphorous coating. When phosphor is exposed to ultraviolet light, it absorbs that energy and radiates it back out as visible light. Only in this way does the light become apparent to our eyes.

So the coating—the "garment" that we give to that light bulb—both obscures its light and slows it down. Only by seeing it through the garment can we grasp it. The commentary of Rabbi Chanoch Zundel ben Yosef of Bialystok, Poland, known as the Etz Yosef, explains Rabbi Shmuel as saying that the light of the First Day is *lo nitfeset be-chomer*—it is not grasped or graspable on the material level, but rather emanates or flows down to us from God. This was not the eternal *or elyon*, or supernal light, the Etz Yosef believed, but a new kind of light, something newly come into being. That is why the Holy One says, "Let there be light."

And what does God wrap Godself in? What does the Holy One use for a tallis? In my study session on the weekly Torah portion this morning, I came across a beautiful word in one of the *Peninei ha-Chasidut*, the pearls of Hasidic wisdom from various commentators. He was talking about the verses of Deuteronomy 26:17–18, which speak of a reciprocal relationship between us and God. The verb used to capture this relationship is *aleph-mem-resh*. In the simple form this means "to say," but here—uniquely in Torah—it is used in a transitive form: *he'emarta* and *he'emirkha*. God "says" us, and we "say" God.

Translators throughout the ages have pondered how best to render this. Everett Fox says "declared." Other modern translators say "affirmed." The King James, more archaic, says "avouched." Rashi understood the unusual form to mean that God "sets aside" Godself for us, and we do the same for God. Onkelos, whose early second-century translation into Aramaic is generally regarded as closest to the source, translates the words using the Aramaic verb *chet-tet-vet*. Here this might mean "to choose or betroth oneself." But it can also mean "to embroider or design," related to the Aramaic word *chutvah*, an embroidered garment.

This is the meaning that the *Peninei ha-Chasidut* commentator favors. We dress ourselves in God, he says, and God dresses Himself in us, enrobing Godself in *Knesset Yisroel*, the ingathering of the people Israel. True, we as God's garment can only reveal God's light imperfectly. Like the phosphorous coating on that fluorescent bulb, we are partly mask, partly hindrance. But by saying that *we* are that garment, we also accept the responsibility of manifesting God as fully as we can.

These thoughts bear further meditation and discussion; that is the nature of aggadic material. But all this is lost on our questioner, Rabbi Shimon. "This is written explicitly in Scripture!" he retorts. "Does it not say: 'You cover Yourself with light as with a garment' (Psalm 104:2)? Why are you whispering?"

Rabbi Shmuel is unperturbed. "*Ke-shem she-sh'ma'atiha bi-l'chishah, kach amartihah lekha bi-l'chishah.* Just as I heard it said to me in a whisper, so I told it to you in a whisper" (Genesis Rabbah 3:4).

Rabbi Shimon comes seeking a *ba'al aggadah*, a master of deep discourse, but he responds to Rabbi Shmuel's teaching strictly on the surface level: he hears a well-known image from Psalms—it's part of our daily prayers, where we put on our *tzitzis* or tallis—and he quotes it back at him. He hears a whisper and asks, "What's the big secret?"

I can imagine how Rabbi Shmuel must have felt. "Oy, did you misunderstand me! Don't be a *shmegeg*. I'm not talking denotative language. This is whisper language. This is secret stuff. This is privileged information." He's saying, "Look, I want you to understand. In that world, the higher world that we're talking about, *this is reality*. You think it is merely a metaphor? I tell you no. It is real."

Why am I telling you this story? Because everything I experience in davening, everything I believe about davenology, is rooted in Rabbi Shmuel's response. Something important is being transmitted here, but Rabbi Shimon is missing it. The imaginal world is a real world. Real things happen in the imaginal world that affect this world in turn. Many traditions, many sources, attest to this. Jewish tradition tells us that *dinim nimtakin be-shorsham*—the divine decree can only be sweetened at its source. We can't do it at this level: we have to go higher. An aphorism commonly attributed to Einstein says, "No problem can be solved from the same level of consciousness that created it." What Jung calls the collective unconscious can be found in that world. The astonishing fact that I myself am conscious calls for me to extrapolate a being, a reality, that is higher and more conscious than I am.

To begin to truly understand what happens when we daven, we cannot remain on this earthly plain. We must deal in matters that concern other worlds, other levels of existence. Some of the things we discuss here may feel like ground you have already covered. Other ideas may seem outlandish, unacceptable to the reasoning mind. The inner meanings, in either case, will only surrender themselves if we ponder them at length. This is not *peshat*-level stuff. These are the whisperings of soul.

Just as I heard it whispered, so do I whisper it to you.

INTENTION
Davening with *Kavanah*

An old story tells of the Baal Shem Tov coming to a synagogue and turning back at the door, unable to enter. Too many prayers inside, he said.

"But Master," asked his disciples, "surely a room full of prayer is a good thing?"

"But all the prayers are stuck there in the building," the Baal Shem answered. "None of them are going up to Heaven."

You might get this feeling today. Clergy and congregants together might be dutifully singing and reciting—but somehow the prayer has no wings. You still feel uninspired. Maybe you've known the peace that can sometimes follow real prayer. Maybe you have prayed until you were drained and exhausted, for yourself or for someone you love. Maybe you've been there when a room full of people have managed to leave their individual preoccupations behind and are singing and swaying and making a joyful noise unto the Lord. If you've been blessed with such an experience, then you may have some sense of what the Baal Shem Tov meant. Sometimes we're transformed, and sometimes we're not.

That's why we talk about *kavanah*.

Jewish prayer begins with *kavanah*. To daven with *kavanah* means to pray with focus, intention, meaning. It means praying from the heart, rather than prayer centered solely in the mind. Celebrating a Shabbos or a holiday with *kavanah* gives that day a deeper, richer texture. *Kavanah* gives meaning to our rituals of marriage and birth and death. It inspires us to perform a mitzvah on a more conscious

5

and ultimately more rewarding level. *Kavanah* lies at the heart of Jewish devotional life. That one word encompasses an entire body of inner work necessary to live consciously in the presence of God.

Our Jewish path to inner awareness begins with *kavanah*. Our meditative lives as Jews could not be complete without it, for it is the steering wheel of all inner consciousness work. Our inner search for *kavanah* might at first be satisfied with a momentary boost of intention. Ultimately, though, we want our *kavanah* to be trans-formational. We seek a complete realignment of the soul, a *mesirut nefesh*—a handing over of the soul to God's work. We wish to become the very intention and *kavanah* of God.

Starting Small

As usual, we must know the Hebrew root to truly understand the word. The root of *kavanah* is the verb *kaf-vav-nun.* meaning "to straighten or direct." Hebrew speakers use this verb today. A sharp-shooter takes aim with *kavanah*. If our words are faulty, it is our *kavanah*, our true meaning, that we ask others to hear. So *kavanah*, on the simplest level, is meaning or aim.

I was in New Haven, Connecticut, in 1946, where we started a little Chabad yeshiva. *Yeshiva* meant, in those days, picking up the kids from public school and taking them to release time, an hour that the schools had set aside for them to go to religious instruction. At these classes, we would persuade them first to come to afternoon Hebrew school, then we talked them into enrolling full-time in our little day-school yeshiva. It was all very basic, aimed at kids who knew very little about Yiddishkeit.

Well, some vinegary old Litvaks at the Orchard Street shul heard that we called our little cheder a yeshiva, and they were all upset by that. For them a yeshiva was where you sit and learn Talmud, not where little children learn their *aleph-bes*. "This you call a yeshiva? It's not even a cheder!" So they made a big tumult about it.

So one day this old Hasid, Reb Leifer, of blessed memory, was collecting funds for the upkeep of the Lubavitcher Rebbe's household.

He was a wonderful speaker, Reb Leifer—he always had a good *moshol* (parable) on hand, like the Dubno Maggid, and they loved to hear him speak. So these guys brought him their big complaint. When it was Reb Leifer's time to speak in shul, he said, "Today, gentlemen, I walked on George Street. And I saw on George Street there was a bus. And on the front of the bus it said CHICAGO. I said, '*Ganef! Sheygetz! Ligner!* [Thief, vermin, liar!] You're in New Haven, why do you say Chicago?'"

He paused, then added, "But the bus is *going* to Chicago! And there is *going* to be a yeshiva!"

That element of aiming, of homing to the place we want to go, is the first level of *kavanah*. *Kavanah* is not attained in a day. We start small and build patiently on every small success. But if we aim our actions and our davening toward a godly place, we will get there.

The Address and the Guide

Kavanah begins at the simplest level. I take a cup of tea, or a little *glezeleh* (glass) of schnapps, and I look at you and raise it up a little, and I say, *Le-chayim!* That moment when I'm drinking to you, or when I say, "I'll drink to that," is an example of *kavanah*, labeling the act and saying for whom I'm doing it. My papa, *alav ha-shalom*, had a custom when we ate meals together as a family on Shabbos. Before every dish that he would taste, he would take the spoon and dedicate it: "*Li-kh'vod Shabbos*," in honor of the holy Shabbos. He learned this from his teacher, the Belzer Rebbe.

Staking out the intent of what you're doing is one of the primary levels of *kavanah*. It's like donating something to a synagogue or charity and saying, "This is to honor so-and-so." This is where we say, "*Le-shem mi?* For whom are we doing it? With what intent do we do it?"

One of the basic *kavanot* you find in the siddur is "*Le-shem yichud kudsha berikh hu u-Sh'khintei*, For the unification of the Holy One, blessed be God, and the Shekhinah": that this holy act bring together the hidden and the revealed, the transcendent and the imminent.

You're saying, this energy that has been gathered here, I want it to be for that purpose. That's what I'm doing it for. You're aiming it; writing an address, as it were. The Buddhist custom of assigning merit is the same kind of thing. The Hindus offer the *prasad*, the food offering to the gods, with *kavanah*. Tibetan Buddhists turning the prayer wheels—that also goes with a *kavanah*.

From an ethical standpoint, we might say that *kavanah* is a Jewish response to instinct. The human animal has powerful drives. We are hungry, we are violent, and we are sexual. These compulsions are written into our blueprint as living organisms.

One of the most difficult tasks we face in trying to do right in the world is discharging these biological drives in a way that builds rather than destroys. It is as if our software were trying to rewire our hardware. We are not only animal, we are human. Once we realize and articulate this *kavanah* for ourselves, we have taken the most important step toward making it real. We can say, "Dear God, the love and well-being of my family means more to me than anything else in the world. Nothing—*nothing*—is more important to me than this, even if it means denying myself something that I would dearly love to have. Please help me do the right thing. I can't do this without Your help." Sharing this with God, or even with friends, can give us new strength to do the deeds we want to do, and to refrain from those that—no matter how enticing—would harm those things we hold most sacred.

Kavanah helps guide our speech as well. We might be relatively righteous in deed and yet our speech is still harmful. Without *kavanah* we say, "I really should change." With *kavanah* we say, "Dear God, please help me to let this thought go. *Netzor leshoni mei-ra,* guard my tongue from evil.[1] I know deep down that sharing this with others would just be a way of aggrandizing myself. And please guard me from impatience. May it be Your will that I not get angry today."[2]

Finally, *kavanah* can give us the compass with which to steer our minds better. Very few people can do mind steering. If you drove a car like you use your mind, you'd bump into all kinds of things. Look at what happens when you try to meditate. You sit down, you try to compose yourself. All of a sudden yesterday's to-do list or last week's argument burps up like the garlic from dinner. No sooner do you have a moment's peace than the flotsam and jetsam of the mind *khap* you and take you to places you don't want to go.

In the coming age we need to move from the realm of *dibur*, speech, into *machashavah*, thought. This is what all the Eastern meditation teachers and Western healers of the mind are telling us. We have to be able to work in *nefesh*, the level of soul. *Kavanah* gives us a compass with which to realign our inner processes.

Is *Kavanah* Necessary?

A Hasidic story: The Rizhiner Rebbe and a *Misnagged* (opposer of Hasidism) are staying in the same inn, and they have adjacent rooms. Both men rise at dawn. The *Misnagged* dresses, davens, and spends almost two hours in the study of Torah. Then he wants to see what the Rizhiner is doing. He peeks through the keyhole, and he sees the Rizhiner still pacing around in his nightshirt, saying, "Oy! Oy!"

At noon they meet downstairs for lunch, and the *Misnagged* says to the Rizhiner Rebbe, "By nine o clock this morning I had davened and learned three *blatt gemorah* [pages of Talmud]. You were still walking around in your pajamas saying, 'Oy! Oy!' What's this *oy-oy* business?"

The Rizhiner says to him, "You are lucky. You can get up and say, '*Modeh ani le-fanekha.*' When I start saying *Modeh ani* [I give thanks], and then I look at the *le-fanekha* [before You], and I see how far apart they are ... Oy! Oy!"

Some might point to this story as proof of how deep and holy the Rizhiner was. Only three words into his morning davening, meditating on the *le-fanekha*, and already he is lost in all the layers of love and awe of the word. *I, with all my limitations, with all my imperfections— before You!* Others might hear a wry warning on the possible pitfalls of being swallowed up by our own *kavanah*. The story reminds us of one of the most basic of all questions in *halakhah*, Jewish law, a discussion begun in the Talmud and continued in the *Shulchan Arukh* and other legal sources. Does fulfilling the mitzvot require an intentional layer of *kavanah*, or is the doing of them alone enough? Is *kavanah* the foundation of all Jewish action, or is it merely icing on the cake?

Halakhic discussions sometimes use the phrase *yatza yedei chovah* when it comes to discharging our duties to God and our fellows. I think it was Rabbi Emanuel Rackman, a lifelong exemplar of open-minded Orthodoxy, who came up with the most elegant translation of this phrase: "he extricated himself from the grasp of obligation." This is not held up as an ideal, but points to the possibility of a mere behavioral fulfillment of the mitzvah: having eaten so many grams of matzah on Passover and drunk so many milliliters of wine, you have fulfilled those duties and can leave it at that.

This emphasis on performance is important and can cover many mitzvot. The Rabbis emphasize it especially in relation to *tzedakah*, the obligation to help our less fortunate fellows with a gift or a loan. *Tzedakah*—unlike many other mitzvot—does not require a blessing beforehand. There *is* no blessing for giving *tzedakah*. We have a hungry person in front of us! We need to act without further delay.

Kavanah is desirable, but—unlike the performance of a specific deed—it is not something that we can ever achieve to perfection. We cannot always attain the Rizhiner's exalted state of *devekut*, or cleaving to God. Hence the halakhic need to show the limits of the mitzvah, to define the obligation it places upon us, so that observance can be a discrete and fulfillable act. We must give the exoterically observant side of us a finite and doable way to live a Jewish life.

Performance, on the other hand, is only the most immediate and exoteric level of fulfilling the mitzvah. Imagine eating matzah on Passover with the mind-set of each of the Four Sons of the Haggadah. The first son, the *chakham*, Wise Mind, wants to do it right at every level. How are matzot made? How much do I need to eat to fulfill the mitzvah? What does this act really symbolize? The *rasha*, Wicked Mind, launches into all the reasons why eating matzah is ridiculous. The *tam*, Simple Mind, asks in wonder, "What *is* this stuff?" And Silent Mind, the one who does not know how to ask, just crunches and swallows, crunches and swallows.

The matzah we eat on Pesach is real, physical stuff, and eating it is a real, physical act. But that is not the only world in which we live. So while Silent Mind unites with the physical, *Tam*, Simple Mind, seeks a simple explanation: What's going on? *Rasha*, Wicked Mind, is way ahead of him. He's working out all the kinks. He hasn't left the table, but he's holding back. He's testing, probing. He hasn't let go of his skepticism. This, too, is valuable. *Chakham*, Wise Mind, is the opposite. He's not satisfied just with eating or with definitions. He wants to know everything about it. A well-known midrash rearranges the word *chokhmah* (חכמה), wisdom to yield *ko'ach mah* (כח מה), the power of "What?"—the wisdom of getting to know *what* a thing is. Wise Mind seeks to understand the mitzvah *lifnai ve-lifnim*, inside and out. He wants to do the mitzvah in a completely integrated and organic way.

Each of the four children may eat from the same matzah! Their individual experiences, though, will each be colored and transformed by the *kavanah* that they bring to it. And *kavanah* is a many-layered thing.

Some mitzvot, moreover, cannot be properly done unconsciously or mechanically. These "duties of the heart," in Bachya ibn Pakuda's famous phrase,[3] cannot be fulfilled without conscious and deliberate intention. For example, the Rabbis recognize the need for *kavanah* in prayer. Saying the words without intent is clearly unsatisfactory; on the other hand, saying every word and syllable with full and true *kavanah* is close to impossible. (Rabbi Seth Kadish discusses the difficulties of praying with *kavanah* in his excellent volume *Kavvana*,[4] including helpful suggestions as to the optimal quantity of prayers that will yet allow for conscious participation.) So a Rabbinical discussion defines a scale, a gradient of sorts.

The controversy goes like this: Is prayer *de-rabbanan*, a commandment that comes down to us from the Rabbis? The Rabbis, after all, were the ones who established the times and seasons for the prayers and the contents of our prayer books. Or is prayer *de-oraita* (*oraita*, meaning "the teaching," is the Aramaic word for Torah)—a commandment from the written Torah itself, as we might expect for such a vital channel of communication between us and God? The question itself admits to a hierarchy: the Rabbis clearly saw their own authority as binding, but a commandment that comes from the text of Torah itself is a stricter obligation. For instance, the Torah says you should eat matzot on Pesach, so that's *de-oraita*. But lighting candles on Shabbos and making *Kiddush* are Rabbinic commands. So there's a hierarchy of importance here. Failing to light candles or make *Kiddush* on Shabbos is bad, but eating *chametz* on Pesach is grave indeed.

A great teacher of my lineage, Reb Shalom Dov Baer of Lubavitch, resolves the question about *kavanah* in prayer in the following way. When you're saying prayers because they're in the prayer book and it's time to say prayers, then you fulfill your Rabbinic command: saying the morning, afternoon, and evening prayers as they are laid out in the siddur is an obligation that comes to us from the Rabbis. But he also points to the verse *Ba-tzar lekha u-m'tza'ukha kol ha-devarim* (Deuteronomy 4:30), which he interprets to mean, "When you are in trouble, you shall find the words." If you pray like you really mean it, he says, and you make the words of the siddur your own, that's scriptural prayer. You're going beyond the Rabbinic commandment: in expressing your inner feelings and need for God, you're fulfilling the words of Deuteronomy. So *kavanah* turns a perfectly adequate fulfilling of a mitzvah into an act that connects us directly to Torah and to God.

Here I Am—Send Me

Kavanah begins at a moment of breakthrough. It blossoms from the seed within us that volunteers for growth. The prophet Isaiah, in one of his most beautiful and fantastic visions, hears the voice of God asking, *"Et mi eshlach, u-mi yelekh lanu?* Whom shall I send, and who shall go for us?" (Isaiah 6:8). *Kavanah* begins at that point when a voice within us responds, as Isaiah did, "Here I am. Send me."

What are those moments in your own life when you felt the clarity of higher purpose? I remember the first time I came to Camp Starlight, Pennsylvania. That was where the B'nai B'rith camp was, and students from Hillel foundations would gather there the last week of the summer. I was about thirty years old at that time, a rabbi at a shul in New Bedford, Massachusetts. I saw how passionate and involved the Hillel students were, and I went out into the field and started to cry and pray to God, "*Ribboyno sh'l oylom*, Master of the Universe, so much one can do with these young people! I hear Your call. Please, give me the opportunity to do it."

This is a "yes" born of an insight: Who am I? "God made us," a verse from Psalms declares. "We did not make ourselves" (Psalm 100:3). I belong to God; I am nothing but an expression of God. On Yom Kippur we sing a hymn that says, "We are as clay in the Potter's hand." A host of other metaphors see us as an expression of godly intent, "like the tiller in the Helmsman's hand, like a stone in the Mason's hand." My entire life and everything I do are nothing but God Godding Godself as Zalman. The best thing I can do, then, is to make my life a good ride for God, to consciously devote my actions to that purpose.

At first our "yes" may be hesitant: "O-kay, I'll do it." Over time, though, as we keep responding, as we keep volunteering for whatever mission God has for us in the world, that "yes" takes on the promise of quality. It says, "Yes! I'll do it! But I so want to do it well. I want it to be noble, I want it to be beautiful." The kabbalist Reb Moshe Chayim Luzzato, in his *Mesilat Yesharim* (Path of the Just), gave this goal a name: *shelemut ha-avodah*. The second word, *avodah*, means work or service. *Shelemut* means fullness, wholeness, completeness, perfection. So *shelemut ha-avodah* captures our aspiration for a completeness or perfection in our service to God.

I am an old man now, and I no longer have the energy that I used to have. What allowed me the strength to begin this work on davening is the urgency I still feel to share the lessons of a lifetime, to complete the mission that I believe God placed me on earth to perform. I recognize that I have been deployed by a purpose greater than myself. "*Libi do'eg be-kirbi*, my heart worries and yearns within me,"[5] to serve my Creator as faithfully as I can. So each of us must determine where our own *kavanah* leads us.

The Practice of *Kavanah*: Exercises and Meditations

We are told that Reb Yechiel Michel of Zlotchov, famous disciple of the Baal Shem Tov, ate his meals from a plate that had the divine name on it. With each spoonful that he ate he got closer to God. This helped him not to forget, and to stay in that connection. Can you imagine eating that way? Our dinner table would become an altar for serving God. My eating would become a feeding of the God within me. And yet there's something almost blasphemous about the thought of covering God's name with beans on a bed of rice. The whole idea seems a little silly. Do we really need to resort to such tricks?

Perhaps the point of the story is that *kavanah* is more easily aspired to than achieved. We want to do right, but our mind wanders. Most of us are freewheeling as far as the mind is concerned. We don't hold onto the steering wheel: wherever our thoughts want to go, we let them go. To do the inner work that *kavanah* asks of us, we have to learn how to steer our minds.

But this is not so easy. I want to be focused. I don't want to be distracted. Saying "I will meditate with *kavanah*," or "I will daven with *kavanah*" or "I will study Torah with *kavanah*" expresses my determination to be totally involved in what I am doing. This is the direction I want to go: this is the direction I *will* go. Yet our determination flags. Our path can get muddied and our intentions confused. A mind that seeks to catch itself at "minding" has tied itself in knots. So it can be with *kavanah*: the more aware we are of our own *kavanah*, the more distracted we have become.

How, then, to achieve true *kavanah*?

First, we need to approach our quest with humility. We cannot have the chutzpah of thinking, *I can figure this out. No problem. I can master this.* Zen koans and other spiritual teachings serve to remind us of the limitations of our conscious minds. In probing the operation of the mind, they remind us not to get too proud of what our mind produces.

One path toward *kavanah* lies in meditating on key verses that express the situation we are looking to create, the spiritual under-standing that we hope to merit. We begin with short moments, quick glimpses of true *kavanah* and of how we can extend those moments over time. Jewish meditation often asks us not to empty the mind but to fill it—to meditate on, to contemplate. Can I keep my *kavanah* on the words "*Shema Yisrael Adonai Eloheinu Adonai Echad*, Hear, O Israel, the Lord our God is One"? Can I, even for thirty seconds, focus on that ONE, merging with the uniqueness, the totality, the All—without going away from that?

On the following pages I offer a few meditations that might help you in your *kavanah*.

שויתי ה׳ לנגדי תמיד
"I set God before me always"

The verse "*Shiviti ha-Shem le-negdi tamid*, I set God before me always" (Psalm 16:8) is one of the great remembrances that opens the door to *kavanah*.

Once there was a Hasid who used to go and study with Reb Chayim Halberstam of Sanz.[6] This Hasid would travel some distance, and on the way there and back he would pass through a small town, where he stayed for Shabbos. The rabbi in that town also fancied himself to be a *shtickl* Rebbe, though he didn't have many followers. "I can teach you," he told the Hasid. "I'm closer, why go to Sanz?"

"Maybe so," the Hasid responded. "But in Sanz they are teaching me also how to be a *yode'a machshovos*"—to possess that near-miraculous power some Hasidic Rebbes have to see into the hearts of those who are sitting before them, to divine their thoughts and concerns.

"Really?" said the local rabbi. "Then what am I thinking now?"

This was easy. "You're thinking, '*Shiviti ha-Shem le-negdi tamid*, I keep God before me always,'" returned the Hasid.

"No!" said the rabbi triumphantly. "I'm not!"

"*Nu*," said the Hasid. "Now you can see why I go to Sanz."

To the Hasid, the question "What am I thinking?" should—on the most fundamental level—have only one answer, whatever the person's other concerns. That is why "I have set God before me always" is embroidered on the covers of holy arks in so many shuls throughout the Jewish world. The awareness that we stand in the presence of the Living God is one of the most important realizations we can install in our operative consciousness.

God is always present. The question is, how present are *we?* We want to stand in that Presence without opacity. Our work is to penetrate, in meditation and in action, to the very heart of being *nokhach penei ha-Shem* (Lamentations 2:19), of being truly present before God. Repeating the *Shiviti* verse throughout the day reminds us to be present in that way.

אדון עולם
"Adon Olam: Master of the Universe"

The prayer *Adon Olam* is often sung as the closing prayer of *Shacharit*, the morning service. It's in every standard siddur. Sometimes the kids come up and lead it. The tune is usually rhythmic and fun, everyone sings along, and the service ends on a joyous note. But *Adon Olam* is also one of the most beautiful devotional poems we possess. Just saying the words slowly, turning their import over in our minds, thinking what they might mean to us, can give us all the contemplation we need.

"*Adon olam, asher malakh be-terem kol yetzir nivra*, Master of the Universe, who reigned before any creature was created…. *Ve-acharei ki-kh'lot ha-kol le-vado yimloch nora*, And afterward, when all is done, alone shall reign the Awesome One."

What would we say today? "From before the big bang and on beyond the last black hole! Your Presence fills creation." Opening yourself to these thoughts is such a mind stretcher. You can go beyond time! You can catch a glimpse of what it's like to see with divine eyes, from the place of God's timeless *NOW*. That moment of oneness is what Meister Eckhart was trying to express when he wrote, "The eye with which I see God is the same eye with which God sees me. My eye and God's eye are one eye, one sight, one knowledge, and one love."

After six cosmic praise-verses, the author of *Adon Olam* brings the focus back to our personal need for help and comfort. *"Be-yado afkid ruchi* ... In God's hand I entrust my spirit. When I go to sleep, I know I shall awake! And with my spirit, my body, too. For God is with me, and I shall not fear."

ה' הוא האלוקים
"YHVH is Elohim; Adonai is God"

People ask me sometimes whether meditation is at home in Judaism. Moses, our teacher, speaks of a unity of the name of God and a knowing of that unity in a way that can only be achieved with meditation and contemplation. He says, "Know ye today, and bring this knowledge back into your heart, that *Adonai* is God, and none other" (Deuteronomy 4:39).

Let's unpack that a little. "Know ye: *Ve-yadata*." This comes from the same root as "And Adam knew [*yada*] Eve his wife" (Genesis 4:1). It's that sort of intimate knowing.

"And bring this knowledge back into your heart." Make it settled there, make it resident.

What should you make resident? "That *YHVH* is *Elohim*"—that *YHVH*, the God of judgment, and *Elohim*, the God of compassion, are one and the same. And that everything that happens is an interplay between the two aspects of the One.[7]

"And none other." Or, more literally, "there is none else but God." Nothing else but God exists; nothing un-God can ever happen. May you know, deeply and intimately, and may you bring this knowledge back into your heart, that all events and aspects of existence are One and that nothing else can ever exist or happen. May you be in the greatest fullness that you can be, may you know God with that way of knowing, and may it happen today.

Simply meditating on the Tetragrammaton, the letters of God's mysterious name, can open a channel to bring down the holy. As in Vipassana or *pranayama,* we can use our breathing to help us get there. Your lungs without breath are like the *yud,* the smallest letter, the vanishing point. Our inhalation forms the *hey,* letter of breath: *hhhhhhh.* At the top of the breath we form the *vav,* straight as an erect backbone. Then we breathe out—*hhhhhhh*—another *hey.*

So we invite *YHVH* to come down and dwell within us. As Jews we are concerned about living in *this* world. Ours is not primarily an *Ein Sof* focus, a preoccupation with the world beyond the beyond, but a Gaia focus. Our fundamental *kavanah* is not to leave the world behind but to bring God into *this* world, to create the "Kingdom of heaven" in the life we live, right here and now.

ואני תמיד עמך
"I am always with You"

One of the most moving things about the psalms is the heights and depths of emotion and devotion that the psalmists knew so well. In Psalm 73, Asaph sings, "I was foolish and ignorant; I was like an animal before You." And yet, he continues, "I am always with You" (Psalm 73:22–23). I love these words. I made up a *niggun* for them once, because they touched me so deeply. What do I know? I don't know anything. And yet one thing I do know is that "I am always with You," and "You take my right hand to guide me" (Psalm 73:23–24).

As long as this creature, this "I," draws breath, I am in intimate connection with the Living God. Even when I decide that I don't want to have anything to do with God, I can't help it: with every passing moment the Creator is fashioning me anew. So I am in a steady state of *devekut,* or cleaving to God. Without *da'at,* though—without awareness—the experience of this closeness is lost to us. So we need to constantly remind ourselves, to open up every room in our minds to the presence and service of the Living God. That is why such a mantra is useful. "*Va-ani tamid imakh.* I am always with You."

דבר בעתו מה טוב
"A thing done in season is good"

"To everything there is a season, and a time to every purpose under heaven" (Ecclesiastes 3:1). Not for nothing did Pete Seeger put these words to music. The sentence resonates with us. We know it is true.

Living in sync with our sacred calendar helps gives us *kivun*, direction. It keeps us from falling into forgetfulness. Living in the flow of time, joining our actions to the signposts and seasons of the year, helps us to connect with the *shefa*, the constant outflow of grace and plentitude that underlies our very existence.

We have a proverb: *Davar be-ito mah tov* (Proverbs 15:23). Usually we interpret *davar* in this verse to mean something that we say: "A timely utterance is good." But *davar* can also mean any object or matter. I like to interpret this proverb as "A thing done in season is good." Aligning my devotion and celebration with the Jewish calendar sensitizes me to the texture of God's will in this time and place.

We can connect to timeliness on almost any livable scale. The sun's path across the sky can connect us to our three daily prayer services: *Shacharit* in the morning, *Minchah* in the afternoon, *Ma'ariv* at night. Every seven days we have Shabbos, the crowning glory of our week. Each month begins with Rosh Chodesh, the first of the month, followed a week afterward by *Kiddush Levanah*, the sanctification of the waxing moon. Our holidays dovetail with the seasons and often begin on the full moon. Every seven years we celebrate the super-Shabbos of *shemitah*, when Torah commands us to let the earth lie fallow and renew itself. And recently, on April 8, 2009, Jewish communities throughout the world recited the *Birkhat ha-Chamah* (blessing of the sun), recited every twenty-eight years when, according to tradition, the sun returns to its place when the world was first created.

Kavanah in Action

Thinking good thoughts and speaking nice words is not enough: my deeds must follow. One of the key purposes of Jewish meditation is to take the gifts that *emunah* (faith) and revelation give to us and put them into operative awareness. This is not so easy. We might accept the Ten Commandments on an intellectual level. But when it comes to a little temptation of "*lo tignov,* do not steal," then my ego begins to make excuses. "*Nu,* the cashier gave me too much change. It's their mistake, and the store can afford it." Other mitzvot give us trouble as well. How many times do Torah and the prophets tell us to care for the poor! But when the homeless guy sticks out his tin cup, we think, "Oh, he's just going to spend it on drugs."

What is an indicator that I am doing it right? How do I know that I am not just spinning my wheels, that my *kavanah* is leading me in the right direction (*kivun*), that I am making real progress in my meditation? Many of our sacred teachings speak of the twin engines of sacred service: *ahavah ve-yir'ah*—love and awe of God. These two words are some of our most basic devotional vocabulary, and they are worth examining more closely.

What does it mean when the first paragraph of the *Shema* commands us, "*Ve-ahavta et ha-Shem Elohekha,* You shall love ha-Shem, your God"? These words are clearly at the heart of what it means to be a Jew. Yet how can you legislate a person's feelings? I once heard in the name of the Maggid of Mezeritch: The *Shema* command, the legislation, is not on the feelings. It is on the mindfulness. *Shema Yisrael!* Listen, O my people, Israel. Hear. Be mindful. *Adonai* our God is One God. If we get that, the Maggid says, then *ve-ahavta* will be the inevitable result. You won't be able to help it. You will love. It is not a commandment: LOVE GOD! Nor is it that I want to tickle myself so I should have love for God, to manipulate myself into feeling those things. Rather, says the Maggid, when I am consciously in *devekut,* my love for God arises naturally from this connectedness. The mitzvah simply urges that transparency.

Yir'ah, awe, is sometimes translated as fear, but neither completely captures the idea. The Hebrew root of *yir'ah* is *yud-resh-aleph* ירא. The root of words meaning sight or to see is *resh-aleph-hey* ראה. *Yir'ah* arises from the state of being seen for what we really are. Imagine I'm in a room, and I think I'm alone. I start doing something that I don't want anyone else to see. Then suddenly I become aware that someone else is there, that I'm being watched. The first spark of *yir'ah* is that startle reflex, the jolt I feel to my *kishkes,* my innards.

There is a story about Juna'id, the ninth-century Sufi master.[8] He has twenty students who each wants to be his successor, and they are arguing among themselves and pressing him for a decision. He is getting older, so finally he says to them, "You go out and each bring a live bird, and I'll tell you what to do." So they each come back with a live bird, and he says, "Now go find a place where no one can see you, kill the bird, and come back." They all go off, and nineteen of them come back with dead birds, but the bird of the twentieth is still alive. So Juna'id makes an angry face. "Why didn't you kill the bird!"

The disciple says, "Master, I couldn't find a place where no One can see me."

The awareness that we are being seen, that we do everything we do in the presence of that Witness—that is the true path to and meaning of *yir'ah*. We're talking about a seeing and being seen that goes beyond the visual. The way we perceive someone emerges not only from the act of seeing but from the insight or intuition that arises from that seeing. Our ability to *regard* somebody, to see them, shares a kinship with our *regard for* them. The Latin *spectāre*, to see, gave rise not only to words like *spectacle* but to our respect for someone as well.

So we need to set aside the idea that our mind is private, and to realize that we are seen and known. Psalm 139 captures this feeling of "You know everything about me, God, more than I could ever know myself." You know my comings and goings, David says; my sitting down and getting up. You understand every word on my tongue better than I could ever hope to. No imaginable place is bereft of Your presence. "If I ascend to heaven, there You are; if I make my bed in hell, You are there" (Psalm 139:8).

Knowing that everything I think and feel is revealed and known to God is, in itself, an important form of divine service, of *avodat ha-Shem*. I want no barrier separating what I feel in my heart from what I'm praying and asking for. I want to make myself transparent of heart, transparent of mind, transparent of body—to say, "O Lord, O Lord, come into my heart, build there your shrine, and never depart."[9] I wish to constantly remember that everything I do is witnessed by that Infinite Witness. I want to invite that witness in and not shut it out. I want my awareness to bring me to the life described in Proverbs 3:6, "*Be-khol derakhekha da'eihu*, Know God in all your ways."

In contrast, the conviction that we have somehow sinned, that we have fallen short of our aspirations, is often accompanied by a sense of being *nifrad*—cut off, isolated. I have separated myself from God. I don't want God to look into my heart. I'd rather God didn't see what I have just done. All our words for sin express this sense of disconnect. We speak of *cheit*, a missing of the mark; *aveirah* (from *ayin-vet-resh*, to pass), a transgression or trespassing; *avon*, a bending or twisting of something that once was straight. In all of these we hear Isaiah's admonition to the people of Judah, "It is your sins that come between you and your God" (Isaiah 59:2). But if even in the midst of failure we can keep a sense of "Dear God, look at this. I'm not pushing You out. I want You to look at this failure of mine. I'm not happy with it. I wish it were different. I'd like to fix it"—then we are already involved in the process of *teshuvah*, of repentance.

Of course, this business of love (*ahavah*) and awe (*yir'ah*) is not only between me and God. If *yir'ah* is what keeps me from doing wrong, *ahavah* is what inspires me to do right. How do I know that I am making progress? When I not only feel *ahavah* toward God but manifest it in the world. When I start to feel more love for *people*—not just for humanity, which is an abstract idea, but for real, flesh-and-blood men and women: my family, my coworkers, my friends; sales clerks, cold callers, other drivers on the road. If I truly make a mind-move, I will become more patient, more manifesting of love, and I will *act* on that love. Only then will I know that *ahavah* is not just a nice idea for me, but that my *kavanah* is for real.

Consciousness Maintenance

Let's say I'm about to teach a class, to speak to people about how to make their Jewish lives more meaningful. Of course, some of my motives are the highest, but I have other motives as well. I want to make a living; I like being in the position of the wise old teacher—all these things are there. And yet, before I begin, I still say, "*Le-shem mitzvat talmud Torah*, I'm doing this for the sake of the mitzvah of studying Torah." I'm not denying the other motives, but I'm wrapping it in the greater motive so it should become a mitzvah. If I need to, I can take this further, and say what's on my mind. I can say, "Dear God, You be my witness that while I'm a bundle of all kinds of motives, still I stand here in Your presence, and I want to do this wholly and completely for Your sake. All the other things are there, but please help me dedicate myself completely to that."

Of course, if our heart stops hearing what our lips are saying, these declarations can also become a trap. I say I'm doing it for a good purpose and with good intent, but as a friend of mine used to say, doing spirituality without having shoveled the inner manure is like putting whipped cream on top of garbage. It starts stinking after a while, because of all the stuff that's unresolved underneath. So we get to the place where our avowed intention is not enough, where we need to resolve and do *teshuvah* for all sorts of things.

This is why, before we go to sleep, we say the bedtime *Shema* and the prayers that surround it, reviewing our day and asking, "What led me to do such-and-such? What were my motives?" and doing the housecleaning that goes along with that. Or you might declare a Minor Yom Kippur (Yom Kippur Katan), a day of fasting and prayer that some observe on *Erev* Rosh Chodesh, the day before the new moon, to reflect on where they are falling short and how they might do better. Or you might keep notes or a journal on how your *kavanot* play out in your life: where your deeds match your intention and where you still have work to do.

All these are important forms of consciousness maintenance, of *kavanah* watching *kavanah*.

Higher-Level *Kavanah*

I want to say a few things about meta-*kavanah*, the primal intention that lies hidden within our psyches. By meta-*kavanah* I mean an alignment that goes beyond whatever specific intentions I might have for what I do. I mean the core orientation of our souls, the force that points us toward either harmony or disharmony with the cosmos.

We want to understand *kavanah* as deeply as we can. We're talking about an understanding that goes beyond knowing how something works or what it feels like when it takes hold of you. We want to know the deepest "whatness" of this thing we are seeking, the kind of knowing expressed by the old saying "*Ilu yedativ heyitiv, ilu heyitiv yedativ,* If I knew it, I would *be* it; if I *were* it, I would know it." We seek a knowing of total identity, a knowing that dissolves any boundaries or borders that stand between us.

Think of a whirlpool. The water that goes through the vortex changes every second, but yet the vortex holds its shape—not a solid shape, but a dynamic and active form. Just so might our conscious *kavanah* change from moment to moment and from hour to hour, yet the meta-*kavanah* within us holds firm. Our real work is to pour into that holy vessel whatever we most deeply want to know or be, as we might pour wine into a cup on Friday night.

Did this *kavanah* originate with me, or was I set on that path even before I was born?

We have alluded to the Hebrew phrase *le-khaven el ha-matarah,* to aim at the bull's-eye. (*Le-khaven* is from the same root as *kavanah, kaf-vav-nun.*) This is a useful metaphor. When I finally embrace a *matarah*—a bull's-eye, a target for my existence—and I say, "Yes, I will go with that, I will collaborate with that, I will invest myself in that," then my embracing becomes a *kavanah.*

We learn from *Zen in the Art of Archery* that if I separate the archer from the bow and the target, I am mistaken. They are one. The Mind that creates the cosmos is more conscious than mine. The bow shot that I'm looking for is one that connects me to that *da'at elyon,* that high and all-embracing knowing. This is what our practice is about.

This direction does not originate with us; it is always and already there, buried and unfolding within us like a DNA of the soul, awaiting our consent. That is the meaning of "*Na'aseh ve-nishma,* We will do and we will hear" (Exodus 24:7), the statement with which Israel, according to our tradition, received the Torah. "Yes, we will do that—in fact we had already started, we were already on that path, even before we heard and understood anything of Torah's actual words."

That is why I like to say that humans are theotropic beings, that we are meant to grow toward God, to follow where God takes us. Not that we are always in harmony with that ideal way. But if we get a little bit more subtle and spiritually cleaned up, then we will get to the place where we, like the needle on a compass, will naturally swing around to align ourselves with our inner core of *kavanah.*

What is the magnetic force that pulls our kavanic needle around and points us in the direction that the Creator, the great All, wants us to go? Deep within us, buried beneath many layers, there is a longing. The *Tanya* calls this the *ahavah mesuteret*,[10] the "hidden love" within our souls whose only wish and desire is to cleave to the great totality of God. This love is well concealed; we have to work to uncover it. But it is never so hidden that it doesn't peek out at us, beckoning us to heed its call. Mind is always playing hide-and-seek with soul.

Our deepest intuition is that we are meant to wake up into a knowing that transcends business as usual. No matter how pressing the *avodah* or service of my daily life, I cannot completely turn my back on this inner knowing. Without it, I would be spiritually destitute. That is why I need *kavanah*: to rededicate myself with every new day to this inner knowing; to contribute whatever is in my power to what the mystics call *binyan ha-malkhut*, the building of the holy kingdom here on earth.

Above all, *kavanah* pulls us forward. At the heart of *kavanah* lies the question: Why? Hebrew has two different words for why, *madu'a* and *lamah*, and each has a slightly different emphasis. *Madu'a* asks, "*Mah yadu'a?* What is known to us?" Philosophers might call this the *what* of etiology. It wants to know about origins and causes. *Lamah* asks, "*Le-mah?* What for?" This is the *why* of teleology. It asks: Where are we going with this? What is the goal?

The *why* at the heart of *kavanah* is not only the *madu'a* of origins but the *lamah* of ultimate purpose. We hear the call from the "takhlitic being" that we are meant to become.[11] The causes that motivated us in the past are not enough to impel our spiritual quest. We need the attractors of the spirit that pull us into the future, a future wishing and waiting to be realized in us. *Kavanah* draws us forward into an *olam ha-ba*—not "the world to come," as the phrase is usually translated, but a world that is, at this very moment, becoming in us and around us.

The book of Psalms conveys this intention with an interesting image. "I come with a scroll-book on me," says the psalmist, "in which there is one thing written"—like a journal, in which you declare its purpose on page one. This is what the scroll says: "My only desire is to do Your will. I want Your teaching in my very *kishkes*" (Psalm 40:8–9).

This is my intent. This is what I want to do. I'm not there yet, but I'm on my way.

NIGGUN!
A Soul in Song

My Rebbe, Reb Yosef Yitzchak, used to tell a story about Reb Schneur Zalman, founder of Chabad Hasidism. The Alter Rebbe (Old Rebbe), as Chabadniks called him, was still quite a young man when he proposed a radical reinterpretation of a technical point in the Mishnah.[1] The discussion concerned domesticated animals and how they may be used on Shabbos. Animals cannot carry things for their masters on Shabbos, the Rabbis say. But they can leave their owner's premises wearing a collar around their necks and even be led by the collar. Most early commentators traced *shir*, the word used for collar, to a rare Hebrew word *sher*, meaning collar or bracelet. But Reb Schneur Zalman saw it on a more profound level.

The word *shir*, as Reb Schneur Zalman reminded his listeners, usually means song. Buried within the usual understanding, that "all [animals who commonly wear] collars can go out with a collar [*shir*] and be drawn by a collar," Reb Schneur Zalman saw a more mystical message: "The masters of song go out in song and are drawn by song." The "master of song" is the soul, he said, which reaches for God in song and is attracted by song.

Early opponents of Hasidism were outraged. Here again were these so-called mystical interpretations that the Baal Shem Tov and his followers were so famous for, taking texts out of context, mangling well-known passages, and claiming to uncover deep things. When Reb Schneur Zalman agreed to speak in Shklov, a stronghold of scholarly opponents to the still-young Hasidic movement, they gathered in force. The Hasidic leader's intellectual reputation was already formidable, and the scholars fired questions at him from every side.

Reb Schneur Zalman did not answer any of them. Instead, he began to sing. They slowly fell silent, and his voice filled the room. He sang a slow, deep melody, full of learning, full of yearning. By the time his voice died away, there were no further questions.

A *Niggun* Is a Wordless Prayer

A *niggun* is a wordless prayer, a melody that a Hasid sings to get closer to God. In the Old Country, if a *chazan* was too much in love with the sound of his own voice, they would say, "That *chazan* is a fool. He frequents the palace of *neginah* [melody, *niggun*], which is right next door to the palace of *teshuvah* [repentance, return to God]—and yet he never goes in!"

At Chabad we had a saying: "Every locksmith has a master key with which he can open many doors. *Neginah* is such a key, for it can unlock all doors." Why? Because a *niggun* sung in the proper way is like doing *teshuvah*, like a moment of true repentance and turning to God. The wellsprings of *niggun* and *teshuvah* are the simple yearnings of the heart that we all share. Not long ago, I was teaching at a Reform synagogue in Calgary on Shabbos morning. "Tell me," I began, "do you sometimes have the feeling that you ought to be better? The wish that you could be different, higher, wiser? Closer to God?"

People nodded.

"Let's take a moment to get in touch with that feeling," I said. "Now, I'd like you to say, 'Oy.' Just like that, from that place of aspiration: 'Oy. Oy. *Oy*.'" So the people did that, and there were some heartfelt *Oy*'s! Then I said, "You know what? We just have done a little *teshuvah*."

Because that's what it is. That sense of longing, that sense that "Oy, if only I were better, if only I could be in a greater place!"—not from some crippling sense of guilt, like Woody Allen, but because we love God, we want to be closer to God—that's *teshuvah*. At that

28

point, because the palace of *neginah* and the palace of *teshuvah* are side-by-side, we are ready to sing.

Even the simplest *niggun* can serve as prayer if sung with the right *kavanah*. The other day, I was doing a guest lecture by Skype to a group of people in Berkeley that is reading *Jewish with Feeling*.[2] We had come to chapter 5, which deals with eco-kosher and the sacred imperative of caring for the planet. Before we started, though, I said to the people, "What I need to share with you, I can't do it cold. So I want you to sing 'Hava Nagilah' with me. Everyone knows the tune, yes? But I want us to sing it without words, and *slow*, really slow. Let's do it as a prayer. And please, ask in this prayer that something should come to you in this sharing that we are doing, something that your soul needs at this time."

That's how "Hava Nagilah" started: the words came later, but the tune was a Sadigura *niggun*, from a Hasidic lineage founded by one of the six sons of the great Reb Yisroel of Rizhin. The Hasidim would sing it very slowly, and as the melody rose heavenward—*DI DI YA MAM, DI YAI YAI YAI YAI*—oy, you would close your eyes, and pinch your face, and make the kind of gesture that wants to storm the gates of heaven! So we sang together on Skype, and we were able to speak of things that otherwise would not have been said.

Molecular Memory

The comedian Lenny Bruce had a great routine on "Jewish vs. Goyish": *Chocolate is Jewish. Fudge is goyish. Fruit salad is Jewish. Lime Jell-O is goyish.* Being a Jew is not just a matter of how we identify ourselves or what we choose to observe. It's cellular. "All my bones shall speak it," the psalmist says (Psalm 35:10).

Hearing a *niggun* sometimes feels like coming upon some faint but strangely familiar path, one we and others have walked before. A Hebrew poet named Fanya Bergstein once wrote a beautiful poem called "Niggunim" (1944). The poem begins:

> *Father, mother, you planted niggunim in me*

Forgotten niggunim and mizmorim [songs, psalms]
Seeds—seeds that my heart carried.
Now they are rising and growing!"[3]

Younger Jews today respond to different songs. But our treasure trove of *niggunim* remains something to be proud of and to pass on. I often urge people: play Jewish music in your home; get so you can *feel* it. We offer a lot of classes that teach everything that goes into the Jewish left brain: *This is what we believe. These are the holy days. This is what you have to do.* Only seldom do we speak to the aesthetic dimension, the right-brain stuff. We need to give our children a cellular connection to these things: Jewish music, Jewish food, Jewish humor.

Niggunim are not just the tunes we Jews sing, a soundtrack to the Jewish movie. They are inalienable to the Jewish spirit, expressions of the God-song that we already carry within us. These melodies trigger an almost molecular memory for me. My parents sang them. So did my grandparents, my great-grandparents—all my Ashkenazic ancestors. *Kol dodi dofek*, says a famous verse from the Song of Songs (5:2): "The voice of my Beloved comes knocking." But, as Reb Nachman of Breslov points out, the word *dofek* (knocks) also means pulse. The voice of the Beloved is always there, pulsing and rhythming under the surface.

Song of the Heavenly Spheres

Chapter 3 of the second book of Kings tells the story of the prophet Elisha, heir to the mantle of Elijah, who one day is visited by three kings: the king of Israel, the king of Judah, and the king of Edom. The king of Israel has persuaded his fellow kings to march against the king of Moab, because Moab is refusing to pay a tribute to the king of Israel. The three armies have marched for seven days and now are parched and without water; the kings are afraid that Moab will defeat them all.

Elisha refuses to deal with them at first. Jehoram, king of Israel, was the son of Ahab and Jezebel, and almost as wicked as his father and mother. "Why do you come to me?" Elisha asks. "Go ask your parents' prophets." But Jehoram pleads for help, and finally the prophet relents. "Bring me a musician," Elisha says. "And behold," the book of Kings reports, "as soon as the musician began to play, the hand of God was upon him" (2 Kings 3:15).[4] Elisha began to prophesy. All would be well.

The commentators were naturally curious about Elisha's response. Why did the prophet ask for music? The great Rabbi David Kimchi imagines a man bereft of his teacher, a man he had traveled with and learned from for years. From the day Elijah was removed from him, Kimchi says, Elisha had been in mourning. The spirit of prophecy had abandoned him, unable to awaken without joy. Rabbi Levi ben Gershon points to a different reason: Elisha's fury at the idolatrous King Jehoram of Israel. Anger, he says, prevents the stillness the mind needs to attain prophecy. Elisha needed some way to let go of his wrath, to attain the expansion of heart that prophecy requires.

Both rabbis agree: the holy spirit rests only upon a person in a state of joy, and music was key to reigniting that joy.

A medieval mystic, David ben Yehudah ha-Chasid, hears deep things at work in this story. The soul, he explains, remembers the *niggunim* it hears when it is joined to God. It remembers the song of the heavenly circles, worlds populated by wheel-angels (*ofanim*) and fire angels (*serafim*) and holy beasts (*chayot ha-kodesh*). When the time comes for the soul to be clothed in an earthly body, *niggunim* become her comfort food. They make her feel peaceful in spirit. That is why a soul in song can open itself to receive the spirit of God.[5]

The phrase "as soon as the musician began to play [*ve-hayah ke-nagen ha-m'nagen*]" (2 Kings 3:15) has been quoted many times through the ages, becoming a code phrase for the connection between music and divine inspiration. An explanation attributed to the Maggid of Mezeritch puts the matter thus: As long as we are busy *doing*, in the active sense, we are not yet receptive enough to receive divine grace. For this end, a person must transform him- or herself into God's instrument, serving only as one acted upon. The Maggid explains the phrase as follows: When the musician (*ha-m'nagen*) becomes like the instrument (*ke-nagen*), then the spirit of God shall rest upon him.

The Musical Dimension of Davening

The human soul needs music. We surround ourselves with music: in malls, in elevators, in the car. Transistor radios were all the rage when they first came out; for the first time, people could carry their music around with them! Then came boom boxes, and now all the *kinderlach* are plugged into their iPods. We all listen differently, of course. Some ears just let the music flow by; others gulp greedily at any sound within range.

Even people who cannot sing a note express themselves through music. Our everyday speech has a music and rhythm of its own that does not come across in print. I lean into some words for emphasis; I drop my voice for others. I pause here, pick up the tempo there. We put in all sorts of extra vibrations when we talk, conveying much more than mere words on a page.

Can you imagine a synagogue service without song? Music adds layers of meaning beyond the original or translated word. It gives our prayers context. It opens up another channel of communication, attuning us with our souls and with each other.

So we have many musical traditions, both written and oral. In reading Torah, the cantillation marks, or *trope*, show us where the commas are and which words belong together in phrases. They highlight repeated elements and moments of drama. Our prayer books do not include that kind of intonation.[6] But generations of cantorial tradition have handed down modes, musical scales, and phrases that we associate with particular prayers and times of year and that communicate with nonverbal centers in the brain. Rosh Hashanah, for example, is where we declare anew God's kingship over us and all creation. For centuries, European Jews have begun the service on Rosh Hashanah evening with a march in a major key. In my imagination I hear it played by an orchestra, the horns ringing out in welcome: a fanfare for the entrance of the King! Tomorrow morning a more pleading tone will come in, asking God to forgive us for our sins. For now, we welcome our Ruler into our midst. The music reaffirming God's kingship on Rosh Hashanah night arouses something within us. If we, as a congregation, sing this tune together with *kavanah* and energy, a palpable change takes place. We begin to move together from regular commodity time to sacred Rosh Hashanah time.

We call these davening modes *nusach*. The word *nusach* can mean both text and melody. It can indicate which prayer rite and textual variations are being used; a traditional synagogue may use siddurim that are *nusach Ashkenaz, nusach Sepharad, nusach ha-Ari,* and so on. But *nusach* can also mean the melody or musical mode of a given time and place, which is what I mean here.

Nusach conveys information. Like the opening Rosh Hashanah tune, it maps us onto a landscape of ritual and time. Jews everywhere know the tune of *Kol Nidre*; when we hear that tune, we know Yom Kippur is beginning. *Nusach* can give us more subtle hints as well. If you listen carefully to the last few words of the *Amidah* on Rosh Chodesh, the first day of a new month, for example, you might notice the *chazan* switch to a different musical mode for the final phrase. This mode belongs to *Hallel,* the additional section of psalms that we sing together after the holiday *Amidah.* This adds a note of celebration; it also reminds listeners to flip forward to *Hallel* in their siddurim.

Nusach also conveys emotion. Few can fail to notice the sadness of the *trope* used to read *Eikhah,* the book of Lamentations, on the Ninth of Av, the day the Temple was destroyed. Reading the book of Esther on Purim, on the other hand, we use a relatively jaunty melody, relating the story of how the Jews of Persia overcame the genocidal plot of the wily Haman. Seven verses into our reading of the *Megillah,* however, we suddenly switch into the Lamentations mode for three words: "and different vessels" (Esther 1:7). The mood change hints that the vessels King Ahasuerus used to serve his great feast had been plundered from the holy Temple.

Keys and modes are important. When Beethoven sat down to write a movement, he wrote it in a particular key. We might reasonably ask, what difference does it make if it's played in the key of A minor of B minor? One is just a little higher than the other! But for the great composers, the different keys touched different parts of their souls. *Nusach* operates on similar principles. It augments the message of the words. It helps us fine-tune our inner being.

A Life in *Niggun*

Music and story go hand in hand. No Shabbos *tisch* (table) in a Hasidic family would be complete without *niggunim* and a *myseh* (story). If someone had a nice *shtickeleh* about the portion of the week, you would talk about that, too. Stories and *niggunim* seem to reach similar areas of our minds, areas beyond the reach of normal discursive thinking. Our people has a whole history of *niggun*, in many different chapters, and each of us, as individuals, could no doubt write our own little memoir in music, modest though it may be. I will try to give a sense of my musical story here, and I encourage you to think about your own. How and where has music touched you? What has your musical journey been like?

My musical life was blessed. I grew up in Vienna, a city that was full of music—and not small music either. Usually we think of the simple, heartfelt Hasidic *niggunim* as the path to *devekus*, cleaving to God. But Vienna had both the simple *devekus* and the "high church": I would daven in a little Hasidische *shtiebel* with my father, but I also used to go to Vienna's big "Polnische Temple," where I sang in the men and boys choir under Obercantor Emanuel Frankl, protégé of Yossele Rosenblatt and one of the greatest of Vienna's many cantors. Our choirmaster was Joseph Millet, who composed tunes that we and Obercantor Frankl would perform. Once I even got to sing a solo that he composed for the *Kedushah*. Many singers and *chazanim* came out of that choir. Oy, how that music would soar! How can I put it? God was not wearing a greasy *kappotte* at that point. You got a real sense of *Malkhut*, of God's kingship.

King of the universe! We still remembered our own kingly ruler in those early days. Not all Christian rulers were despised as anti-Semites. Kaiser Franz Yosef (1830–1916) was a largely benign ruler, highly respected, who kept the states of central Europe together for many years. The Jews of Austria loved him. Reb 'Froyim Yos'l, people called him; *unser kaiser*—our kaiser. He would travel through his realm in his special train, the Kaiser Koenigliche train. When the train passed through a shtetl, a small town, he would come out and stand at the end of the carriage on a little porch, and the priest would come and present the holy relics of the town to kiss. Then the rabbi would step forward with the *Sefer Torah*, the *chazan* singing a prayer for the emperor, praising God who "gives salvation to kings and governance to princes." And *unser kaiser* would give a little bow toward the *Sefer Torah* and say, "Yah, in our archive in Vienna, we, too, have the holy Torreh Scrolle!"

By the time I grew up, Vienna was Socialist, so we no longer had a kaiser. As far as we were concerned, though, 'Froyim Yos'l was still the model of royalty, and royalty was still the model for God. In the big shuls of Europe, you had the sense that "in a multitude of people lies the glory of the king" (Proverbs 14:28).[7] Today, our shuls are much more social, more friendly. People sit and schmooze as we used to do in the old days in the *bet midrash*, the house of study. But I miss that sense of *melekh ha-olam*, of kingship.

Europeans, with their histories of royalty, still summon that sense of awe and grandeur. I once went to Kraków to do a series of workshops. Mozart's *Requiem* was to be performed in the courtyard of Wawel Castle, and the people in charge asked me to introduce it. Speaking through an interpreter, I asked the audience to hear this not just as music but as prayer. Please don't regard yourselves as the final recipients of the music, I said. Instead, offer your ears and heart to heaven. Let your experience of the music go up to God. It's beautiful stuff! It takes you to a different place, somewhere it's hard to get to in jeans. Poland was still under Communist rule in those days, before the Wall came down. This was not the kind of talk they heard often.

As I said, I grew up in the world of *devekus*, as well, a world of *heimisch*, direct, individual cleaving to God, and *niggunim* were always a big part of that. My parents loved singing together in harmony. It was wonderful to hear how they would sing Shabbos at the table. My father, Shlomo Ha-Kohen Schachter, of blessed memory, loved all kinds of *niggunim* and made up some himself.[8] So did my *elter-zaida*, Yosef Hayyim Schachter. He was known as a *yerei shamayim* and a great *ba'al menag'n*, a God-fearing man with a wonderful voice who was chosen to lead the morning davening in Belz for the High Holidays. And he made up some remarkable *niggunim!* So the Belzer *niggunim* were among the first melodies I heard, growing up.

This leads me to a story. Some years ago, I was in Jerusalem, and I decided to visit the Belzer shul, stronghold of the Belzer Hasidim. The Great Belz Beit Midrash is the largest synagogue in Israel, built on a hilltop, clearly visible from most entrances to Jerusalem. In World War II the Nazis destroyed the original Belz synagogue in Ukraine, dismantling its massive walls stone by stone. Today the Belz have recreated their shul in all its former glory and then some. "When the *Mashiach* [Messiah] comes to Jerusalem," the Belzers say with satisfaction, "the first thing he sees on the way up will be our shul."

I was wearing an ordinary suit, not Hasidic garb. It was in the middle of the day, and they said, "The shul is not open for visitors now." So I said to them, in Galicianer Yiddish, "*Azoi redt men tsu a heimeschen Yid?* Is that how you talk to a Jew from the 'home'?" My family's roots in Belz and Galicia go way back, and they realized I was one of them. Then I said, "Do you know this *niggun?*" and I started to sing a tune.

They said, "We sing this for *hakofos!*"—the dancing rounds on Simchat Torah.

I said, "My *elter-zaida* used to sing that *niggun!*"

Oy! They got all excited. That *niggun* became my key to the city, and they came with me to show me around. It's an amazing building. The main sanctuary seats some two thousand men, with special sections for another three thousand women and children. Huge white chandeliers descend from 250-foot-high ceilings. The massive *aron kodesh* of dark, carved wood stands almost forty feet high. They showed me where the current Belzer Rebbe sits and the worn wooden *shtender* where his great uncle, Reb Ahraleh,[9] used to sit. The acoustics are designed so that a single *chazan* can reach thousands of worshippers without amplification. And the walls, they told me, contain some of the old stones from the original synagogue in Belz, Ukraine.[10]

Then they took me down to their office, sat me down in front of a tape recorder. They wanted me to sing the Belzer *niggunim* I had learned as a child. Some of these were known to them, but they wanted to hear how I remembered them: many of the *niggunim* had sped up since the more meditative style of the Old Country. One of the tunes, using words from the personal plea recited by the *chazan* on the Days of Awe, was composed by my *elter-zaida*. They were so happy to hear those old *niggunim* sung in the old way. So that's one story in a life of *niggun*.

The *niggunim* I learned as a child were not confined to the Belz. As I began to near my bar mitzvah, Pop would often take me with him to the Oiseh Chesed *shtiebel* in Leopoldstadt, Vienna's second district, an area known as "Matzah Island" because of the large concentration of Orthodox Jews there. Matzah Island had many dozens of these small, informal shuls, but the Oiseh Chesed *shtiebel* was for the Hasidic *chevrah kadisha*, the "holy fellowship" of volunteers that prepared the bodies of Vienna Hasidim for burial. As a *Kohen*, my father was forbidden to even be in the same room as the bodies themselves, so his contribution to the organization was to keep the books and records. He served as a *gabbai* at Oiseh Chesed, assigning the honors and calling people up to the Torah. On Shabbos, Pop loved to go to the early minyan, so he could linger over *Kiddush* afterward with his friends and sing.

The *chevrah kadisha* was an unusual organization, because it included Hasidim from many different sects. Most of the Hasidim, if they were Bobover, they would go to the Bobov *shtieblach*, and if they were Belzer Hasidim, they had their *shtieblach* as well. If you were a Hassid of a more independent mind, though, you went to the Oiseh Chesed. They all brought their *niggunim* of origin with them, so the *shtiebel* was a wonderful place for me to learn new tunes.

One example I remember was sung by the leader of the *chevrah kadisha*, Avrom Geiger. Back then he was known as "the Geiger" because of the tough reputation he had acquired as *gabbai* and gate-keeper for the Bluzhover Rebbe. But we called him Reb Avrumche, and I remember him as a man with a beautiful beard and a wonderful smile. In a *shtiebel*, where different members took turns leading the davening, you got to know a person for his davening style and his *niggunim*, as well as for his character. When Reb Avrumche davened, he and his two sons would sing "Keil Adon" to a march. When the kaiser came to visit, Reb Avrumche told me, the local kapellmeister would play a little march to honor the changing of the guard. The local Rebbe would say to the *chazan*, "*Khap es marshel*"—catch the march, and teach it to the *meshorerim*, the choir boys. Come Shabbos morning, he went to the davening and said to the *chazan*, "Did you *khap* the march of the emperor?" Yes. "*Mit die meshorerim?*" Yes.

"*Nu*," he says, "then for 'Keil Adon [God, the Lord],' sing the emperor's march." And that's how Avrom Geiger learned it. Because we want to bring the noble music to *ha-Shem*! When I was in school in Vienna, they would teach us how to sing Beethoven's setting of Psalm 19, "The heavens declare the glory of God"—and that was in a *Jewish* school. The whole world of *niggun* borrows in that way.

These happy times came to an end in my early teens. Germany's Anschluss with Austria destroyed Jewish life in Vienna, a prolonged and bitter process that began in the spring of 1938, immediately after the Nazis occupied Austria. We left the country the following winter, shortly after *Kristallnacht*, beginning a long trek that ultimately brought us to the United States.

Niggun Journeys

We came to rest first in Belgium, where we lived for a time in Antwerp. Pop found various places to daven, among them the *shtiebel* of the Vizhnitzer Hasidim, so I learned some of their *niggunim* as well.[11] This was also the age at which I began following my own heart in choosing the kind of Yiddishkeit I was drawn to.

My soul at that time was deeply troubled. Adolescence can be a hyperrational stage at the best of times, and the suffering I was witnessing, including our own, was sorely testing my faith in a God who seemed to have withdrawn from the world. I have often told the story of how I poured theological ridicule on a local class of Orthodox Jewish boys in Antwerp and how a teacher there, rather than argue with me, showed me a passage from Maimonides that expressed similar reservations. That teacher was Barukh Merzel, a warm and gentle man who would change the direction of my spiritual life.

Merzel soon became something of a mentor to me, as he was to so many other boys. After a while that school was taken over by the Gerrer Hasidim, so we moved into the cellar of Barukh Merzel's parents' house. That cellar became our domain, and we had great times. The most wonderful part was on Shabbos afternoon, when the light was fading. We wouldn't talk very much, but we would sing, *niggun* after *niggun* after *niggun*, until it was so dark that it was time for *Havdalah.* I learned so many *niggunim* that way.

Soon Merzel invited me to join a group of diamond cutters he worked with. He had studied Chabad Hasidism at a yeshiva in Heide, a small town west of the city. The dean of students there was Rabbi Moshe Chekhoval, originally from Kishinev in what is now Moldova. Moshe Chekhoval was a diamond merchant. He worked two days at the diamond exchange, to earn a living; the rest of the time he was at the yeshiva. Barukh Merzel and others worked as diamond cutters. Six days a week, I would join a group of young men in a large workroom filled with special lathes. Diamond cutting makes a tremendous racket, and often we would sit around a large table and sing Hasidic melodies at the tops of our voices. I still remember those tunes today. I would often celebrate Shabbos and holidays with them as well, davening and studying and singing.

Maybe transforming rough-cut stones into polished gems qualified Merzel and the diamond cutters to redeem a troubled teenager from his doubts, for the men had a profound effect on me. Until then, growing up, the Hasidism I identified with was more a family heritage and way of life than a spiritual choice. Where else would a boy go but

with his father? Studying and singing in the diamond cutters' fellowship would change that. Their brand of Chabad Hasidism shaped my
own *avodat ha-Shem*, service to God, from that time on.

They added to my store of *niggunim* as well. We have a saying:
"One who attributes a quote to the person who said it, brings redemption to the world."[12] This suggests a similar approach to *niggunim*.
For example, Merzel taught me a *niggun* that he learned from Moshe
Chekhoval. This *niggun* had a special lineage; you will not find it in
the standard collection of Chabad *niggunim*. Moshe Chekhoval had
studied with Reb Avrohom Schneerson, whose daughter married Reb
Yosef Yitzchak, the sixth Lubavitcher Rebbe. Chabad, now associated
solely with Lubavitch, once had other lineages as well, chains of tradition now largely extinct. Reb Avrohom himself was not part of the
Lubavitch lineage; the *niggun* was passed down through the Chabad
lines of Nezhin, once a center of Chabad Hasidism in Ukraine, and
of Kapust (Kopys) in Belarus. The Kapushte people believed that this
was one of ten *niggunim* that Reb Schneur Zalman himself had written, a direct link to the Alter Rebbe, who founded Chabad at the
end of the 1700s. So *niggunim*, like stories, have their journeys in the
world, and that's how this one came down to me.

The name of the *niggun*, Merzel told me, was "A Man's Wisdom
Lights Up His Face" (Ecclesiastes 8:1). The word for wisdom,
chokhmah, is particularly important to Chabad Hasidism, whose
name—CHaBa"D—derives from the acronym for *Chokhmah, Binah,*
and *Da'at*, the three intellectual spheres (*sefirot*) in the classic kabbalistic system of divine attributes. Something about singing this *niggun*,
"A man's wisdom lights up his face," raises your awareness of the
face you show to the outside world. You sing, "*Chokhmas odom to'ir
ponov*," and you want to just *shine* to the *Ribboyno sh'l oylom*, the Holy
One! It's a wonderful *niggun*.

Soon Antwerp, too, became unsafe for Jews, and we were all
dispersed. Reb Moshe Chekhoval survived the war; he came to the
United States on a ship that brought almost a thousand Jewish refugees to an internment camp in Oswego, New York, in 1944.[13] My
family, too, had reached the States by that time. My friend Avraham

Weingarten and I made sure that Reb Moshe had special matzah for Passover and later visited him in Oswego one rainy day. He was released from the internment camp after the war and settled in the United States with his wife, who was also a wonderful person. Sadly, both he and his wife were killed some years later by criminals.

Barukh Merzel was taken to Auschwitz, but he survived and eventually made *aliyah* to Israel. I met him years later in Yerushalayim. He gave me a couple of wonderful *s'forim*, books of Jewish philosophy that he wrote, and I thanked him a great deal for all he had done. He was such a generous soul.

My affiliation with the Chabad-Lubavitch movement would last for the next thirty years, and their teachings have influenced me to this day, especially the profound personal example of the sixth Lubavitcher Rebbe, Reb Yosef Yitzchak Schneerson, whose yeshiva I joined when we came to the United States in 1941. America turned out to be wonderfully fertile ground for the learning and sharing of *niggunim.*

The Songs of Chabad

Unlike the adherents of other Hasidic groups, many who found their way to the Lubavitcher Rebbe in Brooklyn were not born to Chabad families. Often—as with our old Oiseh Chesed *shtiebel* in Vienna—they came from other lineages, bringing their *niggunim* with them. Brooklyn was also home to a large number of other sects, and I would occasionally visit their Rebbes or yeshivot and pick up *niggunim* there.

The Hasidic way of life is almost impossible to imagine without *niggunim.* Typical to Hasidic communities, for example, are *tisch niggunim,* tunes sung at the Rebbe's table. These have many different moods, depending on the occasion. Some, particularly on Shabbos and holidays, are *z'mirot,* poems written throughout the ages. These are matched to different melodies: this one will have a Russian flavor, that one more of a Hungarian feel, a third one a Sephardic melody. Friday night *z'mirot* are generally *freilach* (happy) songs—a lot of waltzes and some great table-bangers. Shabbos morning is a little more calm. Finally, at *se'udah shelishit*, the "third meal" late on Shabbos afternoon, we would go slow, singing those *ga'agu'im niggunim*, the *niggunim* of longing for a *yom she-kulo Shabbos*, a day devoted entirely to peace and rest. Much yearning comes out in these songs, which are very beautiful, special melodies. You're sitting in fellowship with the light fading, as we boys did with Barukh Merzel in his father's cellar, feeling, "Oy, Shabbos will soon be over. How can we hold onto these holy feelings and take them forward with us into the week? Where will we get the energy that we need in order to raise every day to the level of Shabbos?" The feeling that wells up in you at such times can help align your spirit for the whole week.

Hasidic sects differed in their approach to *niggunim*. The *niggunim* of the Hasidim from Galicia make you feel good in the belly; most of them are less inclined to longing than those of the Russian sects.[14] The Modzhitz Hasidim place a great value on music.[15] I once went to visit them in Williamsburg with my friend Avraham Weingarten, and I still remember a tune I learned from the Modzhitzer Rebbe at his *tisch*. Avraham later sang a Modzhitz tune on an album called *Hasidic Tunes for Dancing and Rejoicing* that came out on Folkways.

The Chabad were more inclined to emphasize meditative, *devekus niggunim* at that time. I never saw my teacher, Reb Yosef Yitzchak, get as angry as he did one day when he asked us to sing a certain *niggun* at a *fabrengen*. The person who was leading us speeded up, until the Rebbe banged on the table and said, "*Echad ba-peh ve-echad ba-lev!* One in your heart, another on your lips!" He was saying, "You're already thinking about the next note while you're singing this one here! Don't spoil this *niggun* for me." And he made us sing the *niggun* again, this time with more *neshomeh*, more soul.

Reb Yosef Yitzchak charged a man named Reb Shmuel Zalmanov with the task of documenting the Chabad *niggunim* of his time. The Zalmanovs were a family of Chabad Hasidim from way back, and Shmuel Zalmanov was one of the great singers even back in Otvosk, outside of Warsaw, where the Rebbe had a yeshiva. He was a wonderful person, but he didn't know how to write music, and the guy he collaborated with transposed the *niggunim* exactly as Zalmanov sang them, regardless of the key. This made the notation difficult for people to follow, because instead of using keys that were easy to play in, they often used keys in which all the notes were *a hin un a her,* as we say in Yiddish—here and there. Nevertheless, Chabad's "Book of Niggunim" (*Sefer ha-Niggunim*)—Zalmanov's collection, plus other work that followed—eventually grew to almost 350 *niggunim* in various categories, according to mood and how they were used. These included the following:

- Liturgical *niggunim,* including trope and nusach for Shabbos, holidays, and Days of Awe.
- Special *niggunim* that were composed by one of the Lubavitcher Rebbes themselves and reserved for special occasions.
- Short, catchy *niggunim* for dancing, along with other joyful *niggunim* (*niggunei simchah*) of the kind favored by Reb Menachem Mendel, the seventh Lubavitcher Rebbe. There were even a couple of "victory *niggunim,*" martial tunes that Chabad tradition attributed to the military musicians of Napoleon Bonaparte. We would sing Napoleon's march after *Ne'ilah* at the closing of Yom Kippur.
- *Niggunim* of yearning (*ga'agu'im*).
- *Devekus niggunim, niggunim* for cleaving to God, including one or two known as *hokhonoh* or preparation *niggunim.* Reb Menachem Mendel, especially, before he delivered a *mymar* or discourse, would give a sign to start such a *niggun.*
- *Niggunui hisva'adus* (presence *niggunim*) for *fabrengens.* In my time these were not the huge gatherings that would later take place at "770" (the Chabad headquarters at 770 Eastern Parkway in Crown Heights, Brooklyn) with Reb Menachem Mendel. I'm talking about a *shtiebeleh,* where about twenty or thirty Hasidim would gather to sit in God's presence and talk about how to serve God better. One of the older Hasidim would be the *rosh ha-medabrim,* the speaker. He would begin with a *niggun,* either starting one himself or asking somebody: *Zog a nig'n.* Sometimes he would specify, "*Zog* Reb Hillel's *nig'n,*" if there was one he liked and thought appropriate. A *niggun hisva'adus* is a *tisch*

niggun, but a serious *niggun*, not a banger; its purpose is to prepare the people, to bring everyone into a closer feeling, to slow you down and get you into the deeper way of thinking.

One fall day around 1950, we at the Chabad yeshiva were holding a *fabrengen*, a gathering to celebrate the Hebrew date, the nineteenth of Kislev, the day in 1798 that the Alter Rebbe was sprung from a Russian jail. The *fabrengen* was a little more subdued than usual: Reb Yosef Yitzchak had been ill, and very few people were admitted to his presence. A lot more of us stood along the upper half of the staircase that led up to where he was, singing those wonderful *niggunim* of longing that expressed how we felt, that we were outside and couldn't go in. Along comes Beryl Chazkin, who was one of the *gabbayim* of the Rebbe, and he says, "Shloimeh and Zalman, come in. The Rebbe has asked for you."

I had first met Shlomo Carlebach some twelve years before. Before our travels had begun, when my family was still living in Austria, we used to spend summers at a town called Bad-Vöslau. There was a natural spa there, where the water came out of the ground warm and smelling from sulfur. People from many miles around would travel there for healing, including the Sanzer Rov and some of the other Rebbes.

One day my mother found something suspicious in the liver of a chicken she had bought, so she sent me on the trolley over to a rabbi who lived in the nearby town of Baden bei Wien, a man who was not only a *rov* (rabbi) and a *posek* (a rabbi with the authority to decide questions of *halakhah,* Jewish law and practice) but had a secular doctorate as well. I showed up at his door carrying the chicken, knocked, and said I had a *shyleh*, a question on halakhic matters, for Herr Doktor Rabbiner. So they showed me in. There were two boys there playing ping-pong—twin brothers, a little younger than I. After the *rov* settled the matter with the chicken, I stayed to play ping-pong with the two boys until it was time for me to take the chicken back home to my mother. That was the first time I met Shlomo Carlebach and his brother, Eli Chaim. I did not see them again until we met in the Chabad yeshiva in Brooklyn.

Now the Rebbe had summoned us, so Shlomo and I went in. The Rebbe had a *le-chayim* poured for us, and then he said, *"Kedai az ir zolt onhoybn fohren in di colleges,* It would be a good idea for you to start traveling to the colleges," to spread the message of Chabad.

It was an important moment for the movement, the first time Lubavitch sent *sh'luchim,* emissaries, to the secular academic world. Shlomo and I were in both our twenties at the time. We had each received our *s'mikheh* (rabbinical degrees) and taken our first positions as rabbis at our own little shuls. Now we found ourselves tasked with creating a "wheelchair accessible" approach to Jewish life and liturgy that Jews without much technical knowledge could relate to. We went out together the first few times, to give each other strength, singing and talking and davening with students to whom much of this was new. Music and *niggunim* would be a big part of what we had to offer them.

Adventures in *Niggun*

Back in those early days, at college campuses or working as a rabbi in Fall River and New Bedford, Massachusetts, I used to sing with people and teach them *niggunim.* I noticed early on, though, that people could sing a *niggun* without much conscious content going on. It's like singing "Kumbaya, my Lord" without any notion of Whom we are addressing. Those who first sang that song were saying, "Come by *here,* Lord"—it was real to them. I wanted to show people: *niggunim* are prayers, word-less prayers!

Shlomo Carlebach had the same experience. If you look at all the tunes Reb Shlomo wrote, the words are prayer words. He tried to show people through example: you think you're singing, but you're really davening! He began on piano in those early years, singing subtle and beautiful things. His *"Mimkomcho,"* for example, on the first album, *Haneshama Lach,* is a truly lovely *niggun.* His *"Eshet Chayil"*—I could go on and on. Later he picked up a guitar; he couldn't shlep a piano with him, and keyboards were not yet widely available. He

poured all the *neshomeh* of the old world into a simple tune and a few
folk chords. Maybe that was why his *niggunim* captured so many:
they spoke to both the old world and the new. Shlomo was a remarkable bridge. He created a wonderful transition for us, becoming the
most famous "exporter" of *niggunim* from the Hasidic world.

When Shlomo davened, you stopped thinking about yourself.
Even if you didn't know anything else, even if you knew next to
nothing about Yiddishkeit, you would be thinking about God when
Shlomo davened. He would lead people in a few *niggunim* and then
tell a story in between; that's why I called him the genius of virtuous
reality, because he made you want to live like those righteous people
in his stories. Sometimes, when he saw that people were running away
with a *niggun* and not singing it in the proper frame of mind, he
would stop and show them how it should be sung. Most of the time,
though, Shlomo felt it was enough to get the whole group into a big
WE, instead of *I*.

When I taught a *niggun*, I wanted people to know *explicitly* that
this is a prayer, even if they didn't know any Hebrew. So I tried writing lyrics for a few of the tunes, attempting to convey the *kavanah* of
the *niggun* through words—and in English, so the people I taught it
to would know and understand.

I tried this with several kinds of *niggunim*. One was of the type
we used to call a preparation (*hakhanah*) *niggun*, which the Hasidim
would always sing before the Rebbe would give a teaching. I wrote:

> *For the sake of my soul,*
> *I search for a goal,*
> *and I find none other*
> *than You, O Lord.*[16]

Another *niggun* was attributed to the Baal Shem Tov, and I tried to
get into his mind-set, to write words the soul itself might sing:

> *As I sit and I think*
> *I remember my heavenly home*
> *As I sit and I think*

I feel the nearness of God's Throne.

Lord, my light,
Heart's delight
Thee I seek alone.[17]

I chose another *niggun* by Reb Mikhele Zlotchover, a *niggun* the Baal Shem Tov loved so much that he asked for his followers to sing it around his deathbed. He promised that whenever people sang that *niggun*, he would join them in prayer, even after he had passed from this world. I first heard the story of this *niggun* from my teacher, Reb Yosef Yitzchak, who, just before he died, left us with a teaching called "*Bosi le-Gani*" (I Came to My Garden).[18] So I wrote words to the *niggun* by Reb Mikhele that began, "I came to my garden, from beyond time and space / To meet my bride, my beloved, at our special meeting place."

Finally, I wrote words to a *niggun* by Reb Schneur Zalman himself, the Alter Rebbe.

I believed that writing words to these *niggunim* could convey something of their inner essence to people who did not grow up with this tradition. On the other hand, writing English lyrics to such weighty *niggunim* required a certain amount of chutzpah, so I showed the lyrics to the seventh Rebbe, Reb Menachem Mendel Schneerson, to get his take on it. The first three are okay, he told me. But "*tcheppe nisht mit dem Alten Rebben's niggun*, don't mess with the Alter Rebbe's tune."

Now, the majority of Chabad *niggunim* have no words. Chabad believe that *niggunim* transport us to places words cannot—that, if anything, words limit the *niggun*'s power to induce *devekut*. Most of the Hasidic *niggunim* were prayers in sound. The contemplative *hitbonenut niggunim*, especially, are sung to immerse us ever deeper in the world of spirit and so have no words. Of course there are exceptions, depending on occasion and circumstance. Some Chabad songs, like "*U-faratztah*" (Burst Forth), became famous even outside Chabad circles. And Chabadniks were always open to adjusting their approach as the situation demanded. Once, when I was in New Haven, we had a guest for Shabbos, a Hasid from the Lubavitch yeshiva back in Otwock (Otvosk), Poland. So we didn't sing any *z'mirot*, the traditional Shabbos songs, deferring to the Chabad custom of sticking to wordless *niggunim* instead. "Why don't you sing the *z'miros?*" he asked us. "There will be children in the house, God willing. You have to sing *z'miros.*" And he was right.

Reb Menachem Mendel, too, understood that words could help my people sing these *niggunim* as prayers.

I have not used my words for the Alter Rebbe's tune since then, but I continued to experiment with different ways of leading with song, searching for spiritual gateways that people would find welcoming. Sometimes I'd use recorded music. At the Chavurah in Somerville, Massachusetts, an early experimental minyan from which the *Jewish Catalog* books emerged, we would meditate before we started davening. I would put on the *Lentos* of Mozart and Schubert in the background; at the solstice or equinox, I would play one of the *Four Seasons* of Vivaldi. I believed the music would take people out of their normal discursive thoughts and into a more contemplative and heart-centered place. Leading a Friday night service, I would turn the lights down low, put on a strobe light, and put on a record like *Edge of Freedom*, letting Cantor Raymond Smolover and the NFTY Levites lead the service as our *chazanim* that night. The type of folk-rock they played, and the yeshiva rock that came in a little later, spoke to the young people in the 1960s, as the Viennese choirs had to me.

As a leader, though, I sometimes felt conflicted when the melody clashed with the words. You might have a melody that was very good for getting people to sing, but misleading as to *kavanah*. Even Shlomo sometimes had a problem with that. As demand for him grew, Shlomo became more pressed for time. He would come in, greet everybody, give them a hug; then he would want to get them revved up quick. So he taught them a simple melody, and soon everyone was singing loud and dancing with him. But even Shlomo's *kavanah* could sometimes feel conflicted, the melodies and words facing two different directions. The line from Psalms might be troubled, while the tune was jumpy and hopsy-dopsy, as if we remembered nothing of the psalmist's tsuris, nothing of the *krechts* he felt inside. So everyone would be gaily singing, "Fro-om the strai-aits, I ca-all to the Lord!" But the soul would feel: where are the straits? Because the soul knows despair and hopelessness and needs to express it in the davening. Shlomo knew that himself and felt it deeply, but his service to God lay in reaching people.

So we both experimented, and we both learned, trying to balance between an approach that welcomed all comers and staying true to the deepest *kavanah* and needs of every human soul. I once made a recording called *Your Glory Shines: Prelude for a Rendezvous with the Beloved.* I wanted it to be like a Shabbos *mikveh* for the ears, the aural equivalent of immersing ourselves in the ritual bath on Friday afternoons. I imagined people in the kitchen, preparing for Shabbos, surrounded by Friday night *niggunim,* the yeast already beginning to rise within their souls, which so need the peace Shabbos can bring.

Modern spirituality can leave little place for longing. The deep and unfulfilled yearnings of soul are troubling sometimes; they can remind us of places we're reluctant to go. We seek a calm that is close to complacency, away from the sense in the old spirituals that "God is gonna trouble the waters." *How will I become what I need to become? How will I serve in the way in which I need to serve?* The *ga'agu'im* or longing *niggunim* that raise up these unspoken questions can create a sacred space that all can share.

Getting to the Place of En-chant-ment

Getting into a davening space is easier and more rewarding if you start with a *niggun* or two that you like. Sometimes the heart wants to daven, and the mind starts arguing. But, as the great cantor and educator Max Helfman said once, "you can't argue with a song or a dance!"

Niggunim cause a shift in consciousness. They are a gateway to the world of *Yetzirah,* the world of feeling. Most of the time, on most levels of our being, we live in the prosaic world. In prayer we want to shift our center of gravity toward the right brain, to feel closer to

the soul-unfolding that davening can bring. We can do that through
enchantment—en-*chant*-ment, singing ourselves into a different way
of being.

Only you can know what truly works for you. Start by gathering
a few tunes that help you connect, and sing those. Especially if you
daven privately at home, during the week, it's good to know which
niggunim will get you into your davening space. You go into your
prayer space, where you have your tallis and tefillin and siddur, or
whatever you use, and you just start singing. You drape your tallis
over your shoulder, kiss the fringes. You're in a different place already.
You've already begun.

Making Up Your Own

Sing to God a *new* song, as the psalmist says—and who knows better
than he, who wrote so many? Give yourself permission to make up
your own *niggunim.* "A person should not have an ear only for the
songs of others," said Reb Yisroel of Modzhitz, "but also to hear the
songs that sing from within his own heart."[19] Snatches of tunes will
emerge from your soul and jump to your lips, if you let them, ready
to be sung to God.

Reb Nachman of Breslov teaches that each and every shepherd
has his own special *niggun,* one shaped by the places to which he takes
his flocks.[20] Each place has its own grasses, Reb Nachman says, and
each kind of grass its own song, and from the songs of the grasses the
shepherd's song is woven.[21] A *niggun,* the Breslover teaches, "clarifies
and purifies the spirit." *Niggun* is what makes our souls human.

Making up your own *niggunim* is a very freeing thing. Once you
open your mind and heart to the possibility, you may find that tunes
come to you, as if on their own accord. Many songwriters speak of
the feeling that the tune was already there; their task was simply to
set it down. A *niggun* doesn't need words, of course. But any verse
that touches you can also be the core of a good *niggun,* even if those
words have been set to music before. I once asked a group how many
tunes they knew for the words "*Hinei ma tov u-mah na'im.*" They

sang several. Then someone said, "Let's make up another one!" So I composed one on the spot.

Tunes have come to me in happy times and sad. When my son Shalom was getting married, I wrote a new tune for *"Od yishama be-arei Yehudah*—again shall be heard from the hills of Judea," a famous stanza from the wedding blessings.[22] Another came to me when I was sitting shiva for my father in Boulder. Many people came to visit and support me: all the Jewish Buddhists from Naropa University came out of the woodwork to help me make a minyan. On the last day of the shiva, a melody came to me for *"Nachamu,"* the great comfort prophecy of Isaiah after the First Temple was destroyed.[23] It helped a great deal to console me then, and I sang it again often, on Shabbos *Nachamu,* when we read Isaiah's prophecy, or at the end of someone's shiva or *sh'loshim* (thirty-day) mourning periods.

In welcoming new *niggunim* to emerge, you may naturally be most inspired by the kind of music you know. Your tunes don't need to sound like klezmer. We're not in the Old Country anymore! The psalmist asks, "How can we sing the Lord a new song in a strange land?" (Psalm 137:4). The answer is to adapt the music of the land where you find yourself and to make it holy.

Don't worry about the limits of what you can or cannot do. I made up a tune once that I couldn't finish; it was to the words *"Ki er'eh shamekha,* when I behold Your heavens" (Psalm 8:4). Nevertheless, we included it in the spiral-bound collection *Into My Garden,*[24] describing it as "a tantalizing unfinished sentence which ..." and leaving the rest to our readers' imaginations. *Nu,* so you're not sure where your tune is going yet. Sing it anyway! Maybe "the work is not upon you to finish" (Pirkei Avot 2:21). Someone else may complete your tune someday.

Leading *Niggunim*

How do you lead with a song? My students ask me sometimes. They love the idea of leading a group in singing a *niggun.* They feel the need for it. They realize the transformative effect it can have. But they don't feel qualified; they don't feel they have "permission." Their voice isn't good enough, they can't accompany themselves on an instrument—all the objections that the mind puts up.

First of all, never doubt the effect that a simple *niggun* can have to move people. Every Shabbos I can, when I am at home in Boulder, I go to the local Chabad place to daven. I wasn't happy at first with the way we were going into the davening: we each said our morning blessings at home, then launched right into *P'sukei de-Zimrah* as soon as we gathered. I felt that starting with one or two of the old *niggunim* was important. So from early days I started a *minhag* (custom) that we don't begin davening until we sing a serious *niggun*.

One Shabbat, it was just before Purim, so I started singing a happy *niggun* instead: "*A ganz yohr freylach, a ganz yohr freylach!*"— we should be "all year happy," a traditional *niggun* for Adar, the month of Purim. Afterward the local rabbi said, "That's good—but now let's sing a serious *niggun*." I was so happy that he, too, now felt the need to get into a davening space in that way. Sometimes I could go home right after I sing those first *niggunim*. I feel like I've davened already!

The quality of your voice is far less important than your *kavanah*. Imagine I sing, *Ahhhhhh*, a note on a certain pitch, and you sing with me, *Ahhhhhhhhh*. Sometimes the members of a choir will do that before they begin a song, so now they are attuned together. Singing a *niggun* together is similar: it can attune us to the same soul note, the same spiritual pitch. The whole point of a *niggun* is to take people to a level of soul vibration, if you will, that cannot be reached with words. As a leader, then, I have to do *hakhoneh*, to undergo a certain degree of spiritual preparation, to do a *Shiviti*.[25] I need to be attuned myself, to get my heart aligned, so that when I begin to sing, people can join me in that place. Anyone with the right *kavanah* can do the same.

Repetition is important. The aim is not just to run through the *niggun* a couple of times but to let it build—"soaking in the *niggun* (*er veykt zach in dem niggun*)," we used to say. Body language is important, too. Even if you are just singing on your own, get your body involved. Beat time on the table or your knee. Close your eyes. Sway back and forth if you can. Tell your body where you want to go, and let your body help communicate this to the rest of you. The Baal Shem Tov would sometimes ask his followers to put a hand on the shoulder of the person next to them as they sang. Forming a physical circle, he believed, would actualize the commandment to love your neighbor as yourself. If you're leading a group, modeling such behavior will be important.

As for accompanying yourself on an instrument, I was never able to play guitar, as Shlomo did. As a boy, I would have wanted to play the cello—that was where my heart was—but my left hand was never developed enough to play a typical stringed instrument. I could bow with the right hand but could never get any vibrato with the left: my fingers were never adept enough to do the wiggle right. I got a button accordion for my bar mitzvah, but my left hand wasn't up to that either, and we had to leave it behind in Vienna when Hitler came.

But I've always enjoyed davening with music. I played a little pennywhistle, and from pennywhistle to the clarinet isn't such a big step, so after we'd arrived in America, I bought a clarinet in a pawn shop in Manhattan. It had the Albert system keys, which was the system the old klezmer players used, because it was easier to bend the notes. I would bring the clarinet along to *fabrengens* or weddings of my friends and play. I've played a little flute, too, and keyboard. And I got into playing the autoharp, where one or two fingers could produce a chord, so I'd lead davening or weddings with that. Instruments are wonderful things to sing or dance or daven to. All you need are a few chords!

Outer Structure and Inner Soul

If we go a little deeper, on the other hand, there is no question that the seemingly simple accessibility of *niggun* can be deceptive sometimes. A *niggun* is like a person, with an outer form and an inner soul. You can pick up the outer form simply by listening to someone run through the tune a few times. But touching the inner *kavanah*, the intentionality, is not so easy.

Think about Torah *trope*. The main purpose of the *trope*, as we said earlier, is to help us with the meaning, like punctuation. Yet even adept readers can sometimes work so hard on the *trope* that they don't make sense of the words. For this reason, when I teach people, I ask them to first read the text to me straight, for meaning, and then to include the *trope*, but lightly. A couple of years ago, I read the Purim *megillah* for a gathering at the Boulder JCC—Orthodox, Conservative, everybody could come. I said the blessing. Then, instead of reading the *megillah* with the *trope*, I read it simply as a story, with expression, the way you might to a roomful of kids. One of the rabbis there was really very unhappy about this at first. The *trope* is there, the sticklers say, you have to read it with the *trope*! Later that same rabbi told me, "That was the first time I heard the *megillah* and could understand the story."

Another challenge is that our prayers and texts travel across many different emotional landscapes—sometimes within a single paragraph. I used to do a lab with my students in which I asked them to say Psalm 23 in seven different attitudes. One might be loving: "The Lord is my shepherd, *mmmm*. I lack for nothing! *Ahhhh*." Another might be sarcastic: "The Lord is my shepherd, huh? What, I lack for nothing?" I wanted people to try and paint that picture with different colors. Because "Yea, though I walk through the valley of the shadow of death" comes from a whole different place than "Thou anointest my head with oil"! When they were finished, I said to them, "Read it now one more time, and see if you can say each line with the appropriate affect, with the emotions that you hear behind the words."

We are not merely singing melodies—this is the point. A *niggun* is a path to God, a "song of ascension." But we must set out along that path! We must travel with that intention in mind. If you're not yet ready to sing God a new song, then sing an old one. Get together with friends, tell stories, swap songs. Soak in the *niggunim*. See how far they can take you.

DAVENING IN THE FOUR WORLDS
A Deep Structure of Prayer

One evening, when I was studying in the Lubavitcher yeshiva, some of the older Hasidim got together and had a *farbrengen,* a gathering where songs are sung, stories are told, and spiritual matters are discussed. Our teachers sat at a table with some vodka and fruit. Twenty or thirty *bochurim*—students like myself, eighteen or nineteen years old—stood around them, listening. Conversation was mostly in Yiddish.

Rabbi Shmuel Levitan spoke first. Reb Shmuel had worked as an emissary in the mountainous Caucasus region, teaching the Jews of Azerbaijan and Georgia. He had later been arrested for heading a seminary to train rabbis and *shochtim* (ritual slaughterers) in Belorussia and sent to Siberia. Word was that followers of the Rebbe had sent him a hollowed-out melon filled with wine when he was in prison, so that he should be able to make a seder with four cups of wine on Pesach. Now he was provost and *mashpiya* (spiritual mentor) at our yeshiva, and he was disappointed with our spiritual development. The younger yeshiva students, he grumbled, were not immersing themselves deeply enough in prayer.

When I heard him say this, I took some schnapps, a whole tumbler full. I said, "*le-chayim,*" and drank it down. Then I turned to him and said in Yiddish, "*Ir hot uns keyn mol nisht gezogt, vos's tut zich ba' eich in harts'n ven ir daven't!* How could you blame us for not going deep into contemplative prayer when you have never shared with us what goes on inside of you when you pray?"

He took umbrage at this. "How dare you ask such a question?" I listened until he had finished chewing me out, but I stood my ground. "*Torah hi,*" I said, quoting a well-known phrase from the Talmud, "*ve-le-limud ani tzarich.* It is a sacred teaching, and I need to learn it."[1]

Rabbi Levitan then turned to Rabbi Yisroel Jacobson, who later founded a yeshiva in Crown Heights. Rabbi Jacobson guided us in our inner work, including spiritual feedback sessions with our fellow students. I also studied Hasidic texts with him, for three hours each day. "He is one of your boys," Rabbi Levitan said. "You tell him!"

Rabbi Jacobson sputtered in protest. "I have worked on my prayer my whole life. You expect me to tell it to you standing on one leg?"

Then Rabbi Avrohom Pariz spoke up. He was my teacher as well, a man with piercing black eyes that seemed to be able to see to the depths of your very soul. His power as a teacher lay not in his verbal explanations, but in his utter conviction. The spiritual mysteries were living worlds to him; when he spoke of them, you could see them as if with your own eyes.

"He is right," he said. "He needs to hear what goes on inside."

Reb Shmuel and Reb Yisroel turned to him and said, "All right, then it is up to you to tell him!"

Now it was Reb Avrohom's turn to take a tumbler of schnapps. Even he needed to overcome a natural reluctance, to free himself of inhibition in talking about these things. The schnapps was almost like a protest. *How can I tell you what's going on inside of me in my davenen? It's private. Why should I tell you about that?*

"*Le-chayim,*" he said, and drank it down. Then he closed his eyes, swayed slowly back and forth for a little while, and began to talk to us about his own prayer. He described his own inner, sacred journey, moving through the prayer service from the morning blessings on. Finally, when he came to the threshold of the silent *Amidah,* he stopped. "The rest is between God and me," he said. "I'm not going to talk about it."

True prayer is like the iceberg: little that is visible on the surface, much that happens below. What goes on inside the true and passionate davener? Where does he go? What worlds does he visit? People have asked me to repeat what Rabbi Pariz said that day, but I cannot. His words are no longer in the top drawers of my memory: I have so internalized them that they have become integral to my own prayer. The best I can do is to share with you something of what I have learned in my life about deep prayer, for which the teaching of Rabbi Pariz that evening was a foundation stone. I can only try to do as he did, to tell you some of the things that happen to me in prayer before the living God.

The Deep Structure of Prayer

Many of us think of prayer as a religious duty. Some take this seriously, loping smoothly through the well-worn formulas as a daily obligation. Others draw the line at an hour or two of synagogue on High Holidays. Both approaches have lost contact with the original prayer urge, the irrepressible surge of gratitude or the crushing hopelessness that brings forth true prayer. The idea that we ourselves might stand before God and pray from the heart is almost unthinkable.

But our souls accept only one outcome when it comes to prayer: transformation. We do not wish just to spin our mental wheels: We want to be changed. We want to be moved. We want to end in a better place than where we started. Our souls yearn for this. If we really mean the words we say, how can we help but be moved?

That's why davening takes us on a journey. This is especially true in the morning prayers. The Rabbis imagined us starting the minute we swing our feet over the side of the bed. We may wake up stiff and rumpled and bleary-eyed; we might feel cranky and old, already dreading half the tasks we need to do today. No matter: the invitation to prayer says "come as you are." We will start slowly, rise and go deeper, and return in a better frame of mind and spirit. Prayer properly and truly done—even if we only spend twenty good minutes—will leave us feeling cleansed and at peace, ready to greet the day with gratitude, energy, and purpose.

In order for this transformation to take place, however, we need to understand something of prayer's inner structure. We have already written about this in *Jewish with Feeling*; we'll cover similar ground here but with different emphases.

A graph of our morning prayer journey would be simple, a line that starts where we are and rises gradually to a peak before gently coming down again. Here are the five stages:

Gratitude   We start with the morning blessings (*Birkhot ha-Shachar*), simple statements that give thanks mostly for physical things. The gratitude they express grounds us in our bodies and our world.

Song   The morning blessings are followed by a set of "tuneful verses" (*P'sukei de-Zimrah*) drawn from the psalms. "Sing!" these psalms say. "Praise the Lord!" If we choose to accept the psalms' invitation, we will end this section with our pulse rates humming and a smile in our hearts.

Knowledge   We start to go quieter and deeper as we begin the blessings of the *Shema*. Our thoughts become more contemplative, more cosmic, leading up to the *Shema* itself, the central Jewish statement of God's unity.

Petition   The silent *Amidah* invites each of us to speak directly to God about our wants and needs. With the *Shema* and *Amidah*, we attain the highest peak of our davening.

Descent   We come down off the mountain in the aftermath of the *Amidah*. We end with a prayer like *Aleinu*

58

or a song like *Adon Olam,* leaving us ready to
begin our day.

That is our journey: We get grounded in the physical, conscious
world. Then we get our pulses racing, singing God's praises, making a
joyful noise unto the Lord. Slowly, we move into more contemplative
material, until we rise to stand in silent *yichud* in one-on-one unification, face to face with God. And we descend.

But the trajectory I have just outlined is two-dimensional. If this
road map is to get us anywhere, we need to deepen our understanding of the topography involved, the plains and foothills and mountain peaks of prayer. We will experience a number of different inner
landscapes before we are through: physical, emotional, intellectual,
spiritual. So we need to go beyond a two-dimensional understanding.

We also need to share an understanding of whom we are speaking
to. This is one of the biggest difficulties Jews have today. Much of our
thinking about prayer is uncomfortable about "to whom it may concern." If we are to speak about prayer freely and without restraint, we
need to be clear about Whom we are addressing.

The teachings of kabbalah offer answers to questions like these.
So let us take a short journey into kabbalistic thinking and see whether
that can help us. If you are familiar with such terrain, you may prefer
to treat this as a series of meditations, knowing that an intellectual
understanding is only the beginning.

The Four Worlds

Imagine a glove. If we see an empty glove on a table, we know that it
is just a glove. But if we see a glove at the end of a sleeve, its material
taut, its fingers moving, we deduce the presence of a hand inside it.
We cannot see the hand, but we know it is there.

Yet the hand in the glove is not the end point. It is merely a
physical hand. That hand is controlled by a nervous system and the
nervous system by a mind, the intelligence and volition that move
the hand. And behind that intelligence? Other layers of reality: all

the ideas that the intelligence feeds upon, all the considerations and thought patterns that go into making a decision.

Each level points to a level beyond itself, and each new level is more complex than the last. Even a toddler can deduce the presence of a hand inside a moving glove. An older child will have a distinct sense of a human mind controlling the hand. But any real grasp of the cultural ideas and thought patterns that shape that intelligence will probably have to wait until the child goes to college. And only as fully grown adults, beings who know something of pain and mortality, gratitude and joy, can we gain a deep sense of the great Intelligence that lies beyond ours, the Will behind our will, the Compassion behind our compassion.

In the same way, the "faces of God" that we pray to point to the presence of an Infinite God beyond. None of these faces of God should be confused with the *Ein Sof.* None of them are Godself—yet all of them are God.

Such a layered view of reality is fundamental in kabbalah. Kabbalists sometimes portray this using the four letters of the divine name, the *yud-hey-vav-hey,* standing one atop the other. At the very top is the *yud.* The first *hey* stands beneath it, the *vav* under that, then the final *hey* on the bottom. Each letter represents another level of divine operation in the universe. *Gashmiyut,* what we might call actuality or corporeality, gets stronger as you go down the ladder. *Ruchaniyut,* the dimension of soul and spirit, gets stronger as you rise up. We call these the Four Worlds, and we give each world a name. The worlds rise from the "lowest" or most revealed world to the most formless and abstract:

Atzilut	The world of transcendence, or emanation (the *yud*)
Beriyah	The world of creation (the upper *hey*)
Yetzirah	The world of formation (the *vav*)
Asiyah	The world of action (the lower *hey*)

The kabbalists who imagined this structure were struggling with exactly the same question that we do when we open our lips in prayer: how do we bridge the great divide that stands between our everyday awareness and an unfathomable God? Of course, one does not need a kabbalistic education to pray. Many who live exemplary lives as Jews never give the Four Worlds a moment's thought. But learning something of this metaphoric language will deepen our experience of prayer the way light and shadow bring a simple line drawing alive on the page. Speaking this language will help us engage our whole selves in our prayers. It will enable us to broadcast on all wavelengths.

One of the biggest mistakes we make when it comes to prayer is leaving large chunks of ourselves out of the equation. We tend, as in many other things, to lead with our minds. But mind is not all we have! Our minds deal in concepts. To our bodies, on the other hand, concepts mean nothing. Our bodies speak in movement. The act of rising when the ark is open, for example, means something to our bodies. Standing, bowing, swaying, even dancing—all this is body language. The heart, on the other hand, needs relationship. Our minds might insist that we go directly to the Infinite when we think of God, but the heart doesn't want the Infinite; it wants a You it can confide in and take comfort in. The poetry of *Shir ha-Shirim*, the Song of Songs, speaks this language:

> *As I lay abed nights*
> *I sought the One whom my soul so loves.*
> *I sought Him, but I found Him not.*
> (SONG OF SONGS 3:1)

Oy! That's the heart, sighing and yearning for its Lover.

A Four Worlds understanding helps us see the morning prayers as a journey through four different landscapes, four distinct facets of human experience: physical, emotional, intellectual, and spiritual. Each facet has its own character; each communicates in its own language; each speaks to a different part of us. Learning to navigate the pathways of prayer will give depth and nuance to words that might otherwise seem formulaic. Our theological struggles will become easier as well. Let us examine each world in turn.

Asiyah: **The World of Action**

Asiyah means doing. The lowest level, the world of *Asiyah*, is the physical world, the world of action. When someone is good at getting things done, we say that the person is good in *Asiyah*.

A student of mine told me the following story. It's Rosh Hashanah, several hours into the davening. He's standing in synagogue with his eight-year-old son, and the little one is bored and restless. Suddenly the boy sees some people spreading sheets of newspaper on the floor in front of them. "What is that?" he asks his father. So his father explains: these people are preparing for *Aleinu*, because on the High Holidays, during *Aleinu*, some have the custom of getting down on their knees and prostrating themselves on the ground. "Cool!" the little boy says, enchanted by the idea. His father had never been able to bring himself to perform a full prostration before; something in him always held back, pride getting in the way of humility and submission. His little boy, though, saw getting down on the floor as an opportunity to give his restless arms and legs something to do. Seeing that his son was interested opened the gate for the father as well, and the two were able to do it together. The little boy understood instinctively what his father missed: We can't let the mind control everything. We need to give our bodies a chance to pray as well.

Asiyah is the world in which I do the morning blessings, thanking God for all the things that anchor me to this life. "Wake up," the soul tells the body, "and smell the universe!" Take a look at the list of morning blessings in your siddur, and you will see what I mean. You'll find them early in the morning service:

> Blessed are You, God, for helping us to know the difference between day and night.
>
> Blessed are You for making me who I am.
>
> Blessed are You for the solid ground beneath my feet as I get out of bed.
>
> Blessed are You for—*oy!*—straightening the bent.

Blessed are You for giving vision to the blind. How much sharper the world becomes when I put on my glasses!

Blessed are You for clothing the naked.

Blessed are You for supplying my every need. (The Rabbis understood this as referring to shoes, reminding us that shoes were once a luxury that not everyone could afford.)

Blessed are You for the strength You give to the weary.

Asiyah is the world of *tachlis*, the world of the concrete. One morning blessing that is especially emblematic of *Asiyah* is *Asher Yatzar*, "[The God] who created," which thanks God for helping our bodies function properly. Tradition asks us to say this after emerging from the bathroom.

Asiyah is the realm of the practical and the sensible—the stuff we apprehend with our senses. We're packing for our spiritual journey here, grounding ourselves in our physical bodies and in the here and now.

Yetzirah: The World of Formation

Yetzirah means formation. If we think about the world as a moment-by-moment miracle of renewed creation, *Yetzirah* is the world in which the divine *shefa*, the divine flow coming "down" to us, begins to take shape. In *Yetzirah* and *Beriyah* the sharply defined and bounded realites that we know are forming, but they have not yet taken on the concreteness they will assume in *Asiyah*.

Yetzirah, on a human level, is the world of feelings, the world of passion. It is the realm where love arises in our hearts. When we say, "I love you," we are not conveying information; our loved one has probably heard this before. Instead, we are sharing a feeling. Words are one type of feeling carrier; a hug, a special look, or a smile might convey the same thing. Davening in *Yetzirah* is that kind of declaration of our love for the Holy One.

Yetzirah is where I say the tuneful *Halleluyah*s, the *P'sukei de-Zimrah*. The mood is celebratory:

"*Hallelu!* Let's all praise!"

"*Ashrei yoshvei veitekha!* We're so happy to dwell in Your house!"

"*Shiru la-Shem shir chadash!* Sing unto the Lord a new song!"

The language here is plural. In *Yetzirah*, the realm of emotions and love, the boundaries between ourselves and others begin to feel permeable. What is the mystic experience if not a dissolution of boundaries? Ideally I do this with others. Instead of "I" and my individual wants and needs, I move toward the collective *we*. Something emerges when we sing *Halleluyah!* together, a chorus that is greater than its individual voices. Have you ever been in a synagogue when the room just seems to rise up in song? That is how davening feels when it comes from *Yetzirah*.

Sometimes I get together with my colleagues at Ohalah, the rabbinic organization associated with the Renewal movement. We do wonderful davening together, and I feel so proud of *us*. The feeling is very strong that the Jewish *brit*, our people's special and particular covenant with God, has manifested in the room. I can say, "Dear God, if we please You, we can feel proud of what we have done here today!"

Beriyah: The World of Creation

Imagine a person who has changed inside. Her thinking has evolved on certain things; her worldview is changing. She wants to make real changes in her life as well, but her partner does not understand this. He finds it threatening; he wants things to remain the way they are. But her convictions will not go away. She comes to him again. He says, "I love you," and tries to hold her close. "I'm as attracted to you as the day we were married," he says, but that's not what she's looking for this time. The old love is no longer enough: she needs understanding. She asks not only that his heart be open but that his mind reach to new places, that he support her in what she is trying to accomplish, in being the more realized person that she wants to be.

These are the realms of the lower and middle worlds. In kabbalistic terms, he's saying, "I'm attracted to you in *Asiyah*! I love you in *Yetzirah*!" She's saying, "Meet me in *Beriyah*." Can you imagine if a couple could share such a vocabulary and communicate on that level?

Beriyah is the home of thought. Yet in *Beriyah*, too, our analytical powers encounter the boundaries of anything we can claim to know or understand. *Beriyah* means creation, because the kabbalists imagined it as the world in which the Creator first has the idea to manifest as a created being or physical entity.

"*Beriyah* mind" yearns to tune in to the purpose of life and grasp the whole span of creation. The section of the morning prayers that speaks to *Beriyah* begins with the blessings before the *Shema*. If we are davening in a minyan, the leader begins with an invitation:

> *Barekhu et ha-Shem*—Let us all bless God,
>
> *ha-m'vorakh*—who is already blessed!

We recognize that our blessings are not unique, nor do they begin with us: they are part of a great cycle of blessing, like water that rises from the earth only to fall again as rain.

The scale here is one of systems, of heavenly orbs. Science is our friend here. Gazing at the stars or pondering magnificent photos of galaxies can only inspire us to daven these prayers with more *kavanah*. The stronger our sense of the miraculously improbable physics that underlies our very existence, the more our sense of thankfulness and wonder grows. We first bless the

> *Yotzer or u-vorei choshekh*—Former of light, Creator of darkness,
>
> *oseh shalom*—who makes peace between them,
>
> *u-vorei et ha-kol*—and creates the All.

Ours is not a dualistic vision—light up here, darkness down there. The light may comfort us and the darkness frighten us, but God is the Creator of all: matter and antimatter, black holes and fiery orbs, miracles of every imaginable scale and dimension. From our limited viewpoint, the sheer immensity of our universe can be dizzying, almost terrifying. On a galactic scale, however, the universe is serene and at peace. *Oseh shalom*—to the Creator of that kind of harmony, all is as it should be.

The blessings that surround the *Shema* are no less appreciative than the tuneful verses that precede them. But our thoughts have become more spacious. Did we try to raise the roof with our song in *P'sukei de-Zimrah*? Well, the roof above our heads is higher now, reaching up to the heavens and the stars. Our prayer becomes quieter, more contemplative. We begin to gather ourselves, lifting our gaze toward the great statement of unity that is the *Shema*.

In *Beriyah*, the language is no longer immanent but transcendent. *Beriyah* is the place of *Wow*, the place of wonder. We praise and give thanks for the constant and miraculous regeneration by a Creator who "renews, each day and always, the work of creation." This is not the big bang understanding, in which a single event set the rest of the universe in motion. It is a mystical vision of the entire world being created anew in every instant. A person who sees the universe with such eyes can welcome each and every moment as a new opportunity for praise.

In *Beriyah*, we are still in the group, but what the group does at this stage is to give you a matrix in which to do your individual work. The final paragraph before the *Shema* itself begins, "*Ahavah rabbah ahavtanu*, With a great love You have loved us," but this does not just refer to the totality of Israel. You really have to be yourself in saying that. Most of the time, when we say, "You have loved us with a great Love, and please don't ever take that Love away from us," we hang up the phone right away. We don't give enough time to allow that to happen. If I want to give those words real meaning, I need to sit and feel God's love, the love that loves us no matter what.

This is not a matter of whether I think I'm worthy of love. This comes from an altogether different place. An alternative form[2] of *Ahavah Rabbah* (With a great love) is *Ahavat Olam*—a love of ages, a forever love, a love of the universe. The very fact that I exist is because I am being loved into life—that is how I understand these words. An important part of davening is to just sit *be-nachat ru'ach*, in serenity of spirit, and to allow for that to come in. If I can, I do this in a minyan. But before I can feel it in a group, I have to allow myself to feel it as an individual. I once heard Terry Gross of *Fresh Air* interview Gene Robinson, the first openly gay Anglican bishop. He had endured such controversy, brought so much rage down upon himself from the church that he loved. They were talking about his prayer life these days, and he said, "What I do is I sit quietly, and close my eyes, and—and I let God love me … that's where I remember who I am, and Whose I am."

Acknowledging God's love brings us to the *Shema* itself, the great statement of God's unity, the unity of all existence in God. We have an extraordinary relationship with this sentence. Torah tells us to recite the *Shema* every day, "*be-shokhbekha u-ve-kumekha*, when you lie down and when you get up." Jews throughout the centuries have recited it as their last words before dying. As one halakhic source tells us, "the *Shema* should feel new every day" (*Orach Chayim* 61:2). It is so "heavy" a statement that it can never become rote.

The choreography—the physical things we do in preparation for what we are about to say—is important here. If we are wearing a tallit, we gather together the *tzitzit* from its four corners, symbolizing the ingathering of exile—the physical exile of our people, the spiritual estrangement of our souls from God. We place our right hand over our eyes to shut out all distractions. Many congregations chant aloud and in unison; even a person davening alone is asked to pronounce the words audibly. We slow down: some communities devote an entire long breath to chanting each word. Fervent daveners will give greater weight to that final "One": *ECHAAAAAAAAAAAAAAAAADD!* The final letter *dalet* appears larger in most siddurs: the word does not die away but ends emphatically, leaving a moment of silence in its wake, a whisper of absolute unity.

Atzilut: **The Transcendent World of Emanation**

The word *Atzilut* refers to something that is noble, high, beyond. The world of *Atzilut* transcends our level of understanding. Boundaries are gone, definitions are gone. Individual words and thoughts are gone. We ourselves do not exist. Being as we know it has ceased.

Kabbalistic tradition imagines us davening the *Amidah* in the world of *Atzilut*. For most of us, however, going into *Atzilut* with the *Amidah* is not a reality. I don't think people get to that ideal so easily. Perhaps, in the moment of silence that follows the *"Adonai* is one" of the *Shema*, we might glimpse a moment of cosmic unity. If we stand in silent prayer with eyes closed and hearts open, we might feel our boundaries dissolving. A voice within us suggests that better than the whispered words of the *Amidah* would be stillness—not to talk, not even to think.

But moments of true stillness are fleeting. Most of the time I'm too concerned with the state of my mind, my work, my family, the tsuris that is happening all over the world, and I have to bring all these things up with God. Yes, the *Amidah* can seem like a shopping list. A student asked me, "How can I experience the *Amidah* in this heightened way and at the same time focus on the meanings of all the nineteen *berakhot?* The ancestors, the renewal of life, the needs of Israel, the needs of the planet, the desire for forgiveness, for health, for livelihood, for peace—it all feels too wordy to be spiritual! How can we be so celestial in our davening when these requests seem so earthbound? How could I be in the intuitive place when I have so many concerns that I have to bring to God?"[3]

Maybe the *Amidah* is meant to take us back to the beginning. We start, "O God, open up my lips"—now, God, let me truly begin to pray—and suddenly we find ourselves back at the threshold of our old familiar world. Concerns have a way of floating up just when we are trying to still our minds. This is the natural way of things: we relax our guard, and oops! A worry, a task on our to-do list, floats up like a mind burp. So much to do, so much to ask for! So much *tikkun* (repair) that needs to happen!

But something has changed. We are newly present. We have already come a long way this morning. We have davened the morning blessings, and our feet are grounded in the world of *Asiyah*. We sang and danced in the landscape of the psalms, and our hearts are humming in *Yetzirah.* We have pondered the cosmic mind-stretchers of the universe, our higher minds reaching toward *Beriyah.* In that integration of body, heart, and mind lies an echo of *Atzilut.* Now, with new clarity and presence, we can ask for what we need.

And we need so much. So many people I speak to are in the sandwich generation, where you need stuff for your kids, and your parents need help, and your spouse wants attention, and your work is making all kinds of demands. You're torn in all directions, and you feel, "Dear God, I—I can't, I can't do this. I don't have the strength to carry it all on my shoulders. I need you to lift this from me. I can't manage by myself." So never mind the achievements and attainments; just talk like a friend to God about what you are really concerned about. If a thought comes, turn it into a prayer. These heartfelt prayers are the ones that are really important; these are the prayers we save for *Atzilut,* sending them directly to the highest level.

I start by saying the introductory verse: "*Adonai sefatai tiftach u-fi yagid tehilatekha,* Please God, open my lips and let my mouth declare Your praise." So who's davening? I am asking that God daven through me. I am saying, "Dear God, You know my true needs so much better than I do. Please let whatever comes through be real and true." Then I wait. I try and still my mind and get to the place of intuition. I try to hold on to the All, to that Oneness as much as I can. I don't let my mind cramp up with the effort: I just open myself to these things in a gentle, surrendering way. If my mind wanders and begins to tell me something about how my body feels, then I take this up with God. Something hurts me and I say, "*Refa'einu,*[4] Please, God, help me have a *refu'ah,* a healing." Or I pray for somebody else. Another thought arises—a person I have quarreled with. I say, "*Sim shalom,*[5] Grant us peace; help me to make amends with this person." Then I go back once again to the center, where "to You, silence is praise" (Psalm 65:2).

Please try this if you can. Don't worry so much about saying the proper words, just go into that silent place and see what happens.

When a concern comes up for anything, turn it into a *bakashah*, a request. Then set it aside and go back to stillness.

My afternoon prayers give me the chance to take up with God all the things that happened during the day. I don't always have time to pray when these are happening. I may put out a quick arrow prayer, in the midst of everything else that's going on, but when it comes to prayers for people who need a healing, people who have no livelihood, and so on, I want to take more time. So I record it on my PDA, and when I daven the *Amidah* at *Minchah*, the afternoon prayer, I connect my requests with its blessings. I say, "'Heal us, O God'[6]—that person who is having an operation, and the friend who is now housebound. Please help them." Bringing my shopping list is a more humble way of dealing with the *Amidah*. It's a wonderful opportunity to tell God what I need and to try to be a channel for others.

WINDOW: *Tefillin in the Four Worlds*

I said above that praying with a Four Worlds consciousness can give our davening depth and richness in the same way that light and shadow can bring a simple line drawing alive. Take, for example the experience of putting on tefillin. Many who did not grow up with this tradition find it archaic, even disconcerting. As a young emissary of Lubavitch, of course, it was my job to persuade people to put them on! Most who agreed were embarrassed by this strange ritual and their lack of competence at it. They mumbled the *berakhah* and extricated themselves as quickly as possible. Yet tefillin are a powerful way to bring us into a sacred space; once we pass the competence barrier, the ritual can have a deep and many-layered effect.

This is illuminated by a seemingly picayune question from the Rabbis: How long do we have to wear them? What is the minimal amount of time we must wear tefillin in order to fulfill our obligation for that day? The Rabbis were always concerned with fulfilling *halakhah* to the letter. It's as if they were saying, "Tell me the minimum, so I can be sure I have performed the mitzvah. Once I know the minimum I can make sure I do that and more." So the answer comes: *kedei hilukh dalet amot*, "as long as it takes to walk four ells," an ell or cubit being about the length of an outstretched arm.

Our literal minds might react with surprise. Is that all? A few seconds of tefillin, and I can take them off? But consider the answer from a Four Worlds viewpoint, and the four measures become layers of ourselves and of reality, layers that a ritual like tefillin can give us access to.

I put the tefillin on in *Asiyah*, the world of the physical and the tangible. I feel the leather between my fingers as I wrap it around my arm. I feel the slight weight of the *shel rosh* box as I settle it on my brow and adjust it to the center.

Then I rise to the level of *Yetzirah*, the world of formation, the world that gives shape to my emotions. I meditate on the *kavanot* that we associate with tefillin, the intention to bind my mind and heart to God's service.

I reach for the level of *Beriyah*, the world of creation and of thought, in which shapeless and insubstantial forces begin to gather toward form. I say, "*Adonai echad u-shemo echad*, God is One and God's name is One," and spend a few quiet moments merging those thoughts together in unity.

Can I savor a tiny taste, at least, of the highest level of *Atzilut*? I go deeper into meditation, searching for the space of *achdut*, unity, where my entire self and being merges with this mitzvah I am performing and with the One who commands us to perform it.

That is how I think about the four *amot*, the four spans we need to travel in order to fulfill our obligation. I am recasting a halakhic question in what I call psycho-halakhahic terms, an approach that consults our inner experience and is open to the possibility of transformation. If I really want to be *yotzei*, to perform the mitzvah in the highest sense, then I put on the tefillin in *Asiyah*. I bind myself, heart and mind, to God's service. I meditate upon the unity of God, moving as far as I can toward merging the commandment of tefillin with its source and its end point. Now I can feel that I have done the mitzvah.

Bringing It All Together

A story is told of Reb Schneur Zalman, founder of the Lubavitch movement, and of his early days in the circle of the Maggid of Mezeritch, heir to the mantle of the Baal Shem Tov. The Maggid must have been a person of singular gifts. He attracted a remarkable circle of disciples, known as the "Holy Brotherhood." Eventually, he would send them off to different communities of northern Europe, each according to his own character and abilities, to spread the teachings of Hasidism throughout the land. Many of them became great Hasidic Rebbes in their own right.

Imagine the Maggid's first meeting with Reb Schneur Zalman, who later headed the Hasidic movement in White Russia and Lithuania, center of Jewish intellectual achievement. Schneur Zalman's penetrating intellect, the depth and breadth of his learning, must have quickly been obvious to the Maggid, for he asked the young man to be the *chavrutah* (study partner) of the Maggid's own son, Avraham, a lad of such saintly purity that he was known to all as the *Malakh*, the Angel. "You will teach him *nigleh* [revealed Torah]," the Maggid told Schneur Zalman, "and he will teach you *nistar* [the hidden realms of mysticism and kabbalah]." And so the two began to study together.

One day they ventured into the realms of *nistar,* deeper and farther into the hidden teachings than they had ever been before. Meditating together in silence, they left the world of *Asiyah* behind. Through the worlds of *Yetzirah* and *Beriyah* they rose, toward the realm of *Atzilut* itself, where all worldly things fall away. The *Malakh*'s eyes were closed; his face was whiter even than his usual pallor; his pulse rate had plummeted. Finally he slumped over, barely breathing. Somehow, Schneur Zalman, deep in his own meditation, realized that his friend had gone beyond, that he was near death. He tore himself away from the supernal realms, burst from the place where they had hidden to do their practice, and brought some beer and a bagel, which he forced into Avraham's mouth, bringing him back to the world of the living.

The next morning the Maggid called Schneur Zalman into his study. "Zalmaneh," he greeted him. "Zalmaneh. A big *yasher koyach.* You saved my son's life! But I want to ask you a question," he said, and he looked at him with a chuckle. "How did you manage to find a bagel in *Atzilut?*"

The Angel, tragically, would die young, gone from this world at age thirty-six. Schneur Zalman would go on to become a giant of Hasidism, one of the most forceful and effective of all that wondrous circle, a man whose followers today number in the tens of thousands. The story hints at a reason. Godliness and prayer, it suggests, do not belong solely to the world of spirit, any more than we ourselves do. We have a body, a heart, a mind, a soul. Each dimension of ourselves—physical, emotional, intellectual, spiritual—has its own needs and speaks its own language. I don't want to leave any part of me out. I want my davening, my spiritual life and practice, to integrate them all. How can this holy conversation be real unless my entire self is engaged?

Hardest to integrate, perhaps, is mind. The mind meditates, the mind contemplates, but the mind also analyzes. Once it seizes upon a contradiction, once it detects what it perceives to be a logical flaw in the system, it is hard to appease. Mind examines God as a concept and rises to object. It scrutinizes the language of prayer and finds it wanting. We ask, "What's the theology behind this? What are we saying here?" Many who talk about *ruchniyus* (spiritual matters) from the outside—from a place that is analytical rather than experiential—insist on going straight to the Infinite. "God? Any true God can only be up there in *Ein Sof,* Infinite in all directions and dimensions." *When it comes to God,* we tell ourselves, *accept no compromises! God is not a personality! God is not a will! God is not good! God is beyond, beyond, beyond!*

But when it comes to God, as a famous Aramaic phrase from the Zoharic literature says, "*Leit machshavah tefisa vach k'lal,* No thought can grasp You at all." In his work known as the *Tanya,* the foundation stone of Lubavitch Hasidism, Reb Schneur Zalman repeats this phrase again and again, perhaps because its import is so hard to accept: we are asking our minds to understand that there are some things the mind just cannot do. *We cannot think our way to God.* We cannot reach God by a safe, step-by-step process. We can only get there by a "leap of faith." Not one leap, in fact, but many.

We have to remember the message of *PaRDeS. PaRDeS* is mystic shorthand—an acronym, standing for the increasingly hidden and encoded layers of meaning in our holy texts. We can take a text literally (*peshat*). We can take it metaphorically (*remez*). We can take it allegorically (*drash*). Or we can take it as an esoteric expression of deep and difficult truths (*sod*). The Hebrew word *pardes* also means orchard. The Talmud tells us, in veiled and puzzling language, that of four great sages who entered the *Pardes*, only one emerged alive and with his faith intact. *Pardes* is not easy stuff to handle, even for sages. As for the rest of us, we find it hard to escape the gravitational field of plain meaning. We can't turn off the impulse to draw logical conclusions, to take things literally. So we read the hints of *remez* as *peshat*, the secrets of *sod* as *peshat*, the mysterious allegories of the *Zohar* as *peshat*. In Four Worlds terminology, we come at these things from an exclusively *Asiyah* mind space.

One problem, as we have said, is that this leaves my heart no one to talk to. I want to feel that someone is listening. I want to tune in to a Will that is higher than my own. I want to feel a source of *chesed*, of caring. If we limit God to the ultimate abstraction, then whom are we praying to? But if instead we come at this from a *Yetzirah* heart space, that changes everything. If we attune ourselves to *Yetzirah*, the language of the davening makes sense, and all the stuff that we're talking about here make sense. The feeling that we're "doing the divine thing" makes sense—that's why I like the term *davening* best, to describe what we're doing at prayer.

Think of the prayer known as *U-netaneh Tokef*, "We bow to the power of this day," which we have recited for over a thousand years on Rosh Hashanah and Yom Kippur. The words imagine God's acts of judging and sealing our fate in the coming year: "The great trumpet is sounded. The still, small voice is heard. The angels are dismayed. Fear and trembling seize them as they proclaim, 'The Day of Judgment is here!'" And: "As a shepherd gathers his flock, passing them under his staff, so do You review every living soul and decree their destiny." It is one of the prayers that perhaps best captures why we call these holidays the Days of Awe. If we think about the words, though, we can get into trouble. "Yes," we might say, "that's a nice *myseh* from times gone by, but it doesn't really move me. I don't feel anything happening when I recite that." But this, again, is because we come at it from the wrong mind-set. Asiyah scoffs and says, "It's just a myth." *Yetzirah* understands, "Yes! This is our myth! Please, God, let me walk that mythic landscape. Let it be as real to me as the everyday life I live." That's why I say that unless we live in the Jewish myth, we aren't going to make it.

Myth does not mean fairy tale. I believe there is an empirical reality behind these words. Whether you call it bhakti yoga, as the Hindus do (meaning a form of yoga that emphasizes devotion to a personal god); or you call it the sacred heart of Jesus, as the Catholics do; or you call it *Yetzirah*, like the kabbalists; or you're a Hasid talking about *devekut*, the adhering of one's heart to God—whatever you call it, there's a reality behind it, and each tradition simply finds the garment and the language in which to clothe that reality.

Take a look: When the *Zohar* first appeared, there were other kabbalists—Joseph ibn Gikatilla, Isaac of Akko[7]—writing texts full of "kabbalese," worlds and spheres and so on. The *Zohar* brought it all back into the romance between the Holy One, blessed be He, and the Shekhinah—how She longs for Him, how He longs for Her, all this beautiful language that tells of their coupling. Theologically speaking, this was dangerous ground. But it was the *Zohar*, not the theorists, that became the foundational document of mystic Jewish experience.

Fifty years ago I used to come to New York sometimes from Manitoba to teach a workshop at the Jewish Theological Seminary on Friday afternoons, on how to relate to the Song of Songs. "Let him give me of his mouth's kisses, for your love is better than wine" (Song of Songs 1:2). Oy, do I want such a kiss! "On my bed at night, I sought the one I love; I sought him but could not find him" (Song of Songs 3:1). I wanted my students to experience these verses not as recitation or as ritual but as the outcry of a heart filled with desire.

A person who does not have a romance with God cannot really enter into the mystery. The romantic in us is so amazing. Very seldom is there a couple who, even if they are together in the best possible way, don't feel, "And yet, this still isn't the full totality of intimacy that I crave." You love your partner, you love your kids; regardless, there's a place inside where you can still feel lonely. That place is where we ache for the company of the central Wisdom and Will of the universe. I always think of that wonderful story about the kid who says to his baby brother at the crib, "Please tell me about God. I'm beginning to forget." I don't even want to say it's built in. It's deeper than that.

That's why our davening has to build—why we can't go directly from the tangible world of *Asiyah* to the abstraction of *Beriyah*. The controlling mind is less comfortable venturing into the emotional territory of *Yetzirah*, but we can't skip *Yetzirah*; *Yetzirah* brings the longing. On the other hand, *Yetzirah* can't express our desire unless the body is awake, because the body is such a wonderful vehicle for yearning. So first we thank God for opening our eyes, for straightening us up, for clothing us, for creating us free and in God's image. Only when I am truly in my body can I say, with full awareness, the lines from Psalms in the realm of *Yetzirah*: "Bless God, O my soul" (Psalm 103:1); "I will praise God all my life. I will sing to my God while I draw breath" (Psalm 146:2). And from there, we can go to yet higher worlds and say *Shema Yisrael*, feeling in that One a unity of such depth and dimension that we can't get to it any other way.

I wrote a simple chant once when I was teaching students about the Four Worlds. I wanted to bring home, through singing, the inseparable nature of these four levels of being, how they all merge in us and in the cosmos. So I thought first of nature and how perfect she is. I thought of the heart and how perfection translates there to love. I thought of the mind, which experiences perfection as complete transparency and clarity. And finally, I thought of the world of *Atzilut*, where perfection is knowing that, "*Ahhh*, I am holy. The Divine is manifest in me." So we sang:

> *It is perfect,*
> *You are loved,*
> *All is clear,*
> *And I am holy.*

The chant can be sung as a round, and it goes like this:

The Mystery of In-Between

Reb Scheur Zalman of Liadi uses a wonderful image in the *Tanya*. How, he asks, can we ever hope to cleave to God, whom "no thought can grasp at all"? Only through Torah. As a Jewish mystic, Reb Schneur Zalman saw Torah as the very essence of God's wisdom and will. But in order to become accessible to us, he says, Torah herself must descend through worlds upon worlds until it becomes clothed in forms we can understand. Does this not place a great distance between ourselves and God? No, says the *Tanya*: It is like a man who embraces a king. True, the king is wearing his robe, with more garments under that. But the loving subject feels the same closeness and *devekut* to the king whether the king is wearing one garment or many. Why? Because the king's body inhabits them.[8]

The kabbalists understood that we cannot leap straight from our tangible and disparate world to the formless unity of *Atzilut*. Only in the realm of *Atzilut* does God's presence resemble the Infinite God that our minds insist upon. That God is true, the kabbalists say; that God is real. But the God of *Ein Sof*, of "No-Thing," is also beyond anything we can understand or connect to. We need to travel through other worlds and dimensions on the way. That is why we talk not only about *Asiyah*, the here and now, and *Atzilut*, the highest level of abstraction, but about the intermediate worlds of *Yetzirah* and *Beriyah* as well. The ladder that rises from where we stand to *Ein Sof* has rungs. Our heart must feel God's loving presence in *Yetzirah* if it is to find its path to God. Our mind must meditate on how God manifests in *Beriyah*. The davener needs those middle worlds. For just as we cannot grasp the unfathomable God of *Atzilut*, so we cannot—except in rare moments—pray to that God.

I call this the mystery of in-between.

In the realm of *Asiyah*, God's presence manifests as the totality of everything we can apprehend with our senses: every person, every pebble, every leaf, and every tree. What a wonderful way to experience the world! Yet, in a sense, this leaves us with the same problem as the God of *Atzilut*: no "I" and no "You," no good and no evil, no address for gratitude, no hope of compassion. That is why we need faces for God that are the intermediate worlds, faces that are neither Everything nor No-Thing.

The God that I turn to with love, the God to whom I say, "*Oy, Gottenyu*" or "*Ribboyno sh'l oylom*, Master of the universe" (as I must do fifty times a day) is not the ultimate God, the omni-omni-omni God. How can I have an I–Thou relationship in *Atzilut*, where I don't exist and "I" doesn't exist? Every so often, in deepest meditation, I might glimpse the Absolute in which everything we know dissolves. But our mind is right: in *Ein Sof* there is no Thou.

When I say that the heart needs a "Thou," I mean that something within us is looking for a log-on place for compassion. If God is All, then yes, God can be pitiless, just as nature can. But if we ourselves can laugh and cry in sympathy with what others are feeling, then surely compassion must be a part of God as well. Who is listening when we call out to God? Who is there? The One who populates the intermediate worlds. The mystery of in-between.

People since the dawn of time—all over the world, in every culture, throughout history—have sensed a Reality beyond our reality. That Reality, I believe, is not our creation. It is not just a figment of our collective imagination. But without a face, without a name, I have no "Thou" to talk to, no *ATAH* to whom to say, "*Barukh ATAH*, Blessed are You!" So we each, in our traditions, have dreamed up names and faces for God.

I don't want to imply that the "I–Thou" connection is easy. In May, 1975, Rabbi Arthur Waskow called us to a meeting in Washington to honor the tenth *yahrzeit* of Buber's passing and to celebrate his legacy. Maurice Freedman, who wrote about and translated Buber's work,[9] gave a paper, and others gave papers as well. I said, "I don't want to give a paper. I want to have a workshop on I–Thou-ing." Because I felt like, it's one thing to read Buber's *I and Thou*, but it's another thing to *do* it. How do we go about it?

So people signed up to work with me in the I–Thou-ing workshop. And I said, "I want you to sit and face each other. Look each other in the eyes, and just keep on looking. Try not to block each other out, just open yourself as much as you can to be seen and to see. After about five minutes"—which is a long time to be staring into someone else's eyes—"if you have something to share with your colleague, whatever is happening in your mind, please do that. Please be completely honest: that's very important. Just mention it, and then you can put it away." So one person would say, "I don't want you to keep looking at me, I have a feeling that you're reading everything that's going on inside of me." Or, "I'm looking at you, but suddenly I'm not seeing *you* anymore; instead, I find myself thinking, What can you do for me? What use can you be to me?" And each time they would say it, they would put it aside, so that finally they could get to gazing at each other in a way that was both loving and transparent. But it wasn't easy, and it took time.

Who—where—is your Thou? One way to know when you've found your Thou is that you will feel a listening and understanding presence when you open yourself to talk to God and to be seen by God. My hope, my prayer, is that over time, you will speak more easily and naturally to that Presence. Where in this many-layered universe does compassion reside? Who is the You of God for you?

FOLLOWING THE MAP
A Traveler's Guide

The Hebrew Bible has many examples of people turning to God in their hour of need. They do it naturally, with no text or structure. Hannah is childless; she comes to the tabernacle in Shiloh and says, "Dear God, if you could just grant me a child, I would hand him over to serve You all the days of his life" (1 Samuel 1:11). David is running from King Saul, and he says, "I lift my eyes up to the mountains. Where will I find help?" (Psalm 121:1). The Israelites in the desert are always complaining: "If only we had died in Egypt!" (Numbers 14:2). They all make a connection to God, speaking in their own language about the things that trouble them.

We can do the same. We do not need a prayer book to pray. We don't need a cantor to lead us or a synagogue to pray in. All we need are feelings that we want to share with the listening presence of the universe. If you are not yet used to praying, start by expressing yourself in your own words. You are alive! You have your body, your senses. "Thank you, God, for letting me live another day, for helping my eyes to see and my ears to hear. Thank you for the smell of the fresh-cut grass. Thank you for the birds singing in those trees." Some things may not be going so well. Perhaps your body is hurting. We say, "God, my back is killing me!" All we need to turn the words into prayer is *kavanah*. "Dear God, my back has been hurting. This time it's not going away so quick. I'm worried that I won't be able to work. Please help me do what I can to solve this problem."

Once you start to share your innermost thoughts with God—your gratitude, your worries, your hopes—then a crucial shift has taken place. You have made the core connection that is at the heart of all prayer. You have recognized your soul's desire to get closer to God.

Then the Rabbis come and say, "Let's make that connection part of our everyday lives. Just as every morning we open our eyes and stretch our arms, let us open our hearts and stretch our souls as well." So they set about developing the inner tools and technology of prayer. They gathered songs of thankfulness and praise. They crafted prayers of redemption and repentance. They wrote *bakashot,* requests—for peace, health, livelihood, wisdom, forgiveness. They mapped out whole programs of prayer—journeys of multiple stages to shift us from our everyday awareness toward peace and spiritual

It   is   per - fect,   You   are   loved,

All   is   clear,   and   I   am   ho - ly

transformation.

The manual they put together is known in Hebrew simply as the order or sequence—the *siddur.*

For those who are beginners at prayer, I do not suggest using a siddur or prayer book at first. The language of the siddur can be difficult, especially in translation. The Hebrew of Scripture and davening is full of metaphor. It always points to something a little bit *else;* if we try to read the prayers as information, they will fail us. In the morning prayers we say, "God has established His throne in the heavens, and His kingdom rules over all" (Psalm 103:19). Our minds reject this: *What throne? Why only in the heavens? Why is God male? Why all this*

talk of kingdoms and ruling over us? Only by entering into the psalmist's imaginal world can we reach the places of exaltation and submission to God's will that the language attempts to describe.

For those who seek to draw closer to Jewish prayer, however, the
siddur is invaluable. Unlike our biblical texts, which have been fixed
and unchanging for two thousand years, the siddur has been a work in
progress, responding to the wisdom of rabbis, the inspiration of poets,
and the desires of the people. Today it provides a road map for the
Jewish journey to God.

Davening on a Budget

In 1961, when I served as a "religious environmentalist" at Camp
Ramah, I wrote several davening budgets, budgeting for different
amounts of time that a person might have in which to do the morning
prayers. On the days when the counselors at Ramah had their day off, I
would wake up the kids and bring them out of the *tz'rifim* (huts). I would
give them the budgets and say, "This *tz'rif* has twelve minutes for morning prayers, this one has fifteen minutes"—up to twenty minutes, but
never more than that. And they could choose from the budgets what
they wanted to daven.

The shortest was the budget *de-oraita* ("of the Torah"), the minimum necessary to discharge the Torah-based obligations of prayer:
put on something with *tzitzit* on the corners, put on your tefillin, say
the *Shema.* A slightly longer budget began with *de-oraita* and included
the most important addition of the Rabbis: the *Amidah.* Longer budgets guided the kids in gradually increasing the amount they said,
depending on how much time they had.

I got some flak for this. The pages I assembled were mimeo-
graphed: the custom at Ramah was to share the material that each
branch created with all the other camps, so they could make use of
them as well. When some of the more hard-line people from Ramah
in the Poconos saw my davening budgets, they were shocked. What
did I mean, a twenty-minute davening! My belief was, if the young
people don't learn to do it in twenty minutes, they are not going to do

it. But when they learned how and they were given permission to do a davening that worked for them, then they did it!

I feel the same way today. The Orthodox siddur, especially, has now grown to enormous size. For example, the *de-oraita* obligations for *Shacharit*, the morning prayers, come to only a few paragraphs of text—the *Shema*, a few blessings, a verse or two of Torah study. The ArtScroll version of *Shacharit*, with all the preparations and intentions, the options and variations, comes to almost two hundred pages! Throughout our history, we kept adding. So the kabbalists wanted to include the *Akeidah* (Binding of Isaac), the story of Abraham's ultimate act of faith? Fine, said the redactors. Let's also include the introductory paragraph to the *Akeidah* from the *Zikhronot* (Remembrances) section of the *Musaf* prayer on Rosh Hashanah. Even the *Aleinu* prayer was brought in after the original layers were set. It, too, first appeared in the Rosh Hashanah *Musaf* service, as part of the *Malkhuyot* section, where God's kingdom is proclaimed. (Read the words, and a context of kingship will make sense to you.) Originally, in other words, we said *Aleinu* once a year. But the old congregations loved it, and now we say *Aleinu* three times a day.

The problem is that for many people, a two-hundred-page morning service is simply not sustainable. Not everyone has the time and stamina for an hour-long davening every morning. That's why it is helpful to see the prayers in terms of concentric circles—the *Shema* (which comes from Torah) at the center, a Rabbinic addition like the *Amidah* next, further blessings and psalms a little further out, additional poetry and meditations beyond that—so you can fit your davening to your budget. The siddur's fluid nature over time encourages us to imagine it not only as a bound book but as a loose-leaf binder, a rich source of material from which to draw.

Remember, though, that in order to access the treasure buried deep within our souls, we would do well to follow the map. Even if we take a shorter path over the same ground, the sequence is important. My aim in this chapter is to offer some words of guidance on using the prayer book, based on the countless hours I have spent in its company. We will not cover every corner of it here; I will focus on *Shacharit*, the morning service, the fullest daily expression of the structure of Jewish prayer and of the journey through the Four Worlds. We will talk about key prayers from each stage of the journey. Please read this with a siddur in hand, so we can turn the pages together.

DOORWAY: Covering the Ground

The best way to become familiar with the siddur—to get to know the Jewish treasure chest of prayer in a way no class could teach you—is to go through it in sequence, twenty minutes a day. Don't worry about saying things at the right time. For this educational purpose, it doesn't matter if what you're saying is for morning or evening, weekday or holidays. So today you daven up to *Ashrei*, tomorrow from *Ashrei* to *Yishtabach*, the next day up to the *Shema*, and so on. Do this until you have davened through the whole siddur, preferably out loud.

Actually hearing the words is important. "Voice arouses *kavanah*," the Rabbis said. Daven so your heart can feel what your lips are saying! Try to imagine what these words would feel like if, rather than being recited as a familiar formula, they were bursting forth for the very first time. And—very important— mark the parts that you like, the parts that speak to you: a line of poetry that conveys the joy you feel sometimes; a plea for help that you want to store up for a darker hour. Marking the bits you relate to will give you a map of your own favorite places, sources to draw upon when your heart is moved to prayer.

I have written many times about my teacher Howard Thurman, dean of theology at Boston University, where I did a master's degree in the mid-1950s. Thurman was a great soul and a master of applied religion: it was from him that I got the idea to do labs, to test out in practice what theory suggests we do. At one point I gave him a Birnbaum siddur, so he should see what I pray as a Jew. One day, some years later, I came back to see him, and he asked me for advice. Sometimes, he said, he would be invited to the local Reform synagogue on Friday night, and he would preach there. "But the sermon is always at the very end, when the people can't do anything with these thoughts except go and drink tea! What would be a better place for it?"

I wanted to show him a section from the Mishnah that we say on Friday night, together with the Rabbis' *Kaddish*, so that we experience a little learning together as well.[1] So I said to him, "Tell me, where is that prayer book I gave you?"

He replied, "I don't have it any more."

I asked, "How come?"

So he said, "Thereby hangs a tale!"

There was a young Jew who came to him saying he wanted to convert. He had heard Howard Thurman preach and was touched by the Christianity he embodied. "You're a Jew," Thurman said to him. "You first have to be a Jew before you can become a Christian."

"How can I do that?" the young man asked.

"I don't know, either," Thurman told him. "But here is a Jewish prayer book. Why don't you spend twenty minutes with it each day—make sure it's the same twenty minutes, so your body gets used to devoting that time—and read it from the beginning to the end, however many days that takes. During that time, while you're doing that, you are not to come to my services. But when you're finished, come and check in with me." Then he pulled out a letter and showed me that this young man now conducted a Passover seder for his family and became a practicing Jew, all from spending twenty minutes with a siddur!

Bringing the Body In: The Morning Blessings

Let's begin at the beginning, the moment we open our eyes. Coming as we do from the realm of sleep, we need some preparation before we can even greet God properly. I'm much more creaky at this point in my day; if I try to daven before I'm in my body—if I haven't given thanks yet that my eyes are seeing, that I'm able to move around—then

85

my davening is always very drowsy. It lacks the sharpness that I want to have to be fully in the presence of the One. The morning blessings (*Birkhot ha-Shachar*) get me there. That's why so many of them describe movement and action.

The siddur presents these blessings in a fixed order. But Maimonides stresses that we should say each blessing as we need it, beginning from our first waking moment. This is especially true for the blessings that pertain to physical acts.

So when we first return to awareness: "*Barukh atah, ha-Shem,* Blessed are You, God, for giving me the gift to discern the difference between day and night."

When we open our eyes: "… for giving sight to my eyes."

We stir ourselves consciously for the first time: "… for giving free movement to my limbs."

We stand up: "… for helping me to stand upright."

We put our feet on the ground: "… for the firm ground on which You place me."

We take our first few steps: "… for leading my steps in the right direction."

We wash our hands—*neggelwasser,* as we used to say in Yiddish: "… for commanding us to wash our hands."

We put on our clothes: "… for giving me clothes to wear." (Blessings like this also remind us to give clothes to those in need.)

When we put on our shoes, remembering the days that shoes were a luxury: "… for providing *all* my needs."

And then, when I finally have it together, I tighten all my muscles—tight, tight, tight—and then let go, feeling the energy flowing back to them. Then I thank the God who "*noten la-ya'ef koach,* who takes my weariness and gives me energy."

The morning blessings can speak to matters of condition and consciousness as well. One pair of such blessings is "… for girding Israel with strength," traditionally said when we pull on a belt, and "… who crowns Israel with beauty," said when we put on a *kipah* or some other form of headwear. The first seems to symbolize our readiness and determination, the second the highest consciousness that we can bring to the day. Others may draw different meanings. One of my students told me that he says the first blessing in thanks to God for those who are always watchful on behalf of Israel's safety and security. In the second blessing he thanks God for those who are willing to make compromises for peace.

The first blessing, "for girding Israel with strength," reminds me of a story about Satchidananda, the Indian sage, who was once sitting in a train with a friend of his. Once you have a seat on an Indian train, you don't want to give it up, but when they stopped at a station, his friend went down to buy some boiled water. While he was gone, another fellow came by and asked, "May I sit here just for a moment?" Then Satchidananda's friend came back with the boiled water, and the fellow wouldn't get up! So Satchidananda looked at the man, stuck his tongue out, as in the Lion pose, and gave a *geschrei*—AAH!!—and the guy got up. When in our lives we really need to have that power coming from the belly, to really push, then we can call upon the One who *ozer Yisrael bi-ge-vu-RAH!!*, who girds Israel with strength. But for all the times when we need a smile, and grace, we can say *oter Yisrael be-tif'arah*, thanking the One who crowns Israel with glory.

Three other consciousness blessings appear in different places, depending on the siddur you're using. Most Ashkenazi siddurs place them early, believing that these should be part of the first awareness that we have:

"… for shaping me in Your image."

"… for giving me freedom." (I take a few steps here, to show I can go anywhere I want.)

"… for making me a Yisrael." (I sometimes think of this as, "for giving me the privilege to worship You as a Jew.")

But in *nusach ha-Ari*, the version favored by Reb Isaac Luria and his followers, those blessings appear later in the order. I like that better: once I'm dressed and in my body in the right way, I can bring more *kavanah* to a blessing like "*she-asani be-tzalmo*, who made me in the silhouette and sculpting of God." I say this blessing first of the three. Then I say "*she-asani ben chorin*, who made me a free person." Might there be a contradiction between being sculpted in God's image and having complete freedom of choice? Then I thank God "*she-asani Yisrael*, who made me one of a God-wrestling people," who delight in struggling with such contradictions.

Finally, as the last blessing in this series, we say, "... for removing the last trace of sleep from my eyes."

One good practice in the morning blessings is to single out a blessing that speaks most strongly to wherever you are right now and to stay with that for a little while, to say it with special *kavanah*.

Suppose you are feeling constrained at work. You don't like the place you are in, but you don't feel you have many options. You're hemmed in. You say, "Blessed are You, dear God, *matir asurim*, who frees the bound."

You're getting older and have trouble straightening up these days. You need help remembering to stretch. You call upon the *zokef kefufim*, the God who straightens the bent.

You're having a vision problem. Maybe you have cataracts, or maybe the problem is metaphorical: you can't see beyond the next bend. Or maybe someone close to you is suffering from a blind spot, and it's hurting them or yourself. You call upon the *poke'ach ivrim*, the One who gives sight to the blind, and you say, "Dear God, I need your help with this one."

You feel ungrounded in your life. You don't feel stable; you don't feel safe. You don't have a leg to stand on. You turn yourself over to the God who *roka ha-aretz al ha-mayim*, who spreads the firm ground upon the waters.

You're worried about money; you're feeling poor and impoverished, straitened in your resources. "Thank you, dear God," you remind yourself, "*she-asah li kol tzorki*, who supplies my immediate needs. That's the God I need You to be right now."

DOORWAY: *Breath Meditation*

The morning blessings restore us to our bodies and reunite body with soul. Now we say, "O God, the soul you have placed within me is pure." The word for soul, *neshamah*, derives from the word for breath, *neshimah*. With rare exceptions among the mystics, Judaism has placed little emphasis on *pranayama*, the control of breath. But this is something we can learn from the yogic tradition.

The psalmist says, "Every breath will praise *Yah*" (Psalm 150:6). We can use this as a meditation with the *YHVH*, the Tetragrammaton. First empty your lungs and contemplate the *yud*, the smallest Hebrew letter, closest to emptiness. Then you breathe in, making a *hhhhh* sound; that's the first *hey*. You hold the breath for a moment, sending it to all six directions in your body—that's the *vav*, the sixth letter of the alphabet. Then you breathe out, *hhhhh*, to make the other *hey*. So we can use this prayer to scan our lung capacity and check in with our breath.

The physical space in which you pray will be important. It's good to have a regular space to daven—either a minyan, in a regular seat if possible; or a place in your home, where you can place things that inspire you to enter that spiritual space.

Traditional daveners will wrap themselves in a prayer shawl (*tallit* in Hebrew, *tallis* in Yiddish) and don phylacteries or tefillin. (Many women have taken up these practices as well.) The daily siddur contains the blessings for these, as well as *kavanot*, statements of intention, and some poetry from the psalms to help bring our emotions into it. The *Shulchan Arukh*, classic compendium of Jewish law, recommends that we wrap the tallis around our head and face when we first put it on, "as the Ishmaelites do [*ke-atifat ha-Yishma'eilim*]." This gives us the maximum amount of privacy in which to say the blessing and get in touch with our intentions. We say, "How precious to me is your *chesed*, dear God! We take refuge beneath the wings of *Shaddai*." It's like saying, if I have to be vulnerable to God, I need to be protected from the influence of the environment on me. I had a teacher in Antwerp who used to do the whole davening wrapped in his own private space like that.

When introducing people to tallis and tefillin for the first time, however, I usually don't give them too many explanations. I just say, "Please, put these on, and sit with them for a while. And report back: What did the tallis and tefillin tell you?" I want them to feel and become aware of what the tallis is telling them, what the *tzitzit* are telling them. Putting the tallis over my head before beginning the *Amidah*, for instance, gives me a very strong sense of entering into deeper intimacy.

The traditional intentions, I feel, rely on concepts that a person may or may not relate to. But sit with the tallis and tefillin for a while, with a listening and open heart, and you will gradually begin to have your own nonverbal communication with the essence of the mitzvah. Your soul, your *neshomeh*, will find its own way of understanding what you are doing. Your intentions will arise from your own experience, and I'd rather go with those.

I recently heard a beautiful story about how real this process can be for those who truly inhabit their davening. A man in the Israeli Orthodox community was spending time with his father, an elderly man who was seriously ill. Come morning he brought his father a jug of water and a bowl for *netilat yadayim*, the ritual washing of hands. Then, together, they started saying, "I thank Thee [*Modeh ani*]," the first words of the morning blessings. On this day, however, he noticed that his father did not join him in the sentence "You restore my soul to me." This set off an alarm bell in the son's mind. Such a strange omission, the son thought, could only mean that his father, a deeply devout man, felt his soul had not been fully restored. He immediately began to say *Viduy* with his father, the confession for someone on their death bed, and the father left this world very shortly afterward.[2]

That is why movement and physicality are so important to make these blessings real. In the spiritual realm, the conscious bonding of body to soul is real and necessary. I have pushed for including the morning blessings in shul, for those who might not otherwise get to them at all or might just rattle them off without *kavanah*. But I believe that the morning blessings are best said as we rise in the morning, as Maimonides recommended. Saying them at ten o'clock in the morning in synagogue creates a certain disconnect. *We have long since gotten up and performed all these tasks*, our body says. *Why are we saying thanks only now?*

The more expansive siddurim include many treasures in this first section, along with layers of add-ons that have accrued over the centuries. For those on a minimal davening budget, however, the basic blessings and the crucial *Asher Yatzar* is enough. The blessing of *Asher Yatzar* is a separate paragraph, which we say after we relieve ourselves. It focuses on the functions of our physical body, beginning by blessing God "who fashioned us with wisdom." We continue (in loose translation): "You created a myriad openings and cavities within us. If even one of these were to open or close improperly, we know we could not exist or stand before You for even a single hour. Blessed are You for the healing of our flesh, which is such a wondrous act!" Saying *Asher Yatzar* acknowledges the miracle of even our normal state of health. Sooner or later, though, all of us will have issues with our *kishkes*, our insides, and when you're dealing with the prognosis of illness, your sensitivity and receptivity to such wonders become more urgent and acute. These days I return constantly to the last words, *u-mafli la'asot*, "who acts wondrously," asking God to help my body to function.

Engaging the Emotions: The Tuneful Verses

Now we come to *P'sukei de-Zimrah*, the tuneful verses. This is the section that corresponds to *Yetzirah*, the world of emotion: we offer the feeling space within us to God.

The tuneful verses were not originally part of the morning davening, which focused on the *Shema* and the *Amidah*. But, the Rabbis said, you don't begin to talk to the Master of the Universe without singing some praises first! Psalm 30 opens this section. It's a beautiful psalm, "A psalm for a housewarming, composed by David":

> *Fellow devotees!*
> *Join me in song.*
> *Remembering what is sacred,*
> *Let's give thanks.*
> (PSALM 30:5)

Barukh She'amar

Then comes *Barukh She-amar*, an ancient paragraph that children in Jewish day schools sing from a very young age. Its opening line means "Blessed be the One who spoke the world into being!" My *kavanah* here—even if I don't feel so good—is to say, with real appreciation, "Thank You, God, for making the world." Having thanked God for our own lives and health, we now give thanks for God's creation at large.

Yes, the world is full of suffering. I know that bad things happen to good people. I also know in my heart that the Holy One is Infinite, way beyond good and evil as we know it. Some might say, "Why did You have to create such a world?" Nevertheless, we bless God and say, "Your compassion enwombs[3] the earth. Your caring is kind to all creatures."

Part of our mission in davening is to project into the world the kind of God we want to communicate with. I put those wishes and hopes into *Barukh She-amar.* Just as God spoke the world into being, so we ourselves can give birth to new realities through the heartfelt expression of our lips in divine service. When we say, later in *Ashrei*, "You open Your hand, and each one of us receives what we desire," do we imagine the Rabbis didn't know that some are poor, some are starving? But we're saying, this is the God that we want to have, this is the universe we want to bring into being. I'm not saying that you should fool yourself. But there's also an element in all our prayers of trying to make God behave. In the Song of the Sea we say, "*Zeh*

Eli—this is my God." This is how I want to think of God. This is why I can love God.

Ashrei

The next major signpost is *Ashrei*, the famous prayer that begins, "Happy are those who dwell in Your house!"[4]

If you are ever in pain, and the discomfort ceases, you think, "Oy, *mechayeh*. Wonderful." That sense of bliss quickly fades in our memories, because we don't need it for survival. But this is the place that *Ashrei* would have us be. Think back to moments in your life when you have risen above anxiety, when you have felt healthy in mind and body, when life feels meaningful. *Ashrei* is that state of harmony. It is the meaning that seekers seek. *Ashrei* is the sense of groundedness and holiness that comes from standing in the presence of God without shame or guilt.

Prayer is a path to that state of health and meaning. Why did the psalmist seek to capture the state of *ashrei* in his psalms, if not to provide us with a way of getting there? *Ashrei* is the very first word in the book of Psalms: "*Ashrei ha-ish!* Happy is the person who has not followed the counsel of the wicked." Today we might not call this wickedness; we might call it distraction. Who does not know the temptation to take the second- or third-best option? Who has not felt the urge to give our animal instincts free rein, even though we may cause harm? *Ashrei* is the wonderful feeling we get by setting aside those lesser options, by saying, "No, this time I will go with what I know to be good and true."

Psalm 145, which makes up the bulk of *Ashrei*, is an acrostic, each line beginning with the next letter of the Hebrew alphabet. This made the psalm easier to remember; it takes us back to the times when written manuscripts were rare. I knew a man who had an heirloom siddur. It was written on parchment, by hand, and bound like a book. You can imagine how precious such a book would have been in ancient days. The ordered lines of *Ashrei* are also a beautiful way of grounding us in language, of saying, "Each letter sings Your praises!"[5]

Realizing the bliss of *ashrei* is a mitzvah, just as the euphoria of putting aside our responsibilities to simply *be* on Shabbos is a mitzvah. After running frantically all week, we put down our burdens on Friday afternoon and say, "*Barukh ha-Shem*—thank God. At last! Now I am free just to sit and enjoy. I don't need to run; I don't need to make, do, fix, or change. For one day, I can just be." If we pause from running through our day to offer a prayer, we find that we have created a little piece of Shabbos—of *ashrei*, a haven of peace in the middle of our busy lives. That is why the first sentence here says, in effect, "Oy, how good it is to be at home with You."

Halleluyah!

Ashrei's final sentence is borrowed from Psalm 115, so that its final word is *Halleluyah*, meaning "Praise God, y'all!" This is the key word of *P'sukei de-Zimrah*; the five psalms that now follow (Psalms 146–150) begin and end with *Halleluyah* as well. Together, these six psalms symbolize the six days of creation.

The last of these, Psalm 150, reminds us of something important. We davened with music in Temple times. The Mishnah, in tractate Pesachim, describes the Levites as playing music and saying *Hallel* in connection to the Passover sacrifice. We know the names of many Levitical instruments, including something called a *magrefah*, whose sound was said to be so loud it could be heard all over the city. But we know nothing about what the music was like. All we can do is go there in our imagination! I have a suspicion, for example, that Psalm 150 (last of the series here) was actually a tune-up. It says, "Let's hear this instrument; now let's hear that one":

> *Praise God with the sound of trumpets,*
> *Praise God with the strings and harp.*
> *Praise God with drum and dance,*
> *Praise God with organ and flute.*
> *Praise God with crashing cymbals,*
> *Praise God with cymbals that ring.*

Finally—now that we have you all together, now that you're all tuned in—it's *tutti*:

> *Let all who breathe praise Yah, halleluyah!*

Other psalms are dedicated "*La-menatze'ach,* to the conductor" (for example, Psalm 4). So we know that *somebody* was in charge!

We knew how to celebrate in Temple times. The Sukkot ritual, for example, included a special water-pouring ceremony, a celebration that was legendary even then. The Levites would stand on the steps and play cymbals and trumpets and stringed instruments. Sages juggled knives, burning torches, glasses full of wine. The celebrations continued throughout the night. One famous source says that "whoever hasn't seen the water-drawing celebration doesn't know the meaning of celebration!"

We can understand how all the persecutions in the centuries since then might silence a community's music and rejoicing. The Rabbis have forbidden instruments on Shabbos since the *churban,* the Temple's destruction. But we of our generation have much to sing and dance to God about. If the Rabbis had wanted us to be all somber and silent, they would not have picked these six psalms for *P'sukei de-Zimrah!* Reb Shlomo Carlebach and others have set many lines of the *Halleluyah*s to song. Some of the tunes are lively and joyous, some sad and yearning, some somber and thoughtful. The *Halleluyah*s are an invitation to sing. Even if you can't handle the Hebrew, sing your own song to God, whatever that song may be. Sing "Amazing Grace." Just sing! Let your soul express itself in song. Soul stuff comes out in song that doesn't come out any other way.

Verses from Chronicles and Nehemiah

Of the paragraphs that follow the *Halleluyah*s, I always enjoy saying the one from 1 Chronicles 29:10–13, which begins, "And David blessed." He says, "Yours is the greatness, the strength, the splendor...." These are not just words but refer to all the kabbalistic spheres and faces of God that manifest in the lower worlds: "the *gedulah* and *gevurah*, the *tiferet*, the *netzach* and the *hod*"—all the *sefirot* and faces of God.

The next section, from Nehemiah 9:6–11, begins:

> *You, Yah,*
> *You alone made the heavens*
> *and the heavens beyond our heavens,*
> *the earth and all that live upon her,*
> *the oceans and all that they contain,*
> *the hosts of heaven bow before You*
> *and you infuse them all with life!*

—and here I always put some money into the *pushkeh*, my box for charity, as if to say, "I, too, wish to give life to someone." I always keep some singles in the ashtray of my car as well (sanctifying the profane, as Rav Kook would have us do). When I come to a street corner where somebody's collecting, I stop and give the person one of those.

Yishtabach

The last major signpost of the everyday Songs of Praise section is known as "*Yishtabach*, Your name be praised." *Yishtabach* seals these songs with a blessing. My favorite part is the sentence in the middle that lists fifteen (*yud-hey*, or *YAH* in gematria) different kinds of praise we would like to bestow upon God. I translate these as musical terms:

> *Music and celebration,*
> *Jubilation and symphony,*
> *Fortissimo,*
> *Anthem,*
> *Victory march,*
> *Largo,*
> *Forte,*
> *Paean and hymn,*
> *Sanctus and maestoso,*
> *Laudo and aria,*
> *Celebrating*

Your divine reputation
In every realm.

During the davening, we don't usually think of it that way. But when you hear a piece of classical music, you see: Here comes a sanctus, that's the *Kedushah.* Here's an anthem, that's the *Malkhut,* the part about God's kingship. Here is a fortissimo—that's *Gevurah,* the *sefirah* of severity and awe. Here is a hosanna, a *shevach.* This way I can bring my aesthetic appreciation of all these varieties of music into my davening!

Once I was leading the Shavuot prayers in Oregon. It was the second day, so I felt we had some more flexibility, having already discharged our obligations on the first day. Aryeh Hirschfield of blessed memory, the rabbi of Portland's P'nai Or, was playing the guitar. Yitzchak Hankin[6] was playing the cello, and I was tootling around on a flute.

Instead of using the siddur, I suggested, let's explore all the different ways of praying to God that are laid out in *Yishtabach.* "First, let's do *shir,* 'song,'"—and I asked for suggestions: what do you think we should play?

For the next word, *shevachah,* a praise song, I think we did *Ha-Aderet ve-ha-Emunah,* one of the acrostic hymns that's fun to do in English, taking turns to see what praises come out: Adoration and Admiration! Beauty and Beatitude! Charity and Compassion! Devotion and Delight! Excellence and Effulgence! *Zimrah,* to us, meant instrumental music, no words. For *oz,* a word suggesting strength, we did drums and percussion. *Memshalah* means government, rulership, so we did a march, like a processional. We devoted the whole day to it; I no longer remember everything we did. But I thought that just once, we should take this list of prayer modes that we recite and actually experience it musically.

The different parts of the morning prayers are sometimes given different weights. If you go to a typical Orthodox shul for Shabbos morning prayers, you will notice that one *chazan* sits down at the end of *P'sukei de-Zimrah* and a new person (generally someone better versed or more tuneful) comes forward to lead, beginning with the blessings that lead up to the *Shema*. It's as if we need a more serious leader to take our prayers to a new level, like a coach sending in a heavier hitter. I always thought that a pity. The original intent was to get more people involved in leading prayers. But this had the unfortunate effect of emphasizing the *Shema* and its blessings and diminishing the joyful warm-up to them.

True, the blessings of *keri'yat Shema* (the reading of the *Shema*) require a very different energy. The scale here is vast. We invoke the angels (*malakhim*) and the great fire beings (*serafim*). We say, "*Kadosh, kadosh, kadosh*, holy, holy, holy," with the heavenly hosts themselves. Other prayers, like "Light up our eyes with Your teachings," are more suited to quiet contemplation than to a rousing chorus.

In comparison, the tuneful verses seem like "davening lite." As full of praise, full of song, full of "*Halleluyah!*" as they are, they lack the theological weight of the great *Shema* statement. Yet imagine we sent in the *chazanim* the other way around, first sending up our strongest and most confident souls to really raise the room in song and dance to God. The structure of the morning prayers tells us that if we put in the energy to really daven *P'sukei de-Zimrah* in all its liveliness, we can ride that energy into the blessings of the *Shema*. Through our heartfelt *Halleluyah!*'s we earn the *zekhut*—the merit, the permission, the privilege—to pass through the gate into a more higher and more contemplative space. That gate, or boundary, is marked with a *Kaddish*.

WINDOW: *Poetic Paths to Prayer*

The obligatory prayers, which date back to the Talmudic age and before, would not produce a very thick volume. But spiritual poets, like poets everywhere, have never been content with the words of others. Throughout the centuries, the *payyetanim*—Jewish writers of spiritual poetry (*piyyut, piyyutim*)—have sought new ways of declaring their love for God. Some of their work made it into the standard liturgy. The majority was lost to today's daveners, buried in old sources, but now you can search for *piyyut* on the Web and find projects dedicated to bringing them back.

The forces that inspired them can speak to us today. Reb Avraham ibn Ezra says, "Don't jump into *Nishmat* so fast. Here, I wrote you a *piyyut* to get you in the mood and expand your awareness." *My soul thirsts for* Elohim, *for the living God*, it begins. *My heart and my body rejoice to the living God.* The words *life* and *living God* are repeated throughout. "And look!" Ibn Ezra continues. "At the very end I included the expression '*Nishmat kol chai,*' to lead you naturally into the prayer that follows, which begins with those same words." I used to sing this with the diamond cutters in Antwerp, when I was a boy.[7]

The placement of the *piyyutim* is important. Imagine your name is Mozart, and you have been commissioned to do the *Missa Solemnis*. Now you have to figure out where you're going to put things in—different moods, different emotions. So you know you have a Kyrie, a Gloria, a Credo, a Sanctus—all the different parts of the mass. That was the model for the church service. When the *payyetanim* sought to inject beautiful pieces of poetry to enhance the davening, they, too, saw before them a kind of structure, finding many a foothold in the landscapes of prayer that our siddur traverses.

A poet moved by God's manifestation in the natural world would express himself in the first part of the *Shema* section, known from its blessings as *Yotzer*, Creation. Two such poems, *Ha-Kol Yodukhah* and *El Adon*, have become part of the traditional Shabbat morning service. Other beautiful examples can be found in some of our holiday prayer books (*machzorim*), particularly the older ones.

Payyetanim inspired by Torah and the revelations our people have received would write something for the second part of the section, called Revelation. Because revelation was seen as proof of the love God has for us, the final paragraph before the *Shema*—and the first paragraph of the *Shema* itself—begins with the *ahavah*, or love.

And we have some beautiful *ge'ulot* as well—*piyyutim* relating to the third great theme of this section, known as Redemption (*ge'ulah*). We might ask: Why does revelation come before redemption? Didn't the Exodus from Egypt precede the giving of the Torah on Sinai? The answer is that we haven't been redeemed yet! Yes, in the desert, redemption came before revelation. But still we yearn for our ultimate liberation, and this is the feeling the poets tried to capture in their redemption songs.

Let the yearnings of long-ago poets whisper in your ear today. Turn your davening into poetry for God.

Meditations of Mind: The *Shema* and Its Blessings

The morning blessings have spoken to our body's desire for groundedness and movement. Singing the tuneful verses speaks to our hearts. How, now, do we engage our contemplative sides? If our emotions thrive on connectedness, our more contemplative side seeks to push beyond its own boundaries, if only for a little while. It wants to immerse itself in the totality of the universe and of our people. This is the part of ourselves that we seek to engage through "the reading of the *Shema* and its blessings" (*keri'at Shema u-virkhoteha*). Moving into the *Shema* after the morning blessings and the tuneful verses, we find ourselves in a very different landscape.

If we are davening in a minyan, we begin our next section with an invitation. *Barekhu!* This is a summons and an invitation to everyone in the room. The *chazan* bows and says, "Come, everyone, let us bless our blessed God!" Why do we not issue this invitation at the beginning of our davening? Because the *Barekhu* is where congregational davening probably began in ancient days. The *Shema* appears in Torah; the duty to recite the *Shema* and its blessings are discussed as far back as the Mishnah, the first layer of Oral Torah. The obligation to recite them is heavier and more ancient. *P'sukei de-Zimrah*, as we noted above, came later.

Barekhu's root, *bet-resh-khaf*, also gives us the word *berekh*, knee. So *Barekhu* also evokes knees and kneeling, as if to say, "Kneed-to are You; worshipped are You." I'm saying, "For You, dear God, I get on my knees." We think of kneeling as a Christian thing, a form of anatomical apostasy. But imagine you're truly in a time of trouble or hardship. "Dear God, listen to my prayer, please; I'm praying for my child." If you're alone, and nobody is watching you, and you feel you have an urgent request to make, don't be ashamed to go down on your knees. Our devotional literature is full of Rebbes and other leaders prostrating themselves full length on the floor, arms and legs spread out, when they or their congregations were in distress. Unlocking the knees can unlock the heart as well.

Barekhu is where we begin looking at cosmology. It's where we go into creation. Before that, we are in the place of praise and thanksgiving. Then we say, "You created the sun! You created the moon! I want them also to join in praising You!" It's like pulling off the road to watch the sunset: the entire natural display becomes words of prayer.

Davening helps us live in the texture of time. On Friday evening at Camp Ramah, we used to sing a beautiful song by Chayim Nachman Bialik, "The sun has just gone from the tops of the trees, come, let us go greet the Sabbath queen. Behold, she descends, the blessed one, the holy one...." Bialik understood the texture of time that we experience on Erev Shabbat.

Once in a while, go out and watch a sunrise, and your davening in the morning will make sense. When you stand and watch a sunset, praising the One "who evenings the evening" (as we do in the evening prayer) feels natural. Dawn and dusk give us the equivalent of a *neshamah yeteirah*, the extra portion of soul that the Rabbis believe we have on Shabbat. The daytime understanding is denotative: watchful and objective, direct and precise. With night comes the other consciousness, the connotative stuff—softer, mellower, more absorbing. At dawn or dusk we find ourselves between the two. Holding such a vigil occasionally, witnessing that mingling of daytime and nighttime consciousness, cannot help but affect your davening.

Creation, Revelation, Redemption

The *Shema* and its blessings meditate upon three great themes in our human relationship with God: creation, revelation, and redemption.

We address God as the *Yotzer or*, Shaper of light, Creator of luminaries—that's creation. We say, "Our ancestors trusted You, and You taught them the laws of life—Torah and mitzvot, *chukim* and *mishpatim* (edicts and statutes)." That's revelation. Then comes the *Shema*, which ends with "I am the Lord your God, who brought you out of Egypt to be your God." The paragraphs that follow thank God for redeeming us as a people. That's redemption, completing the triangle of God, Torah, and Israel.

We start with thoughts of creation. The poetry here stretches toward the cosmic:

> And the ofanim [wheels], the planets turning in their orbits,
> and the chayot, holy beasts of the sky,
> constellations of the zodiac,
> with thunderous noise rear up toward the serafim,
> the blazing ones, the galaxies.
> All in concert sanctify Your Name in dread and awe,
> chanting:
> **KADOSH!**
> **KADOSH!**
> **KADOSH!**
> Holy, Holy, Holy are You
> Yah of multitudes,
> of infinite diversity.
> The cosmos is filled
> with Your radiance!

A sense of moving up and down the spiritual ladder, like the angels in Jacob's dream, is especially true and important in this section of the davening. The angels could have said *Kadosh* only once. Instead they say it three times. Why?

In the past I used to think of it this way: There's a *kadosh*, a holiness, that we feel in the body. When you're present at a death or a birth, you feel this kind of awe; Catholics might cross themselves at that point. That's the first *kadosh*. The second *kadosh* is our best understanding of *kadosh*, the highest degree of holiness that we can possible grasp. And the third one is: If *kadosh* were only what I can understand, it would not be *kadosh*. The third *kadosh* has to be beyond our understanding. So I would go *kadosh* below, the second *kadosh* higher, and the third *kadosh* way high.

Now I go the other way also. I start with the highest *kadosh*. The first *kadosh* is the holiness of galaxies. It emanates from the *serafim*, the chanting fire angels of Isaiah's dream, where this verse comes from (Isaiah 6:2). These beings live in the world of *Beriyah*, on fire with desire to gaze upon God's presence. Then I come down a little lower, to the *chayot ha-kodesh*, the signs of the zodiac, the holy creatures who populate the world of *Yetzirah*. Finally, I come down to the *ofanim*, the planets turning in their orbits in the world of *Asiyah*. At that point, addressing *Adonai tzeva'ot*—the God of multitudes, the God of infinite diversity—makes sense. Saying that "the whole earth is full of God's glory" makes sense.

What do these different angels say? Next line: *Barukh kevod ha-Shem mi-mekomo*. Usually this is translated something like, "Blessed is the glory of God from God's place." *Mi-mekomo* (from God's *makom*, place) is the highest place, where God is really at home, but there we haven't got any connection. *Kavod*, the glory of God, is the part that we can handle somehow, but that glory has to be *nimshakh*, pulled down through the worlds. So *barukh* is the process by which it's drawn down. We are saying, let there be an effulgence, a radiance, a shining forth. Let that *kavod*—that reflection of God, the reputation of God—be drawn down to us, so when we look at anything, we can say, "Oh! Here is God, but disguised now in this way." *Barukh*, blessed, as we said above, has to do with knees. But *barukh* also calls to mind the word *bereikhah*, or pool. Just as we can draw water down from a high place to a lower place, so can our prayers draw godliness down to our level of existence and understanding. It's as if our prayers were bringing it all down, bringing it all down, from that exalted place of aloneness and beyondness, all the way down to our level of existence here.

Then we say, "*Le-El barukh ne'imot yiteinu*," let us offer pleasant things to that God who has been drawn down. Let us offer You pleasure in worship, as the angels do. Why? "For God alone [*ki hu levado*] is *marom ve-kadosh*, way beyond the world, and holy." So we're back in *Atzilut*, the highest world, and the drawing down begins again. A long list of epithets for God follows. God is *po'el gevurot*, for example: a Doer of great things. *Gevurah* (plural: *gevurot*) is the kabbalistic sphere of boundaries and limitations. So I translate *po'el gevurot* as "condensing and focusing," the *tzimtzum* process of God withdrawing Godself, as Lurianic kabbalah tells us, to make way for the created world. Then comes *oseh chadashot*, praising God for constantly creating everything anew. And so on. We end with praising the One "who renews in goodness, each day and always, the work of creation"—again, drawing God down to our level of understanding.

At that point I say, "Oy, please, *Ribboyno sh'l oylom*, when I look at what's coming out of Eretz Yisrael, please—'*or chadash al Tzion ta'ir*, shine a new light upon Zion'—and let us merit that light soon, dear God, *please*. We need it soon." With the blessing that ends this first section, "*yotzer ha-me'orot*, Creator of luminaries," we conclude our meditations on creation.

The second theme that runs through the blessings that surround and embrace the *Shema* is revelation. If the emotion most closely associated with creation is wonder, the emotion most closely associated with revelation is love. In the traditional davening, we say that those who serve God

> *lovingly give permission, one to the other,*
> *to sanctify the One who formed them,*
> *calmly and in clear, sweet language.*

One Hasidic interpretation[8] says it very beautifully: If I truly love the Beloved, then I don't care who gives the Beloved pleasure. But if I love *myself* loving the Beloved, then I want to be the one. Usually the word for "those who serve God," *meshartim,* is translated as "the ministering angels." Angels are selfless beings, so they "lovingly give each other permission," because for them the important thing is "to sanctify the One who formed them." But I like to imagine all the godly men and women of every religion giving each other permission in this way. Those of different faiths who are truly in touch with the will of the Beloved could not be at war with one another! They all want to serve the Beloved.

The image of God lovers giving each other permission can extend to the cosmic spheres as well. Take a look and imagine: if we think of the *ofanim* as the planets, the *chayot ha-kodesh* as constellations, and the *serafim* as galaxies, and we say they "give each other permission, with love," what is the *ahavah,* the love? My Rolfer, Joe Heller, had a wonderful explanation. One day he was making me stand on the floor, to really *feel* the floor underneath me. Gravity, he said, is the basic law of the universe, and gravity is the law of love. Because two bodies in space attract one another! It's so wonderful, when you go to astronomy, the movements and coincidings of the heavenly bodies, the way each shapes the orbits of the others—it's as if there were a certain permission being given. There is a certain *ahavah* that the sea and the moon have. So the *ahavah* is like the gravitational force. They turn toward each other, each recognizing the other's place in the cosmos.

Revelation is something that comes with intimacy. In the siddurim that go according to the *nusach* of the holy Ari, Reb Yitzchak Luria, we say, "*Ahavat olam ahavtanu.*"[9] I like to translate this as "From ever You have loved us into life." Because the loving that we thank God for is not merely a feeling; it is the creative force that brings us into being, into this *olam,* this world.

We go on to say, "*Ve-ha'er eineinu be-Toratekha,* Light up our eyes with Your teachings." It's like saying, we want to celebrate the intimacy of that moment in which the Beloved gives to the lover a glimpse of how the Beloved wants to love and be loved. I like to translate it this way:

When we study Torah,

may we see clearly
what is meant for us to know.
  When we do Mitzvot,
may all our feelings
sit harmonious in our heart.
  Focus all our hearts' longing
on that moment,
when we stand in Your Presence,
in awe and adoration.

Finally, we seal the paragraphs leading up to the *Shema* with a blessing, "*ha-bocher be-amo Yisrael be-ahavah,* blessing the one who chooses us in love" or, if you prefer, "who relates to us in love."

The *Shema*

In the center, after the statement of love, comes the *Shema*—the *yichud,* the unification, a moment we've been building up to since we started.

  LISTEN, Yisrael—
  Yah, our God,
  YAH IS ONE.

Who is saying this? Moses, our teacher (Deuteronomy 6:4–9). "Listen!" he says, meaning us. The instruction comes in singular, not plural: *shema,* not *shim'u.* Listen, Yisrael—*you individual member, here and now, of an ancient God-wrestling people: Yah Eloheinu*—the god you think of as your God; and all the gods that all the peoples of earth imagine, each with their own imagery and language, as *their* gods—all those "our Gods" (*eloheinu*) are ONE.

  Unique.

  All-There-Is.

  In the heart of that *yichud,* that unification, we are all one. In *Atzilut* I am not I, and you are not you. And yet we do not lose our Yisrael-ness. The statement is addressed to us as Jews, recognizing the role and tasks that we have been placed here to do. So now we have to figure out: what are we going to do with this teaching?

Many years ago, in a booklet called *Gate to the Heart*, I suggested a way to say the *Shema* more deeply and truly. I suggested reciting the same sentence four times:

The first time, hear Moshe Rabbenu saying it to all of us. "Hear, O Israel"—all the souls who are assembled before me today; all of their descendants, and their descendants' descendants, until the end of time.

The second time, hear it as if Moses were addressing only you, as if the message were coming to you over all that distance of time and space. "Listen, [your name here]; this message is meant for you."

The third time, think of someone you want to send it to. I send it out sometimes to one of my children, when I have the feeling that it would be important to them to experience that. Or when I hear that a grandchild or someone I know is confused. Put yourself in Moses's place, and send the message out with love and compassion.

For the fourth and final time you say it, imagine you are on your deathbed, saying your last *Shema*. Your soul is slipping away from you, about to rejoin the great ocean of consciousness. At that moment, all the *Shema Yisrael*s of your lifetime—all the *Shema*s you have ever sung, and recited, and meditated on—will all join together in a fullness and a glory and come to your aid.

The *Shema* is the quintessence of *Beriyah*, the world of knowledge and thought. We are not giving thanks, we are not praising, we are not blessing, we are not asking. We are simply trying to wrap our minds around the statement that holds up the ceiling of our Jewish existence: God is One. This is harder to grasp than it sounds. The *Tikkunei Zohar* marvels, "You are One, but not in the sense of enumeration"—not "one" as an alternative to two, three, or four, but a Unity of infinite existence and infinite potential.

And yet no matter where you go in the siddur, no matter which *olam* (world) you find yourself in, you're always in the place of *Yetzirah*, the feeling world. Because after all, the act of davening is an act of

loving! The theme of revelation brings the two worlds together—
Yetzirah within *Beriyah*, heart and mind. The love we speak of in the
Ahavah Rabbah and *Ahavat Olam* prayers is love in its highest form,
what Spinoza called *amor Dei intellectualis*, the higher mind's love for
God.

    We continue the *Shema* in the words of our teacher Moses:

> *Love Adonai, your God,*
> *With all your heart,*
> *And with all your soul,*
> *And with all your being.*

Our *kavanah*, then, is to hold nothing back, to love God with everything we have, everything we are. Of the words "With all your heart,"
Rashi wonders, why does it not say, *be-khol libkha*—with all your
heart, in the singular—but rather *be-khol levavkha*, using the intensive
form? What this means, he says, is "with both your good and your evil
inclination." I think of this as meaning, "Love God with everything
your heart desires."

    Rashi goes on: "*be-khol nafshekha*, with all your spirit"—even if
God takes your spirit from you. Even in death. The next phrase, "*be-
khol me'odekha*," Rashi interprets as with all your wealth, "since some
love their wealth even more than themselves." Or, he says, with every
measure (*midah*) of your being.

    I have translated the lines this way:

> **Love Yah,** *who is your God,*
> *In what your heart is,*
> *In what you aspire to,*
> *In what you have made your own.*

Sometimes I think of *me'odekha* as "With all your 'very,'" from *me'od*,
the Hebrew word for very. Love God superlatively! Think of the
adjectives good, better, and best: there is a base form, a comparative
form, and a superlative form. In the last one, the superlative state,
there is nothing else. That's the *me'od*. There's no one else. I don't

have any distractions. I don't have any side issues. That's the way I want to love God.

Of course, I know that without God's help I cannot hope to attain this level. So my words have a subtext. When I say, *"Ve-ahavta et ha-Shem Elohekha,* Love *Yah,* who is your God," the subtext is *Oy, halevai*—please let it be so. "With all your heart, and soul, and being"—*Oy, halevai, halevai.*

On a thematic level, the *Shema* moves us from love—with which the *Ve-ahavta* begins—to the section's final theme of redemption. The *Shema's* last two sentences hark back to our redemption from Egypt, and we continue to celebrate that in the paragraphs that follow.

There are times when I don't know how long I can hold onto that *Echad,* that One. The paragraphs of the *Shema* can take me back into the stories, distracting me from the precious moment of unity, the meditative oneness with all things. The paragraphs that follow the *Shema* can seem like unnecessary verbiage: "Established and enduring and fair and faithful and beloved and cherished and delightful and pleasant ..." The *Zohar* makes a whole *gesheft* about the importance of these fifteen adjectives. But in their zeal to provide the *Shema* with a proper setting, the Rabbis may have detracted from its depth and simplicity.

If I have time to daven at length (*be-arikhut*), then I can give the *Shema* crown all of its proper retinue. But if my time is limited, or I'm swept up in the *Shema's* final words—

> *I Am Yah, who is your God,*
> *the one who freed you from oppression to be your God.*
> *I am Yah, who is your God.*
> *Emet—That is the truth!*

—and I'm really feeling that, then I skip the intervening material between the *Shema* and the *Amidah.* Instead I say simply, *"mi she-ga'al et ha-avot, hu yig'al et ha-banim,* You, *Yah,* who saved our ancestors, may You soon bring redemption to us also." I say the final blessing of this section, sealing the theme of Redemption: "*Barukh atah Yah, ga'al Yisrael,* Blessed are You, *Yah,* Redeemer of Israel."

And I go right into the *Amidah.*

Asking for What We Need: The *Amidah*

Now we come to the *Amidah.* We often call it the "Silent *Amidah,*" which reminds us to look first on the level of *Asiyah.* Imagine you are an observer in a synagogue, seeing this for the first time. What do daveners do with their bodies during the *Amidah?* They are standing, feet together. Some place their tallis over their heads to create a more private prayer space. Many are swaying back and forth or from side to side. They are forming the words with their lips but praying in silence. The entire room, though full of people, is quiet.

What are they saying? The daily *Amidah* seems like nothing but a series of blessings and requests, but there is more. No prayer is more sensitive to the texture of time. No single prayer tells us more about where we stand in the sacred cycle of our Jewish year. The *Amidah* is like the prayer service in microcosm. The picture frame—the first three and last three blessings—barely changes, but the inner content is determined by the sanctity of the day.

The First Three Blessings

The *Amidah*'s first and last three blessings are always fixed: we say the same thing for weekday, Shabbos, and holiday alike. The middle blessings vary with the type of day. A person who knows the siddur could wake up during the *Amidah* and tell you whether it is Shabbos and, if so, whether we are saying the morning, afternoon, evening, or added *Musaf* prayer. A special paragraph reveals that today is a pilgrimage holiday (Pesach, Shavuot, or Sukkot) or a Rosh Chodesh, the first of the lunar month. Another announces that today is Chanukah or Purim. So the *Amidah* reflects the season as well as any mirror. It acknowledges where we are on the calendar and sets us up for that particular day.

Three blessings serve as our gateway to the *Amidah*'s inner contents. Our relationship with God has always come wrapped in two basic emotions: love and awe (*ahavah* and *yir'ah*). Both are vital to the *Amidah* and its framework.

Our connection to God goes back thousands of years, and we acknowledge that history first. The first blessing is known as the blessing of the *Avot*, the patriarchs or ancestors. (More and more congregations are adding the *Imahot*, the matriarchs, as well.) We say, "God, you have been with us since the days of Abraham and Sarah, Isaac and Rebekah, Jacob and Rachel and Leah. You remember the *chasadim* that they did, the righteous deeds. Please draw that merit down to us, and look after us as you did them."

The second paragraph of the *Amidah* blesses God for sustaining life and helping the sick and the fallen, even to *techiyat ha-meitim*, resurrection of the dead. Here our minds rebel. The resurrection of the dead is an ancient principle of the Jewish faith, one that Maimonides included as one of the Thirteen Principles of Jewish belief. Yet in what way can I affirm this? I do not believe that the crypts will open up in cemeteries and corpses will crawl out of them. I do not believe that the individual cells of my remains will be reconstituted at the end of days. How many bodies have I worn out in only one lifetime already? How can I praise God for "enlivening the dead" and mean it?

And yet, just as rationalism makes that idea impossible to swallow, science comes to the rescue. As Albert Einstein is supposed to have said, we can either live our lives as if nothing is a miracle—or as if everything is. Take a look: Once we thought of our planet as a lump of sand and rock populated by living beings. Now we have learned that even the balance of our planet's atmosphere depends on living interactions. The call to collaborate as cells of a greater global intelligence is urgent and unmistakable.

Nor does the miracle of life stop there. Computer memory is now a crucial ingredient of our collective mind. We talk about "machine learning" now. And what are DNA and RNA if not strings of information, encoding the genetic wisdom of a species? So our whole awareness of matter and the physical world is changing. The boundary between the living and inert is becoming blurred. That which we once considered dead is coming alive. What a miracle! And so I praise God with all my heart for giving life today to what yesterday we thought dead.

The last of the three fixed blessings that introduce the *Amidah* is "You are holy [*Atah kadosh*]." Some people object to this basic Jewish vocabulary word, "holy." Dividing things into holy versus unholy brings us to dualism and polarity, and we're not comfortable in that place.

But take a look: My toenails are a part of me, but not at the same level as my brain cells. So there's a difference in gradation and level. We learn this from organismic thinking: Unity and non-duality do not mean homogenized. If you put me into a blender and blend all my cells together, I won't be alive anymore. In order to be alive, I have to maintain the differentiations between systole and diastole, between white corpuscles and mitochondria. They all have to work together. They're all part of the holistic One—but at different levels. So we acknowledge with this blessing that even in a non-dualistic world, we have different levels of meaning, existence, connection.

Ancestors, life, holiness: that is the three-blessing foundation the *Amidah* rests on. That is our gate. The theme of the ancestors reso- nates in more subtle ways as well: we are, in fact, invoking each of the three in turn. Our faith began with Abraham, so we seal the first paragraph with the blessing *Magen Avraham*, Shield of Abraham. In thanking God "for reviving the dead," we think of Isaac, who was a moment from death as he lay upon the altar in the *Akeidah*, the Binding of Isaac.

Finally, in speaking of holiness in the third blessing, we think of Jacob. The figure of Jacob in Torah is beset by troubles for most of his life. Oy, does he suffer! And yet of Jacob we say, *mitato sheleimah*, "his bed was complete." Why? Because Abraham had Ishmael, who split off from our faith and our history. Isaac had Esau. But all of Jacob's children—all of those who came from his bed—were part of *Benei Yisrael*, the Children of Israel. (That's why, in the *Amidah* of Shabbat

Minchah, the afternoon prayer, we say, "Abraham is joyful, Isaac will rejoice, Jacob *and his sons* will rest in it." In what do they find their rest? On a *peshat* level we would say that they rest on Shabbat, but I think of it as resting in God.)

Jacob was the *balabos*, the homemaker. He was always embroiled in family life: his wives, his many children, their squabbles, making sure they had enough to eat. In the *Amidah*'s third blessing we say, "*U-k'doshim be-khol yom yehalelukha.*" This is usually translated as "holy beings praise you every day." But I like to read it that those who praise you are *kedoshim be-khol yom*—holy in the everyday, rather than a holiness that sets itself apart from the world.

The Middle Blessings

The first three blessings lay down a framework for our prayer. They are included in every *Amidah* that we say throughout the year. The middle section of the *Amidah*, however, varies with the type of day. On Shabbos and holidays, which are days of rest, this section is shorter and more celebratory. On a weekday, when we are beset with cares and concerns, we take this opportunity to turn to God and unburden our hearts.

In Europe, in the days when ordinary people were just beginning to be literate, they used to have something called a *briefenshteller* (or *brivnshteler*), which was like a manual that showed people how to write letters.[10] I think it was Sholem Aleichem who wrote a story about a young couple who bought a *briefenshteller* to learn how a groom should write to his bride and how a bride should write to her groom. Then they copied the letters out word for word and sent them to each other.

Someone who is focused on just saying the words of the *Amidah* and fulfilling the obligation is like that young couple: they didn't understand that the *briefenshteller* was just to show a template. You have the form. Now you have to put in your own details!

My single most important message about the *Amidah* is to make it your own. Prayer will never truly be part of our lives until we address our real concerns. This, from a davener's point of view, is really the moment of truth. And yet asking for what we truly need is the hardest part of prayer. We throw up all sorts of obstacles. Whom am I praying to? Who am I to ask for anything? Will it help? We have written extensively about these questions elsewhere, but here is a summary.

Whom am I praying to? I am praying to God, however I understand and experience that word right here and right now. I may not be praying to the God that is All, but simply sharing my *tsuris* with the face of God with which I am most intimate. Perhaps I am praying to whatever it is that listens in the universe. I don't need to do any more than that.

Who am I to ask for anything? I am a creation and manifestation of godliness. I am a wave in the ocean and a world unto myself. The infinite potential for creativity and love in the universe manifests in me and *through* me, as it does in every other creature.

And will it help? We know some parents pray with all their hearts for a child to be cured of a life-threatening disease, and yet the little one dies. We pray daily for peace, yet we are still at war. Prayer is not a switch with which we can control the universe. But I do believe that we can, with our prayers, reach dimensions of existence that we do not otherwise have access to and that the openings in those higher worlds bring blessings down to us. And don't forget the more immediate benefits at home. Prayer waters thirsty souls like rain on flowers. Prayer may not bring world peace, but it gives my heart peace. Prayer may not cure the sick, but it helps us find healing. Prayer may not guarantee me a job, but it helps me rise up with renewed energy and purpose to address the obstacles before me. A prayer truly prayed is the beginnings of its own answer. So yes, prayer helps.

The Rabbis well understood how hard it is to say what's in our hearts. Now that it is time for us to speak, what can we say? Where do we begin? So they began the *Amidah* with a sentence that seems to capture the resistance we must overcome: "O God, open up my lips, and let my mouth speak Your praise." Even old hands at davening can rush through this phrase too quickly. *Open up my lips!* Just a quarter-inch of movement, but how hard that opening can be!

If that opening is hard for you, know that you are not alone. Don't try to force your way through. Take the opportunity to dwell on this most difficult hurdle. Ask for help with just this one thing. Rabbi Hanna Tiferet Siegel wrote a beautiful tune to her own translation of the words: "O God, open up my lips, as I begin to pray." (Called "S'fatai Tiftach," it appears on her album *Olamama.*) Singing is a wonderful way to ease into prayer, as well as an opportunity to repeat a given sentence many times, deepening your *kavanah* a little each time.

Another thought. This first sentence reminds us that prayer begins with silence. Think back to the silence that follows the last, enlarged *dalet* of the *Shema* statement's final *ECHAD*. This is not a silence of absence but a silence full of the presence of the One, a silence of infinite potential. So let us stand, just for a moment, in a silence so deep that *only* "God [can] open up our lips and let us begin to pray." Then, when we can't hold the quiet any longer and issues come up for us about our lives, we can open our lips and hearts and ask for what we need for the day.

How do you make the *Amidah* your own? You'll find that once you begin to really inhabit your prayer, you may start to come up with all kinds of teachings and insights about it. "Once I was really struggling with a work problem," a student told me. "The next morning I was saying the weekday morning prayers with a friend. We sat out in his backyard, which has a stream running through it, and for the *Amidah* we stood by the stream, each in his own thoughts. I got to the fourth blessing, the paragraph that says, '*Atah chonen le-adam da'at,* You favor us with knowledge and teach us understanding,' and suddenly I really felt the faith of that statement, that I could trust God to give me the wisdom I needed. And very soon after that I found an answer to my problem!"

Here's another example: A student told me that instead of saying, "Desire, O God, Your people Israel *u-vi-tefilatam*—and their prayers," as his Ashkenazi community does in *Retzeh,* the seventeenth blessing of the daily *Amidah,* he loves to use the Sephardic variation: "... *u-li-tefilatam she'eh,* and turn toward their prayers." The reason this small change is important to him, he said, is because of a teaching he'd once read from my Rebbe, Reb Yosef Yitzchak, who told a story[11] about a man who came to see the Baal Shem Tov. This fellow, whose name was Reb Mordechai, was attracted by the charisma and depth of this seemingly unlearned man and became one of the Baal Shem's disciples.

Reb Mordechai had trouble with prayer, as so many of us do. Learning Torah was no problem; Mordechai loved to learn. Indeed, he begrudged any time taken away from study. Joyful exercise of his intellect in God's holy name was like standing on a mountaintop. But prayer, the service of the heart—this was hard for him. He just couldn't open himself up to it.

What turned things around for him, as so often happens, was a seemingly small thing: the right word at the right time. He heard the Baal Shem Tov quoting a story from the Talmud (Shabbos 10a) in which one rabbi, Rav, sees another, Rav Hamnuna, prolonging his prayers. "They forsake eternal life [*chayei olam*]," Rav said disdainfully, "and occupy themselves with the needs of the hour [*chayei sha'ah*]." In other words, "He's spending too much time davening and not enough time studying." The Talmudic rabbis often valued study over prayer; Rav's put-down was a classic expression of that.

But the Baal Shem Tov, centuries later, turned Rav's response on its head. To truly understand the Talmud's message, the Baal Shem suggested, we must focus on the two key terms that Rav used. In Biblical Hebrew the word *olam* typically meant antiquity or eternity. In that sense, interpreting the expression *chayei olam* as eternal life makes sense. More recently, however, *olam* has most frequently meant "world." This gives the expression new meaning: *chayei olam*, life of the world. And living in this world, said the Baal Shem, is precisely what Torah comes to teach us about.

Chayei sha'ah, on the other hand, should not be understood as "the life of the hour," the Baal Shem Tov continued. True, this is the more common understanding. *Sha'ah* means hour. As Rashi explains, prayer is concerned with our daily needs: health, peace, sustenance. But the Baal Shem Tov reminded his listeners that *sha'ah*, when used as a verb, means something completely different: it comes from the root meaning "to turn toward."[12] What *chayei sha'ah* really means, said the Baal Shem, is "a life of turning"—turning to God. Far from dismissing Rav Hamnuna for prolonging his prayer, the Baal Shem Tov said, we should understand that Rav was praising him for setting aside the life of this world (that is, Torah study) for a life of turning to God.

And that, said my student, is why he says "... *u-li-tefilatam she'eh*, and turn toward their prayers"—because every time he says it, it reminds him of the Baal Shem Tov's message about prayer and turning toward God. He thought that was a beautiful teaching, one that helped him overcome his own difficulties with prayer.

Daveners often collect little thoughts and teachings here and there to give their davening more *kavanah*, even if they're not completely conscious of doing so. There's a wonderful series called *Peninei ha-Chasidut* (Pearls of Hasidism), which has little teachings from all kinds of Rebbes and books on the different holidays. Imagine having such a siddur as well, with teachings that appealed to you and with your own experiences, or to have a little insight journal, in which you wrote down moments of awareness that you got from your davening during the week. That would be a wonderful thing to reflect on from time to time!

The blessings of the daily *Amidah* might seem like arcane formulas and stilted phrasing at first, particularly in translation. But they are wonderful opportunities to ask for things to concern us. I have tried to paraphrase them here in direct, everyday language. This will give you some sense of how to make the blessings your own, how to add the things that most concern you at this point. Here they are in order, beginning from the fourth blessing, which follows the three fixed blessings at the beginning.

> *Atah chonen*—You give us wisdom. Help me align my intellect with clarity and purpose. Give me inspiration. Help me realize my highest intentions.

Hashivenu—Oy, dear God, return us to Your ways. Help me to serve You. Bring me back, so that I might turn toward You again.

Selach lanu—Forgive us, God, for the things we have done wrong. If there's anything I can do to correct them, please let me do it. And if I can't fix it, please wipe the slate clean and help me to do better next time.

Re'eh—Please, God, see where I hurt and when I'm in trouble. Use the power of *Gevurah* to see me through.

Refa'einu—If You heal me, I know I'll be healed. I place myself in Your compassionate heart. Please grant healing to me and to all Your people.

Barekh aleinu—*Ribboyno sh'l oylom,* I'm worried that I won't be able to make a living for me and my family. Please bless all my "crops" this year, and let the earth be bountiful to us as well.

Teka be-shofar gadol—Dear God, you know that we are scattered and our efforts are scattered. Please bring us together and awaken us to our common purpose. Point us always to higher things and to our ultimate redemption.

Hashivah shofeteinu—So many people in the world suffer from injustice. Please bring justice and fairness to them, and give each of us the judgment to know what is right.

La-malshinim—Dear God, much as we strive for the good, yet evil still survives and thrives among us. Please disrupt the plans of those who choose the paths of violence and malice.

Al ha-tzadikim—On the other hand, thank God, there are those who do the right thing, who act in fairness and *chesed.* Guard all those who trust in Your name, and help me to be one of them.

Ve-li-Y'rushalayim ircha and *Et tzemach David*—Please help to bring us, as a people, to our highest destiny. Dwell among us as You promised, and rebuild the city of Jerusalem on earth and in our hearts.

Shema koleinu—Hear our voices and have pity on us. Receive our prayers with compassion. I know that even if I had no one else to listen to me, You are there and listening. (The Rabbis recommended this blessing as especially suited to saying anything that's in your heart and that has not found a place in the rest of the *Amidah*.)

The Final Blessings

The *Amidah* closes with three final blessings. The first, *Retzeh*, is called the blessing of *avodah* (service). It is couched in the language of sacrificial ritual: "Restore the *avodah* to your Holy of Holies; accept the fire-offerings of Israel and their prayers with love." But what we are really saying? "Take pleasure, God, in our way of praying. Teach us to encounter Your presence." We are saying, "Everything that we have been praying about—please, receive that." We want to be certain that we didn't talk to the wall!

Retzeh is only one of many places in the traditional davening that look back to Temple times with yearning. Oy, if we only had access to our *Beit ha-Mikdash!* Yet I do not yearn for Temple times as a means to offer sacrifices. I'm a *Kohen*, a priest: I would eat good steaks in a rebuilt Temple, but that's not what I want.

In Boulder, Colorado, where I live, we have the Cesium Fountain Atomic Clock, a clock so precise that even after sixty million years it would not be off by so much as a second. This, the U.S. Government's website claims, is "the nation's time and frequency standard": other atomic clocks we use attune themselves to that one.

Can you imagine having such a soul calibrator, a place from which there would be a going-out, as there is from Boulder, by which broadcast I could recalibrate my *neshomeh?* This is what we yearn for, and this is what the Babylonians and the Seleucid Greeks and the Romans tried to wreck for us: to tear down the broadcast tower that was our Temple, to stop the beating heart of the people. They succeeded, but only physically. We may not have a single center, accurate to the point of godliness. But we have our community, our Torah study, and our davening to recalibrate ourselves to who we are and what we need to do.

We seal *Retzeh* by saying, "Blessed are You, God, who restores your Shekhinah to Zion"—and then right away we start the next paragraph: "*Modim anachnu lakh*, we thank You."

Reb Levi Yitzchak of Berdichev used to tell a wonderful story about such juxtapositions. He asked: Why do we bless God, in the *Amidah*'s sixth blessing, as the "the merciful One who pardons us so frequently [*chanun ha-marbeh li-s'loach*]"? How can we be so sure that God has forgiven us? Imagine, he says, a child who wants to eat an apple before dinner. The child's father says, "No. Wait until after dinner." But this child is a smart one: he quickly rattles off the blessing for fruit. The father, not wishing to violate the Rabbinic precept against saying a blessing for no reason, has to give his son the apple. In the same way, the Berdichever says, we quickly thank God for pardoning us. That's why we say "who restores Your *Shekhinah* to Zion" and then go right into "We thank You."

Where does the Shekhinah dwell today? In our hearts. We each have a place that we go to lick our wounds when we get hurt, when somebody hurts our feelings. Others may never see that place inside us; it's not a place where we feel at our most adult and confident. It's nobody else's business, so we don't let anybody in.

But we can let God in. A famous *piyyut* (devotional poem) says, "I will build a sanctuary [*mishkan*] in my heart"—the word *mishkan* stemming from the same root as *shekhinah*. Into that place I want to put my *shekhinah*. So if you can, when you say, "Blessed are You, God, for restoring Your *shekhinah* to Zion," put your hand over your heart for a moment, and say, "Thank You for giving Your *shekhinah* a home in my heart. Thank You for being the awareness that I have in my heart, the awareness that I've prayed for."

Then we give thanks. "We thank You" (*modim anachnu lakh*), the paragraph that comes next, is where we truly count our blessings. An attitude of gratitude is such a wonderful way to greet the world. Gratitude is perhaps the single emotion most closely aligned with happiness, whatever the circumstances of our lives may be. The paragraph, in loose translation, says this:

> *Thank you for being our God and the God of our ancestors.*
> *You are the rock of our lives.*
> *You are our shield and our salvation in every generation.*
> *We will thank You and tell Your praises—*
> > *for our lives, which we place in Your hands;*
> > *for our souls, which we entrust to You;*
> > *for Your miracles, which are with us every single day;*
> > *for Your wonders and Your goodness, which are constant:*
> > *morning, noon, and night.*
> *Your goodness never ceases;*
> *Your compassion and chesed never run out.*
> *Our hopes have ever turned to You.*

We seal this paragraph with "For all these, *ha-Shem*, our God...." It's as if we were saying, "*Beyond* all these, we thank You for being our God." The blessing's final words are "*lekha na'eh le-hodot*—it is not only fitting; how pleasant it is, how good it feels, to give thanks to You!"

The last blessing of the *Amidah* begins "*Sim shalom*, Grant us peace." Why does this come last? Because, as the midrash tells us, "There is no vessel better than peace for containing blessing."[13] Some communities today pray not only for peace for Israel but for "*kol yosh-vei teiveil*," for all the world as well.

Finally, we come to *Elohai Netzor*. It is in fact an addition to the *Amidah* proper, appearing after the final blessing. Yet it is best said slowly, and with great *kavanah*. The rest of the *Amidah* is phrased in terms of "we" and "us"—it's plural, though I phrase it in terms of my own needs, above, to personalize it. The *Elohai Netzor* is the only part of the *Amidah* said in the first person singular; it is strictly between me and God. "My God, guard my speech from evil or deceit.... Open my heart to Your teachings, and let my soul pursue Your commandments."

If you are, God forbid, in a work or social situation where you fear the actions or even the malice of others, this prayer offers you comfort. "If any would rise up against me, unravel their plans and spoil their plot." Yet one sentence can be troubling: "And to those who curse me [or, as some interpret it, 'those who make light of me'], may my soul be silent; let my soul be like dust to everyone." We don't always want to feel like we're such a *shmatteh*!

The Sephardim have a nice variation: "May it be Your will that no person be jealous of me, and that I be jealous of no one; and that I not get angry today, and that I not anger You...."

Elohai Netzor leaves room for improvisation. It originated, the Talmud tells us, in the habit various sages had of adding their own thoughts to the end of the *Amidah*. *Elohai Netzor* is based on one such paragraph. This suggests that those who wish to enhance the standard *nusach* with their own thoughts can do so. The penultimate sentence is the source of the famous line from the song "By the Rivers of Babylon": "May the words of my mouth and the meditations of my heart be acceptable in Your sight, O God, my Rock and my Redeemer" (Psalm 19:15). This is clearly an appropriate place to add anything personal that you want to say to God. So you'll say what works for you.

Bringing Down the Abundance: Closing Prayers

We've risen up; now we have to come down.

We began our prayers with a series of morning blessings that bring us into our bodies and help us inhabit our physical selves. We aroused our emotions with the tuneful verses, moved to song by the "*Halleluyah*s." We moved into our higher minds with a contemplation of God's creation and unity in the *Shema* and its blessings. Then finally we reached for the lofty abstractness of *Atzilut*—and at the same time, finding ourselves newly present and awake, we searched within ourselves to speak of our deepest hopes and dreams. Now it is time to re-engage with the world and—this is a crucial point—to bring something from our davening back into our lives, to make sure that we were not just spinning our spiritual wheels. If we want our prayers to be answered, we have to make sure not to hang up the phone too quickly.

When Jacob dreamed his dream of the ladder, he saw the angels "going up and coming down it" (Genesis 28:12)—not coming down first, as we might think, but rather ascending first, then descending. Spiritual ascent is relatively easy. Holding onto some of the insights you got there, bringing back with you some of the fruits of your journey and putting them to use: that is the hard part. So the morning prayers, before they are through, give us the opportunity to ask ourselves: What will remain after I close my siddur? How long will my determination to live in a more ethical and loving way last? How can I do a better job of putting my resolutions into practice?

After the *Amidah*, it is important to find a moment to search your heart and conscience. This is especially important in the evening prayers, toward the end of the day. If you find something that needs repair—perhaps something you did that troubles you—make your commitment to fulfill that *tikkun*, and ask for whatever help and grace you need. What I'm really asking myself at this point is: Where was I in my davening? What did I learn today, and what do I need to bring back into my life?

The daily morning prayers usually include a section at this point known as *Tachanun*—confession and supplication. Some of the more abjectly humble and self-chastising language may not work for everybody: "We have scorned, we have rebelled ... we have been perverse, we have acted wantonly." Some might rather say Psalm 6 or 25, which speak from the same place. I also wrote a *tachanun* for the English siddur I published.[14] The feelings at the core of these variations are the same: "Dear God, I need help. I've got problems. These are the things that I did wrong. Help me with them. Help me to right them. And if, God forbid, I cannot right them, please wipe them off my slate."

This is also a good opportunity to reflect in writing. During the week, you can take a piece of notepaper and a pencil. Reflect for a few moments after your davening and see what comes down. "So what do I have to do today, *Ribbono shel olam?*" Write down what comes to you, and try to refer to it during the day or before you go to sleep at night.

Kaddish

In some minyanim you may notice that the final stretch of the morning prayers includes a number of repetitions of the *Kaddish*: a Half *Kaddish* after the *Tachanun* (supplication), a Full *Kaddish* after *U-Va le-Tzion* (A redeemer shall come to Zion), a Mourner's *Kaddish* after *Shir shel Yom* (the Psalm of the Day), a Rabbinical *Kaddish* after *Ein ke-Eloheinu* (There is none like our God), and finally another Mourner's *Kaddish* after *Aleinu*. Why? What's going on?

Kabbalists think of the prayers that we say after the *Amidah* as part of the *yeridat ha-shefa*, the "descent of the abundance"—the process by which God's grace becomes manifest in the world. Imagine I'm in a house. The house doesn't have a staircase; if I want to go up or down a floor, I have to use the elevator. The *Kaddish* serves as that elevator: when a minyan goes from one world to another, it always does so with a *Kaddish*.[15] This is true earlier in the davening as well—when we're on the way up, as it were. When we leave the world of *Asiyah* and the morning blessings, the mourners say a Rabbinical *Kaddish*, and everyone responds with "Amen!" It's as if we were saying, "Now that I'm about to leave this level, '*Yitgadal ve-yitkadash shemei rabbah*, magnified and sanctified be God's great name.' Let the world of *Asiyah* be filled with God energy, and I'm about to go to *Yetzirah.*"

We spend some time in *Yetzirah*; then, after the tuneful blessings and before *Barekhu*, we say the Half *Kaddish* before entering the world of *Beriyah* for the *Shema* and its blessings. We would say *Kaddish* before the *Amidah* as well, but the Rabbis asked that our davening "follow redemption with prayer" (*somech ge'ulah li-t'fillah*), going into the *Amidah* immediately after the blessing of "who redeems Israel."

The elevator image applies after the *Amidah* as well. We're on the top floor of the building; the air is almost too pure for a working pair of lungs. We want to go back to street level, to resume our normal lives. So we go down a floor, then another, then another, bringing the connection we made with God back to our everyday lives. That's why we have so many repetitions of the *Kaddish*, and that's why we connect this section to *yeridat ha-shefa*, descent of the divine abundance.

Aleinu

The *Aleinu* is the last major signpost of our davening. It's like turning around for one final wave before taking leave of God in our prayers. My sense with *Aleinu* is that we're saying, "Now that it's time to stop praying to You, I feel as if I haven't even started! Despite everything I've already said, still, *Aleinu le-shabe'ach la-Adon ha-kol*—what can we do but offer praise to the Master of all?"

As we mentioned earlier, *Aleinu* was originally embedded in the Kingship (*Malkhuyot*) section of the Rosh Hashanah davening; it has some very triumphalist moments, which the tune only serves to emphasize. Many modern daveners have trouble with lines like "who has not made us like the nations of the world, and has not placed us like the families of the earth." Some prefer to read it as "who has made us for Him, like the nations of the world, and has placed us for Him, like the families of the earth," replacing *lo* with an *aleph*, meaning no or not, with *lo* with a *vav*, meaning "for Him."

Both paragraphs of *Aleinu*, however, end with thoughts that take us back to one of our prayers' highest moments. *Aleinu*'s first paragraph ends with "*Adonai* is our God, in the heavens above and the earth below—*ein od*! There is no other!" The second paragraph ends with a quote from the prophet Zechariah: "And God will be king over all the land; on that day God will be One, and God's name will be One" (Zechariah 14:9). So we end on a note of Unity, the all-encompassing Oneness that is God alone. We end, in other words, in the same place as the great *Shema* statement that rises like Sinai from the landscape of our prayer: "Hear, O Israel, the Lord our God is One."

The Psalm of the Day

Like guests who can't tear themselves away, though, we add a coda: *Shir shel Yom*, the Psalm of the Day. These are the songs that the

Levites sang in the Temple. Not all the text is easy to relate to, but I think it's important to recognize, at the end of our davening, that Monday is not the same as Tuesday, and Tuesday is not the same as Wednesday, and that each day has its own texture. Helping to weave that texture with our prayers is part of what davening is about. Try to devote this corner of your prayer to the day, even if you just pick one sentence. For example:

> Sunday: "Earth and her fullness are Yours, *Yah!*"
>
> Monday: "God is vast, and God's fame is glorious, in God's city, on God's holy mountain."
>
> Tuesday: "God is present in a godly gathering."
>
> Wednesday: "When my legs fail me, Your *chesed* holds me up."
>
> Thursday: "Make music to God, the Source of our strength."
>
> Friday: "*Yah*, You rule, robed in majesty!"

These six songs find a parallel in *Kabbalat Shabbat*, the service with which we welcome the Sabbath. We begin there, too, with six psalms, one for every weekday. The first five are Psalms 95 through 99. We don't say Psalm 100, because that's the psalm that was said with the *korban todah,* the sacrifice of thanks in the Temple. This was not offered on the Sabbath, so the Rabbis thought it inappropriate for Friday night. Instead, for the sixth psalm, we go to Psalm 29: "God will bless us with peace" is a nice way to end the week! If possible we use these psalms as an opportunity to look back on our week, to think how we might improve the way we spent each day. We say Psalm 95 and think, "What did I do on Sunday? *Oy.* Oh, dear. 'Forty years I was angry with that generation' (Psalm 95:10)." So in saying every psalm you reflect on the corresponding day. Then we say *Lekha Dodi* (Come, my Beloved), bowing Shabbos in with "Enter, O Bride! Enter, O Bride!" And finally we say the seventh psalm: "*Mizmor shir le-yom ha-Shabbos,* A psalm, a song for the Sabbath day."

Davening on Twenty Minutes a Day

So how do I daven on a budget? How can I make the journey we describe here if I'm hemmed in on all sides by demands on my time?

I begin in *Asiyah*, putting on my tallis and tefillin first, creating the prayer space that I need. I check in with my body, and I say *Asher Yatzar*, acknowledging the miracle of the limbs and organs that sustain me. Then I look out of the window and see the world outside, the people and the buildings and the trees, the sun or the rain or the snow, and I say, "Thank You, *Ribbono shel olam*, all of these are wonderful, and I thank You."

I want to spend a little time in *Yetzirah* if I possibly can, giving my emotions a voice. Three key prayers here are *Barukh She-amar*, *Ashrei*, and *Yishtabach*. If I have time, I say those. The Rabbis recognized that many working people do not have the time to rejoice in God at length, so they provided a digest prayer that appears just before *Ashrei* called *Yehi Khevod*. Eighteen different psalms contribute verses to it, many of them gems from elsewhere in the davening. All of the emotions we express in the tuneful verses are to be found here. Another good one for those on a tight davening budget is Psalm 100, "A psalm of thanksgiving," which is only five verses long. I translate the first lines as, "This is how you sing a 'Thank You' song to God: join the whole earth symphony!" The psalm includes the famous injunction to "Serve God with joy," four words that summarize the *kavanah* we bring to our davening.

If I really have very little time, I go straight to the *Shema*. I say *Shema Yisrael* and *Barukh shem kevod malkhuto*, and I say, "Dear God, I'll do the best I can to love you with all my heart, with all my soul, with all my might." Then I say, "*Ribboyno sh'l oylom*, here's the *Amidah*," but I go right away from the three opening blessings to the sixteenth blessing, "Hear our voice," where traditionally we pray for what we need. I say, "Dear God, please listen. This is my list for today. These are the things that are on my mind. I pray for my parents to get well. I pray for my children to do well. I pray for a decent livelihood. I pray that my partner and I will have the strength to love and to stay together. *Please* help; give me the strength to see this through. 'For You hear with mercy the prayers of Your people, *Barukh atah ha-Shem*, who hears all prayer.'"

Then I go to the final three blessings. In "For all these," the seventeenth blessing, the blessing of thanks, I say, "I thank You for my life, our lives that are given over into Your hands," because I know that without help I'm not going to make it. I close with the *Amidah*'s final thought: "*Oseh shalom*, just as in the heavens everything works out as it should, so please, bring peace and tranquility upon us as well."

I take my leave with *Aleinu*. If I can, as I'm taking off my tallis and tefillin, I say a sentence or two from the psalm of the day, reminding myself of this day's place in the texture of time. Sometime during the day, now or later, I try to study at least one sentence of Torah. (I use *Chok le-Yisrael*, a source available free on the Web, which includes daily, bite-sized portions of Torah, Prophets, Writings, Mishnah, Gemara, *Zohar*, Jewish law, and *musar*, Jewish ethics.)

Conclusion

Davening, like daily life, is a multi-layered experience. We bring the body in with the morning blessings. From this point on, our body and the world of *Asiyah* will be part of our prayers: We stand or sit, we sway back and forth, we bow or rise up on our toes. We place our tallis over our head to give ourselves more privacy, kiss our *tzitzit*, feel the comforting weight of the tefillin on our hand or arm.

We arouse our emotions with the tuneful verses, but in truth, no matter in which *olam* (world) we find ourselves, we are always in the feeling of *Yetzirah*. What is davening if not the act of loving!

We focus our minds on the great themes of creation, revelation, and redemption and on the *Shema*. Yet in some sense we are always in *Beriyah*, always wrestling with and taking comfort in the great ungraspable conundrum of unity that lies at the heart of all we do, all we know, all we believe.

And finally we look toward *Atzilut*, to the very essence of mystic awareness, and we say, *Oy, halevai, halevai*. If we could only get there! We strive to make our prayers a vessel for our own experience—and yet, at the same time, to transcend all that heart and mind can grasp. We aim to be most truly ourselves, to stand in our fullness before the living God.

AT HOME IN SHUL

The Synagogue Experience

A davener may not enter a synagogue in the same state as the person who crosses the same threshold right behind him. Entering a synagogue is one thing. *Being* there is another.

Many people today experience shuls largely as facilities for life-cycle celebrations: bar mitzvahs, weddings, funerals. If these are the times that your life path brings you to the synagogue door, *gesunterheit*: you have shown up, you have joined the congregation in these moments, and that is important. But, as moving as these rituals can be, you may not be seeing the synagogue at its best, nor may you be experiencing prayer at *your* best.

The davener who likes prayer deep and rich thinks of a synagogue differently. This person comes more often, and in a different frame of mind. He or she might enjoy synagogue most when *no* special event is being celebrated, on the "ordinary" Shabbat in which only the shul's most dedicated God lovers join together in prayer and study and song. The davener, too, approaches prayer as a life-cycle event, but in a different sense. Just as a computer microprocessor goes about its business with every cycle of its inner clock, so does prayer pulse with every beat of the davener's heart.

How can we create a receptivity within ourselves for whatever the group davening experience has to offer? How can we, too, feel at home in shul?

Shedding Our Expectations

The first problem that many of us encounter upon entering a synagogue is one that we bring with us: our expectations. So many of us seem to have an ideal shul in our minds. Perhaps we can't quite articulate it, but we know that the seats in today's synagogue—or the ark, the color scheme, the windows, the rabbi, the cantor, the way people dress here, the service itself, the tunes they use—are not exactly what we had in mind; they're not what we feel most comfortable with. So the first task before us is to empty ourselves of our expectations—to free ourselves of the hold they have over us. I always quote Swami Satchidananda, who would say, "Don't make any appointments, you won't have any dis-appointments!"

A story: It was 1959, and I was teaching Jewish studies at the University of Manitoba, Winnipeg, where I was the Hillel director as well. The Hillel directors' group took a trip to Israel, and I was with them, the first time I had ever been to Israel. Comes Friday evening in Jerusalem, and we have met Schmuel Hugo Bergmann, who was a philosopher at Hebrew University, a friend of Martin Buber's and a wonderful human being. We asked him where we should go to daven, and he said, "Why don't you come with me to a Reconstructionist service?" So we went to Beit Ha-Chalutzot on Ibn Gevirol Street in Rechavia.

Reconstructionism was still quite new at that time. Less than fifteen years had passed since Rabbi Mordecai Kaplan, founder of the movement, had been excommunicated by the Union of Orthodox Rabbis. When I came out of the service, some of the other Hillel people said to me, "Come on. What kind of davening was this? How could you be so involved in it?"

I said, "It took me five minutes to give up any expectations I had. Once I joined in, I really got into it!"

Their hesitations were understandable. On the one hand, the davening that day was what I call a Protestant service. A Catholic mass builds; it goes up the mountain and comes down the mountain, just like the traditional Jewish davening I grew up with. A Protestant service is flatter; it's very left-brain. You rise for a hymn, sit down, do a reading, hear a sermon. You might sit in silence. But it doesn't have that same sense of building to a climax, then release.

Other aspects were more welcoming to me. The Reconstructionists used the Kaplan siddur, of course, and I found that Rabbi Kaplan had made sure that everything in English was also in Hebrew. If he wrote a prayer for *licht benshen* (candle lighting), for example, he wrote it not only in English but in Hebrew as well. So most of the Reconstructionist service was davened in Hebrew, and very seriously. A man named Ben Chorin Friedman was leading the prayers, and it was a beautiful service—a real waker-upper, without all the usual trappings that put you to sleep. We read about the prophet Elijah going to Mount Horev and hearing the *kol demamah dakah*, "the still, small voice" (1 Kings 19:12). The leader invited the people to sit in silence and meditate. I had published *The First Step*, a book about Jewish meditation, only the year before, so the silence was music to my ears. I was in seventh heaven!

Emptying myself of expectations is largely a matter of approaching the experience in the right frame of mind. Whenever I go to a different shul, I always ask myself the same question: How can I place myself in the closest *kirvat Elohim*, nearness to God, that I can be in this particular setting? I have davened with organs, choirs, everything. I'd be at Temple Emanuel on the Upper East Side in New York, overlooking Central Park, and I would say to myself, "Zalman, you're not in a *shtiebel*. This is an Appolonian experience, more mind-centered than heart-centered. But you can allow yourself to go to that place!"

Feeling at Home

Adjusting our expectations is important in visiting unfamiliar settings, but we gravitate to places in which we feel at home. How to find a shul where you like the way they do things and feel close to the other people there? In the old days, people used to go to a *landsmanschaft*. You belonged to Anshei Hotzenplotz, a benevolent society of immigrants from that particular place, because that's where they spoke your *mamaloshen*, ate the food you ate, and davened the way you were used to. The *landsmanschaften* are mostly gone now, but the desire to daven and celebrate with our own kind has not abated. If you're a young, single person in Manhattan today, for example, the Park Avenue Synagogue may not be for you; you may feel much more at home davening at B'nai Jeshurun or Romemu.

If you're an occasional shul-goer and have not yet found a home, ask your friends, people you feel are on the same wavelength as you. Go shul hopping! Find out which shul you like most. You can't know what your local synagogues have to offer until you give them a chance. Sometimes you'll find yourself drawn to more than one congregation. This one has a wonderful Shabbos service, that one has a great carnival on Purim, a third has a *yahrzeit* minyan at the right time when you need one.

Don't be ashamed to ask for help. Let's say I come in to a shul, and I don't know anybody. I'm trying it out for the first time, and the service is unfamiliar to me. I look around, and I make eye contact with someone. I go over to that person, and I say, "I'm new here. Would you be kind enough to let me sit with you and to show me how things are done here? I'd appreciate that greatly."

If you *do* have a shul where you're a regular davener, then I ask of you a *gemilat chesed*: please make sure that the visitors, the shul hoppers, the guests who are in town for the weekend and need a place to daven, are welcomed. Many of our shuls are less good at *in*-reach than they are at outreach. They work harder on attracting new members than on reaching out to people who are already in the door. It's a terrible thing to be a guest and nobody looks at you, nobody greets you at the door, nobody makes you comfortable or invites you home for a Shabbos meal.

Another story: It was Sukkot 1984, and I went to the Great Synagogue in Jerusalem to daven. It was a strange experience in some ways. When we got to the *Kedushah*, the choir director faced the *aron kodesh* and directed the choir backwards—silly stuff like that.

After a while I noticed a small group of African Americans, their *kipot* perched in funny places on their heads. The prophet Zechariah says that you're supposed to come to Jerusalem on Sukkot, so there's always a procession of non-Jewish pilgrims at that time. But nobody was sitting with them; nobody was showing them anything. They had no idea what was going on. So I went to beg a few siddurim with English translations from the other people there, promising I'd return them at the end of the service, and I went to sit with those visitors. When it came to "*Kadosh kadosh*," I said, "This is the Sanctus," connecting the prayers to their experience as best I could.

You can do this anywhere, in any setting, where you see a guest who does not know the ropes as well as you do. The other day a bar mitzvah was going on here in Boulder, Colorado, where I live. A mother was there with four children, one of whom was a classmate of the bar mitzvah boy. So I gave them siddurim, and I asked a woman from the shul, "Will you please sit with them and show them what's going on?" I feel that this is a form of *kiddush ha-Shem,* a sanctification of the name of God. Imagine how our father Abraham would have greeted those visitors!

Entering the Room

One thing that is very strong in Jewish Renewal, as you have probably seen in these pages by now, is attunement to the different dimensions of our beings: physical, intellectual, emotional, spiritual. Setting foot in a synagogue brings our bodies into the room, but in truth we probably are not fully there yet, even physically. We are not yet at the point where we can say, as the davening begins, "*Mah tovu ohalekha Yaakov,* How good are your tents, O Jacob; your dwelling places, Israel!"—and mean what we say. Judaism is well aware of the need to create a physical space for ourselves, a davening space in which we can begin to feel truly at home, and it offers us tools to do that.

The Torah says that before the priest, the *Kohen,* can enter the sanctuary in the *mishkan* (tabernacle), he must first wash his hands and feet. The Jews of Yemen retained that custom, washing their feet as well as their hands, just like the Moslems do, because they came to shul barefoot. Imagine if we, too, took the time to make that stop before we went in. You see it a lot less now, but a regular part of entering a synagogue in old Europe was *kiddush yadayim,* a ritual washing of hands, sanctifying the act with a blessing:

> *Barukh atah Adonai, Eloheinu, Melekh ha-olam,*
> *asher kideshanu be-mitzvotav ve-tzivanu*
> *al netilat yadayim.*
> *Blessed are You, our God, Sovereign of the world,*
> *who sanctified us with the commandment*
> *to wash our hands.*

I'm always grateful to synagogues that have sinks and vessels prepared for that. I would like to see every shul install a wash basin in the entry, offering a ritual to cleanse our hands from the doings of the outside world and prepare ourselves for prayer.

I used to take some of my students to church sometimes to show them some things that churches have borrowed from us. Have you ever seen a good Catholic coming into church? There is a font with holy water when they come in. They dip their fingers and sprinkle some on themselves or make a sign of the cross with the water. Before Vatican II, the priest used to wash his hands as part of the Mass before he began with the Sacrament. He would say, "I wash my hands among the innocents." A psalm attributed to David has a similar thought: "I wash my hands in purity and circle Your altars, O Lord" (Psalm 26:6).

When the Catholics enter the church itself, the first thing they do is genuflect in the direction of the altar. They bow down. In some Jewish congregations, too, people lower their heads toward the ark upon entering, acknowledging the presence that abides there. We say the whole world is filled with God's glory, but God's presence here in the sanctuary seems more palpable than on the outside. Our footsteps slow as we enter: we walk more lightly, more quietly. "*Be-veit Elohim nehalekh be-ragesh,*" the psalmist says (Psalm 55:15): We walk in God's house with feeling, sensitivity, receptivity.

One of the first things we do upon entering a shul is to take the books we need. I also like to see synagogues that have some inspirational books on a bookshelf in back, so that someone can come in, take a siddur, a *Chumash*, and one of those books as well. Then, if they need to space out for a little while, they can look into Heschel. Bringing such a book from home can serve you well if you sometimes have trouble staying with the service.

We gather books, tallis, yarmulke, and find a seat. The Rabbis urged each davener to have his or her own regular place in shul, and there's much to be said for that approach. When you sit in "your" seat, you are home. Your davening paraphernalia might be stored there; your usual neighbors are beside you; the fellow who sings those nice harmonies is right behind you, as he always is.

Yet there is something to be said, too, for allowing your present frame of mind to guide you in taking your place in the room today. Maybe when I come into shul today I don't feel quite up to joining in fully. I have something to work out on my own. So I won't sit in front: I'll sit toward the back someplace, or closer to a window, so that I'm in touch with whatever happens in shul, but I'm not fully immersed in it. I need to do my own homework and be with my own inner space.

Other times I feel like I want to daven strong with everybody. I know that the congregation needs my support, my song, my "Amen!" and I feel able to make that contribution this morning, so I sit closer to the person who leads the prayer. It is like putting a log in the fireplace. Logs that burn separated from each other will not make a good fire. But put a minyan of people with some prayer in their hearts close together, and you're likely to get a good warm blaze going, with some real singing, some Amens, some swaying and hand clapping. Never be embarrassed to contribute to the congregation in that way—not taking over, not leading with your ego, but making a contribution to the greater good, the davening circle that you have come to be part of today.

Now that we have found our seat, it is time to put on our tallit. Those with an advanced or traditional prayer practice will also don tefillin for morning prayers during the week. We do so with blessings, of course, but the traditional siddur also includes some wonderful verses and meditations associated with these special acts. A davener putting on her tallit might spend an extra moment or two with the tallit wrapped around her head, alone in her own special prayer space. Some put on their tefillin in the businesslike way in which we might approach any daily task; others will move more slowly, taking an extra thoughtful minute to bind the straps on their arm and themselves to God.

Think how deeply a davener has already advanced into prayer space. The fringed and knotted *tzitzit* surround us in each of the four directions. The words of the *Shema* rest on our forehead and upper arm; the strap wound around our middle finger betroths us to God. We sit quietly and prepare for prayer, softening the heart and preparing the mind to receive whatever messages will emerge in prayer today.

We can also enter with a certain quality of intent. What do I want to do today? I want to give thanks for the week. I would like to pray for my friend who is mourning the loss of his mother. I want to pray for my friend who is sick. I want to pray for the victims of a terrible incident that's been on the news lately. I even want to pray for our government, that our president, lawmakers, and judges will be blessed with courage and wisdom. Then I want to give thanks for the present day and moment. I might say, "Ahh, *Ribboyno sh'l oylom*, it's Shabbos. How happy I am to be spending these hours with my family and friends in Your presence!" Setting our intention in this way can help us become part of the prayer that's happening all around us.

Praying for the You in Me

Praying in a minyan is praying in community. You never walk into a shul without looking around. You want to see who is there. This, too, can be a challenge. The likelihood is that I may have some judgment on people. In Chabad we would follow the morning blessings with a *kavanah* from Lurianic kabbalah: "I take upon myself the commandment to love my neighbor as myself." This gave us an intentionality with which to proceed. I can say, "Dear God, whatever jealousies and resentments I might harbor in my heart, please remove this judgment from me." In that first look-around I want to be able to say, and mean in my heart, "You, and you, and you—all of you—may your davening this day achieve the highest possibility, may it bring you to the highest realization." By opening that up for them, I open it up for myself too.

Reb Pinchas of Koretz, the great Hasidic master, wondered how we can pray for other people to become better. Are we not depriving that person of their choice and free will? The answer, he says, is that we are all part of each other. You are in me, and I am in you. Praying for the "you in me" to be better—the "you" that resides in my heart—somehow helps the "me in you" to do something good for you, and the "you in you" to become better. This is not a moral vision but an organismic vision. On a prayerful level, we are all part of each other and of the greater whole. So look around and open yourself to *ahavat ha-beriyot*, love of your fellow creatures.

Spacing Out

So here we are in synagogue, surrounded by a davening community. The seat we occupy, the view we have, the books in front of us, the tallis and *kipah* and maybe tefillin we are wearing, the rabbi and the cantor and the people near us singing, all help to anchor us in this space. We have opened ourselves to the davening and to our fellow daveners. "One thing have I asked of God; that will I seek," says the psalmist: to sit—to truly be present—in God's house and to gaze upon God's countenance (Psalm 27:4). We want to ascend far enough up the holy ladder to achieve some moments of real prayer. We want to open ourselves to an I–Thou relationship with the *Ein Sof*, the Infinite One. We want to talk to God. These things are not always easy. But they are within our reach, and the rewards are great.

One delightful part of shul-going is giving yourself permission to space out. The *P'sukei de-Zimrah*, the "tuneful verses" that the Rabbis ordained as the best way to warm ourselves up for the more contemplative sections that follow, are a wonderful place to do that. Comes a beautiful line: "*Kol ha-neshamah tehallel Yah*, Everything that breathes praises God—*Halleluyah!*" All of a sudden I get a glimpse of what that might look like. Everything that breathes! Elephants trumpeting! Grasshoppers rubbing their legs together! Geese honking as they flap across the sky! Each one making a sound; each one offering something. I don't want to go any further right now. So I give myself permission not to stay with the people. The congregation will go on, but you might just decide that you need to take time out. You'll catch up with them when they next announce the page. Not a problem.

There is a wonderful psalm that we say on Shabbat morning. It begins, "A prayer of Moses, the man of God." I imagine Moses sitting alone during those forty days on the mountain, waiting to be called again to receive revelation. He is looking over his life, and he says, "God, you have been our dwelling place *be-dor va-dor*, from generation to generation" (Psalm 90:1). I translate it more mystically: "In each incarnation I was at home with You. Before the worlds, before the mountains were born, You were there. A thousand years in Your sight is like a day gone." And I decide to put the siddur down. I don't need anything more at this point. I give myself the luxury to go in my imagination to how Moses may have felt in that moment.

These are the kinds of imaginary visits that I can make. We say, "God of Abraham, God of Sarah." If I can just get into their heads and feel what they must have felt back then, walking the pasture land of Canaan with the knowledge of God fresh in their hearts, I would get such a different take on what it means to be a Jew, descendant of the patriarchs and matriarchs. I can ask myself, what must it have been like when the Baal Shem Tov was praying? If I were to allow my imagination to take me to Ibn Gabirol in the Golden Age of Spain, what was it like when he was praying? When Yehuda HaLevi was praying? What must the word *Echad*, the Oneness of God, have felt like to the brilliant philosophical mind of Maimonides? Such musings can only deepen our experience of prayer.

So does song. Sometimes, I don't feel like being that much in my head. Instead I'll go with a melody, lifting my voice with the others, swaying in my seat or moving my feet, clapping my hands, helping to create a wave of song that will float every vessel in the room. Or I might close my eyes and drift along on the efforts of my fellow daveners, held up by the sound of all the voices around me, feeling, "I'm a child of the universe. I have a right to be here. I'm embraced by the Shekhinah, the divine presence. Underneath are the everlasting arms. I don't need to do anything. I can just let myself be loved by the God who is coming through this melody here and now."

So if you find a goody that is significant to you, stay with it. Connecting to the words and sounds and people in this way is a crucial part of the spiritual work. When such a bulb lights up in my mind, the last thing that I want is to rush heedlessly onward. I want to savor the gift of that moment. I'm not a train, which must always stay on track. I'm driving my own vehicle and can go off on a byroad if I feel the urge. To be truly in *kavanah*, you have to have the freedom to improvise.

Joining In

Now, you may feel: *I'm having such a good time connecting to God on my own, following the muse of my soul. Why indeed should I move in lockstep with the congregation? What might motivate me to join the collective, to become another little tile in the larger mosaic?*

Davening in a minyan reminds me that no person is an island. It gives me a much stronger feeling of *K'lal Yisrael*, the greater body of the people Israel. Each of us is a link in a chain of tradition that stretches back thousands of years. The God of my ancestors becomes more real to me in shul. We all share the same patriarchs: Abraham, Isaac, and Jacob. We all share the same matriarchs: Sarah, Rebekah, Rachel, and Leah. (Jews by choice may not share the same biological lineage, but their souls have an equal share in our ancestors.) Each of us here today is a living cell in the organism of *K'lal Yisrael*.

As I look around the room, my experience becomes a lot more inclusive. There sits a person looking thoughtful as she prays. Another seems sad. A third looks joyful. A child is hopping up and down. The insights that come to me when I'm *be-kahal ve-eidah*, in community and congregation, are different than when I'm by myself. My social persona feels more motivated to act in the world; I feel an obligation there. As Hillel said (Pirkei Avot 1:14), "If I am not for myself, who will be? But if I am only for myself, what am I?"

True, davening with our fellows can be distracting, especially if they themselves are talking or otherwise distracted. If you daven near a real davener, on the other hand, you can align yourself with their davening. Or, if you daven with a little *kavanah*, you yourself might be the davener that others align with! We sing together and answer "Amen" together. We rise to our feet together for the *Amidah*, imagining God Godself rising with us, singing, "*Kumah be-ezrat Yisrael*, Rise to the aid of Israel!"

"*Elohim* stands among a godly congregation," the psalmist tells us (Psalm 82:1). The Rabbis interpreted this verse to mean that wherever ten Jews gather for prayer or study, the Shekhinah stands among them (Talmud, Berakhot 6a). Was this to encourage people to daven in a minyan? Or were the Rabbis trying to capture the wonder and synergy of studying Torah in fellowship? Probably some of both. A critical mass of divine manifestation can happen when we gather together to study or pray. We cannot take this for granted. But the more aware we are, the more committed we are, the more we feel the presence of Shekhinah.

Sometimes I get sidetracked during the *P'sukei de-Zimrah*, those "tuneful verses" that offer us a chance to sing. The devotional poetry there has so many marvelous verses that I go off in my own thoughts. But then, when the *chazan* goes to *Yishtabach*, I join right back in. Why *Yishtabach*? Because that is the point at which we shift into *Beriyah*, beginning the section that leads up to the reading of the *Shema*. When we have been warmed up with the sound and the feeling around us; when all the neurons in the room turn to say *Shema Yisrael* together, there's a great power, there is a flow from one to the other. I am no longer an isolated individual: I have become a member of the great "we" for a little while. So wherever you have been in your imagination, whatever flights your soul has taken, rejoin your fellow daveners at *Yishtabach*, so that you all converge on *keri'at Shema* together.

WINDOW: *Investing Ourselves*

The other day, three of my rabbinical *chaverim* (comrades) who study with me were here: one Orthodox, one Conservative, one Reform. We were learning *Derekh ha-Melekh*, a work by Rabbi Kalonymus Kalman Shapira, the Piacetzner Rebbe, who preached in the Warsaw Ghetto before he died at the hand of the Nazis. The Piacetzner was talking about Psalm 100:3, "*Hu asanu ve-lo anachnu, amo ve-tzon mar'ito*," a verse that, as written, translates "He created us, and not we ourselves; [we are] His people and the flock He shepherds." It is a famous verse, for the way it is traditionally understood changes its meaning. The word *ve-lo* is written with an *aleph*—"and not." But the Masoretes, ancient editors of the *Tanakh*, asked us to read the word as if it were rendered with a *vav* instead—"to him." The two words sound the same: *ve-lo*. But the different spellings change the meaning from "He created us, and not we ourselves" to "He created us, and we are His" or "we are for Him." The Masoretic version incorporates a greater sense of belonging, of giving ourselves over to God.

The Piacetzner interprets the verse in yet a third way. If we are passive, he says, if we feel no yearning and experience no growth, then we fulfill the meaning of the verse in which *ve-lo* is rendered with an *aleph*: He created us, but—God forbid—we are *not* His people and the flock He shepherds. But if we invest ourselves, if we exert ourselves spiritually and put ourselves out there, then *ve-lo* (with a *vav*) *anachnu*, we are God's and for God.

Amen!

One single Hebrew word can help us more than any other to join the community in prayer: *Amen!*

Tradition asks that we respond with *amen* to every blessing that we hear. *Amen* derives from the Hebrew verb *aleph-mem-nun*, meaning to be firm or trustworthy. *Amen* means "So be it. May your words come to pass." It is prayer and affirmation in one. When King David is dying, the question of which of his sons will succeed him is very much in doubt. The country is divided; much blood has already been shed on the issue. So he calls to him his most loyal followers—Tzadok the priest, Nathan the prophet, and the warrior Benayahu—and instructs them to enthrone Batsheva's son Solomon to rule after him. "Amen!" Benayahu cries out. "May *Adonai*, the God of my lord the king, say thus!" (1 Kings 1:36). This is no mere dutiful response. Benayahu is declaring his allegiance. It is a matter of life and death.

Now, there are many ways to say *amen*. The grunted *amen* of the old-timers in the little *shtieblach* is the half-conscious affirmation of a person who shows up for davening three times a day, year in and year out. Not that the feeling isn't there, but it's a lifelong intentionality. They are the veterans of a million *amen*s. They don't allow themselves to be overcome with emotion; they pace themselves.

A person who davens in community more rarely can use that very unfamiliarity, the specialness of the occasion, to respond differently. Just by saying *amen* we start to align ourselves with the *kavanah* that we aspire to. The gospel tradition knows this, and we can take a leaf from their siddur. We want to say "*Amen!* Right on! Count me in! This *chazan* speaks for me!"

Saying *amen* out loud is like going through a gate. When you entered the room you had your own thoughts, your own internal conversations. Now you are putting those aside, if only for an instant, to register your vote audibly with those of the daveners around you. Once the word has crossed your lips a few times, you can start to lean into it a little. *Amen* is a spiritual practice in itself. We want to say it without false piety, without ego, without showmanship, and yet we want every *amen* to be a heartfelt and palpable contribution. We want to support the *ba'al tefillah*. We want to offer our *amen*s in a way that does our bit to help lift up the davening in the room.

Supporting the Leaders

We often forget how much our leaders *need* our support. It can be hard, as a *chazan,* to hold on to the sense of "*Shiviti ha-Shem le-negdi tamid*, I place God before me always." Many shuls have this sentence embroidered on the cover of the ark, but it is not so easy to achieve! If I lose the *Shiviti*, then I'm no *ba'al tefillah* ("master of prayer" or prayer leader)—I'm just a performer. Whenever you daven with your own shul's messenger, singing along or answering *amen* or even listening actively, you're helping that person to keep the *Shiviti* in mind.

Many times I have felt torn between my role as leader and my role as davener, a person who wants and needs to talk to God. Sometimes, in leading High Holiday prayers for people less familiar with the ritual, I would tell them, "When you see me with the tallis over my head" (during the silent *Amidah*, for example) "then you have to understand that I'm not focusing on you. I'm focusing on God." I needed them to respect the I–Thou moment when I was addressing *ha-Shem* in such a way. Then I would bring the tallis back down to my shoulders and resume my role as *shaliach tzibur*, the messenger of the congregation, leading them in singing and reading and so on.

Being such a messenger, trying to lift the room up in prayer, not knowing if you're reaching people or not, can be a lonely experience. Sometimes when I lead davening, I ask people, "Would you please move closer? Please come and stand around me." It makes a big difference.

Where we stand matters. I used to lead the evening prayer when Shabbos goes out. We would eat *se'udah shelishit* together, the celebratory third meal when we'd sing songs and tell tales of yearning, sitting in the waning light. Then I'd ask people to come up on the bimah and surround me there, and I would do the whole evening prayer in English. When I came to the *Amidah*, I would say, "If there is anyone here who would like to join and say a prayer out loud, please say it at this point." So people would rephrase a paragraph in words that meant something to them, and then I would end with "*Barukh atah Adonai*" and give the *chatimah*, the "signature" of that blessing. At such points I wanted the people to stand very close, to bring themselves into the middle of it. There's more collaboration, more shared stuff happening when we do it together.

The direction we're facing matters. If we stand in a circle, the focus is the center. When we are facing the *aron kodesh*, the focus is there, even if the ark does not face east. Sometimes, when people are davening in some temporary situation, they face the *aron kodesh*, wherever it happens to be, and then for the *Amidah* they turn away and face what they think is east. I think that's a mistake: it spoils the spirit of the davening in that place. The same when people do this at the *Birkat Kohanim*, the Priestly Blessing. Jewish law asks us not to look at the *kohanim* while they're chanting their blessing. Some people cover their eyes, or put their *tallitot* over their heads and the heads of their children. But others turn their backs! As a *Kohen*, I point out how, "Hey, you're showing me your *tuches* at this point! If you want to cover your eyes, cover your eyes, but please stand there in a receptive way, rather than turning away."

You can pray for the *shaliach tzibur* as well. In the *Musaf* prayer of Rosh Hashanah, before the *chazan* starts repeating the section of the *Amidah* that is devoted to God's kingship, the congregation says a beautiful *tefillah*, a prayer for the *chazan*, asking God to "be with the lips of the messengers of your people Israel"—those who are leading us in the davening on this day.

I often tell the story of doing a session on eldering in a church. I asked to be at the service as well, and before the sermon the minister asked people to pray that he should have something to say that speaks to their condition. I thought that was such a beautiful thing to do. So whenever you come into shul and begin your davening, you can do a silent prayer and say, "Dear God, I hope the *shaliach tzibur* will be a messenger for my soul and my issues as well. Please help her in this way, so I might feel that she represents me as well."

The rabbi is about to give a sermon. The more you can open yourself up to what he is about to say, the better the chance that it will have meaning for you. You can say, "Dear God, please help the rabbi's words be a conduit for meaning in my life. Let them help me with the issues I am struggling with." The rabbi may be entirely unconscious of your receptivity and active listening, but often something will sneak through to you anyway, because you have opened a channel for it. The same is true with Torah reading. The texts of Torah or haftarah can mean so much more to us if we listen with open ears, listening not only for details of biblical life but for metaphors that speak to the life we find ourselves living today.

Sing!

Another obvious way to join in, as we've said, is by singing. Not all of us think of ourselves as having good singing voices. We ask a person, "Do you sing?" He responds, "Only in the shower!" What does he mean? That when he's by himself, with the sound of the shower to cover for him, and with hot water flowing over him and opening up his every pore, then he can open his heart, too, and sing freely.

How wonderful! Please, let davening be such a place for you as well. Let prayer be your hot shower! Think of a song like "Happy Birthday to You." Of course you can sing this on your own. But even better is warbling it out loud together with a roomful of people. Birthday parties are one of the few times that *everybody* sings along, whether we think we have a good voice or not. Our heads know it's a silly song. But our hearts feel it! Our hearts give us permission. We all want to participate in this joyful and loving moment, wishing the best for this person on his or her special day.

This, on the simplest level, is what prayer in community can offer. Just as a parent walks in bearing a birthday cake and candles, so does the leader walk among us with the Torah, and we all lift our voices in song. Some may be a bit off-key; others may know enough to offer a harmony. This person may need to follow the words in the siddur with her finger; that one can close his eyes and lose himself in the meaning. It doesn't matter. The tune and our emotions come together, and the delight of *tefillah be-tzibur*, davening in community, fills the room.

Lifting our voices is so important. In Orthodox shuls, especially, people sing not only during the singing bits; even in between, many will murmur the words out loud and at their own pace, wherever they happen to be in the prayer. Anyone who walks into the room can tell immediately that prayer is happening, and not just up where the leader is standing. I used to ask people to do this with me when I led davening back in the 1970s, and I did the same thing on one recent Rosh Hashanah in Los Angeles. I simply said, "If you can recall seeing people daven when they raise their voices, and in the whole congregation there is this murmur that's rising as people express themselves, please do that with me now." And I suggested they hold the siddur in one hand and use the other to gesture, to underline what they were saying. So they raised their voices a little bit, in Hebrew or English, whichever way they wanted to do it. And that made a difference: they felt that they were really davening! It was so much messier and more alive than those responsive readings in unison.

One *talmid* (student) of mine, a wonderful person who *nebech* died very young, Rabbi David Wolfe-Blank, knew this from being in Chabad: he called it "chaotic davening." Rabbi Larry Kushner calls it "cacophonous davening." He remembered doing this at his shul in Sudbury, Massachusetts, when I used to visit. "We didn't know that it was okay for different people to say different things at the same time," he said. "When we really did the cacophonous davening, it was a din. You couldn't hear yourself in the room!" Try it sometime and see.

WHO AM I TO GIVE BLESSINGS?

Every one of us has inherited from Abraham, our first Jewish ancestor, the power to give blessings. When God first appears to Abram (he is not yet Abraham) and tells him to leave his birthplace and go to the land that God shall show him, God makes Abram a few promises in return: "I will make you a great nation, and I will bless you and make your name great, and you shall be a blessing. And," God continues, "*avarekhah mevarakhekha*" (Genesis 12:2–3). The usual way to translate these two words is "I will bless those who bless you." But we can also understand it as "I will bless those whom *you* will bless."

The question of blessing is simple. Can we say "God bless you" and mean it? I don't wait for people to sneeze before I say that. It's more than a habit; when I'm in a warm-hearted relationship with somebody, it's a necessity. I have a feeling in my heart that needs to find release in blessing.

A blessing is a special kind of prayer. Blessing another person requires that we summon all the *chesed* we can muster at that moment—all the gentleness and compassion, all the shared humanity and connectedness. In Yiddish we called this *farginnen*. There's no one-word translation for this in English; it means the opposite of begrudging, to truly want the best for that person. That's what we do when we bless someone: We wish the person well in the most active sense. We pray for their well-being.

I knew a fellow in Israel by the name of Michael, a tall, blond guy. Michael was the *gabbai* at the shul in Mevo Modi'in, the settlement

founded by Shlomo Carlebach. Michael would call people up to the
Torah and then give them a *mi she-beirakh* ("God who blessed"), the
standard blessing that you recite for a person who's been given an *aliyah*. They called him "Michael of the thirty-five *mamesh*-es," because
of the way he did those *mi she-beirakhs*. *Mamesh* (Hebrew: *mamash*)
was one of Shlomo Carlebach's favorite words. It means palpably,
touchably, really, in truth—as if to say, I'm not just saying words: I
really mean it! Usually the *gabbai* just runs quickly through the standard *mi she-beirakh* formula, but Michael would always add a heartfelt
list of things he wished for that person in particular. "You should
mamesh have *parnasah* [livelihood]," Michael would say, "and you
and your wife, *mamesh, mamesh*, you should find happiness in each
other, and your children…." He felt it that strongly.

Watching such *anshei chesed* (people of kindness) in action helps
us summon the quality of *chesed* within ourselves. I know a guy named
Barry Barkan, who founded two organizations for elders in Berkeley,
California: first the Live Oak Institute and then the Elders Guild. This
guy is such an *ish chesed*! He has a generosity of spirit that is truly
unusual. I learned from him to always have money in the ashtray of
my car, so when I see someone begging on the street, I can open the
window and give him something. Whenever Barry would walk down
College Avenue and see a person in need, he would always do a high
five with them; he would stop and talk with the sole purpose of spending a few minutes just being kind. He would look at somebody and see
what was missing in their life and call down a blessing for that. I call
Barry and others like him *ba'alei berakhot*, masters of blessing.

But *chesed* is not the only quality we need to give blessings. The
act of blessing asks us to be sensitive, to receive and transmit on the
wavelengths of blessing. When Isaac is getting ready to bless Esau, his
firstborn, he first sends him on a little mission: "Take your bow and
arrows. Go out to the field and hunt something for me. Make me the
delicacies that I love" (Genesis 27:3–4). He's a simple man, Isaac, old,
blind, and tent-bound, and he wants the taste of the wild one more
time. He needs to get into the mood! He needs to feel, to the very
depths of his cells, "Oy, *mechayeh*. What a good son! I want to bring

down the very best for him." The blessing that Isaac intends to give Esau is first and foremost a blessing of the gifts of nature: "May God give you of the dew of the heavens and the fat of the earth" (Genesis 27:28). Before Isaac can call down the blessings of nature, he needs to get back in touch with them himself. Just before blessing his son (who, of course, is actually Jacob, wearing the skins of a goat), Isaac draws him near, and kisses him, and breathes him in. "Behold," he says, "the scent of my son is like that of a field blessed by God" (Genesis 27:27). And with that beautiful phrase he starts the blessing.

So the act of blessing invites you to become transparent, to become a channel. *Berakhah*, the Hebrew word for blessing (*brokhah* in Yiddish), resonates in different ways. Some, as we have said previously, hear a relationship with the root *bet-resh-khaf*, meaning knee. Blessing God—*Barukh atah, Adonai* or *berukhah at, Yah*, whatever opening you prefer—is like going down on our knees, bending our knees in supplication. The letters of *berakhah*, blessing, are also identical to those of *bereikhah*, a pool. Imagine a reservoir of blessing, waiting for the person on some high level. All it needs is someone to be the pipe, the conduit, to draw the blessing down to this plane.

Once there was a man, Chanina ben Dosa, who used to pray for the sick (e.g., Mishnah Berakhot 5:5). He was a very poor man, but wise and righteous—a giant of his generation. "Every day a voice goes out from Horeb [another name for Sinai]," the Talmud tells us, "and says, 'All the world is nourished for the sake of Chanina my son'" (Talmud, Berakhot 17b, Taanit 24b). The Baal Shem Tov had a beautiful teaching on this. Rather than interpreting the Hebrew word *bish'vil* as "for the sake of," as the context suggests, he pointed out that *shevil* also means path or pipe. What the holy Chanina's prayers did, said the Baal Shem, was to open up a channel or path for God's outpouring of goodness (*shefa*). The heavenly voice is saying that "all the world is nourished through the path or channel [*bi-shevil*] of Chanina my son."

I received a third important lesson about blessing from Reb Menachem Mendel Schneerson, the last Lubavitcher Rebbe. When he got older, the Rebbe took up the practice of giving out dollar bills for charity on Sunday afternoon, and people would line up for hours for the chance to exchange a few words. The Chabad people took a photograph of each person who came up, and I still have the picture from the time I joined the line. Someone whispered my name to the Rebbe, but he didn't need it. He looked at me with a smile and handed me a dollar. And then he said to me, "Reb Zalman, you're a *Kohen*, a priest. Please keep me also in mind when you're reciting the Priestly Blessing during the High Holidays."

I want to tell you, never have I felt such empowerment as a *Kohen* as I felt at that moment, when the Rebbe asked for my blessing. But I didn't understand his request as saying that he needed my help. He was offering a teaching: When you get up there, and raise your arms, and begin the blessing, don't do it as a routine, just because the *chazan* is prompting you to say, "*Yevarekhekha!*" Keep specific people in mind. Bring blessings down for them. He was offering himself as a model for that.

The Rebbe was equally specific himself. Any of his followers could write him a letter and say, "I need help, I need a prayer for such-and-such." And the Rebbe would say, "I will remember him at the graveside" and include that person's particular request when he went to pray at the grave of his father-in-law, Reb Yosef Yitzchak, the previous Rebbe.

What was the power of praying at the graveside? Reb Schneur Zalman once wrote to comfort the people after Reb Menachem Mendel of Vitebsk died.[1] He quoted the *Zohar*, which says that "when a *tzaddik* departs, he is to be found in all worlds more than during his lifetime" (*Zohar* 3:71b). During his lifetime he was only in his body. He couldn't be everywhere at once! But once a righteous person is no longer on this plane, he is available in many more dimensions than he was during his lifetime. Many of the mystics among our people have ascribed a special power to the places where the righteous are buried or to Rebbes' *yahrzeits*, the anniversaries of their deaths, to draw down blessings.

I found a book called *Sefer ha-chassidut* (The book of Hasidism) by Yitzchak Raphael. It contains brief biographies and a selection of teachings of a hundred Rebbes. I wanted to get copies of it for my students, but it was out of print. So I ordered a program that does optical character recognition, so I could scan and edit it. The book is arranged historically, from the Baal Shem Tov to the Rebbes of our day, but I'm rearranging the entries according to the calendar, so my students can look up a Rebbe on his *yahrzeit*, when the teaching might have more power, more resonance in the higher worlds.

One thing I found is that the personality of each one of the Rebbes shines through in the torah that he gives. This is true even when he's emphasizing something that is contrary to his own inclinations! So we recently had the *yahrzeit* of Reb Menachem Mendel of Kotzk. It was wonderful to find the Kotzker talking about not getting angry, that you have to teach gently. The Kotzker himself was not the most patient person; he felt the need for that teaching himself. So—happy heavenly birthday to you, Reb Menachem Mendel of Kotzk. What can you share with us today?

Today we are more rationalist and egalitarian. Many of us are not comfortable with the notion that certain people—or places or dates—are more empowered or auspicious than others. As a *Kohen*, for example, a descendant of the tribe of Aaron, I sometimes feel that we in the liberal Jewish world have become overly democratic at times. More conservative congregations still preserve the special status of the priestly descendants: The first and second *aliyot* to the Torah are reserved for a *Kohen* and a Levite, respectively, if any are present. The *Kohanim* still recite the Priestly Blessing (though in the Diaspora this is done only on important holidays) and observe certain behavioral restrictions. More liberal congregations, however, have dispensed with these distinctions. People say, "Come on, we don't have *Kohanim* any more. We don't want this hierarchical stuff today."

But this bringing down of blessing can be very powerful at times. It's worth going to Jerusalem when Aaron the High Priest's *yahrzeit* comes up on the first of the month of Av, or on that day of Sukkot when it is Aaron's turn among the *ushpizin*, the ancestral guests in our sukkah. The Kotel (Western Wall) is filled with rows upon rows of *Kohanim*, all swaying beneath their tallitot. It's amazing when you hear them all calling out together: *YE-VA-REHHH-KHE-KHAAAA!* I feel that's a very special thing that I can do for people, as a *Kohen*, and I wouldn't want to lose that. People misunderstand our roles as priests. My job when I get up there is not to bless people. My job is "They [the priests] shall place My name upon the people of Israel," as God says in Numbers 6:27, "and *I* will bless them."

Some congregations have expanded the priestly category, inviting all the people who could originally eat of the *terumah*, gifts of food that were brought to the priests in Temple times (Mishnah Yevamot 6:3). These included not only a *Kohen* but his wife and children as well. In Jewish Renewal we invite anybody who feels a sense of priesthood to come up and raise their hands over the people. But the understanding is always that they are not the ones who are blessing; they are the *vehicles* to bring blessing down.

I keep saying, at every opportunity that I have, that the world is under-blessed. We need blessings! If you feel yourself called to give someone a blessing, then I hope the thoughts I offer here might be helpful. Summon the *ish* (or *eshet*) *chesed* within yourself, to become a fount of kindness and a prayer for another's well-being. Make yourself a conduit for blessings that are waiting on higher planes than we know. Remember that a prayer for blessing needs not only a mailing address, but a return address as well: do not be afraid to name specific people and outcomes. If you can offer your blessing at an occasion or place that might open a special passage into a more blessed future, so much the better.

May all these come to pass for you, so that you, too, might become a channel for blessing. And please say with me: *AMEN!*

ADVANCED PRACTICE
Prolonged Prayer

Dov Ber had a friend, and the two young men would learn together and daven together. Years went by, and Dov Ber became known as the Maggid of Mezeritch, heir to the mantle of the Baal Shem Tov himself. The other fellow, meanwhile, settled down as a *balabos*, a homeowner in a town. His wife took care of the day-to-day running of the business, and he sat in shul, davening and studying Torah. Once a year he closed his books and traveled to Leipzig, where he bought enough goods on the wholesale market to supply their business for the coming year. That's how the couple made their *parnasah*, their living.

One day he comes to visit his old friend the Maggid, looking forward to renewing old times. "Let's daven," he says, "and then we'll learn together." So they put on their tallitot and tefillin and start davening. Pretty soon the fellow is finished, but the Maggid is still davening away, davening away, davening away.

Finally the Maggid finishes. As he's folding up his tallit and tefillin, his old friend says, "Why does it take you so long to daven now? Surely it doesn't take that long to say what you need to say?"

The Maggid looks at him for a moment. "Let me ask you a question. You travel to Leipzig every year. It's a long journey. Takes you a lot of time, no?"

"Yes," says his friend. "Of course."

"So why don't you just go there in your mind?" the Maggid asks. "Imagine yourself going to this town, then the next town, then finally you come to Leipzig. Then have the *kavanah* that you're buying what you need. Then focus your mind on returning, and you're home!"

The friend says, "What are you talking about? I can't just *think* these things. This is my livelihood we're talking about. I have to actually *be* there!"

"That's why it takes me so long to daven," the Maggid replies. "Just thinking about it is not enough. I have to *be* there. And getting there takes time."

The soul, too, wants to be there. If we're lucky and we're open, we have a peak experience sometime in our life. We catch a glimpse, and then *op!*—it's gone. After a while another peek, another experience. We see enough to know this is real. Still the soul wants more. It wants more than just a momentary connection with God. It wants to *linger*.

So if you say, "Look, I've had some experience davening now. I'm at a place where I've started to have a real conversation with God. I've worked to make the meaning of the words my own. I've found that, yes, prayer helps me. It's hard for me to imagine negotiating the challenges in my life without being able to ask God's help. But I've found myself wondering: What would it be like if I could *really* take the time, if I could stop and meditate for a while on some of the phrases I feel drawn to, instead of hurrying on? How deep can it go, the relationship of the Jewish soul to God?"

Contemplation in Chabad

I too had these questions, and I want to share with you something of what I learned.

I was raised among Hasidim from many different sects. As a boy I saw good people from many lineages studying, keeping the mitzvot, living a halakhic life. I witnessed people davening with great fervor. But their arousal seemed to me like a branch caught fire: burning brightly, yes, but from the outside. I wasn't satisfied with a God we had to noodge into forgiving us on Yom Kippur, or with the paterfamilias watching his *kinderlach* dance on Simchat Torah. I was looking for an inner blue flame, and I didn't see it in the Hasidism I knew.

The Chabad (Lubavitcher) Rebbes spoke to those who longed for a deeper experience of God. "I don't want your world to come," Reb Schneur Zalman, founder of the lineage, would cry out in his davening. "I don't want your Garden of Eden. I want You, You, You and only You." My blossoming soul answered strongly to such yearning. Davening at the yeshiva proceeded at a different pace than most people are familiar with today. Don't let the businessman lead davening during the week, Reb Schneur Zalman wrote in the *Tanya*,[1] because a businessman needs to hurry. We were encouraged to daven slowly, giving each word, each sentence, each paragraph its due; leaving "space between one flock and the next,"[2] to borrow a phrase from a very different context. Our davening proceeded at a pace not of recitation, but of conversation with God. You can imagine what this did for our *kavanah*. We would often spend an hour and a half or two hours at our weekday davening, simply to allow the meaning of the words to sink in.

The meaning of the words (*perush ha-milot*) is the first benchmark standard for davening. The *Shulchan Arukh*, our most famous compendium of *halakhah*, begins its discussion of *kavanah* in the *Amidah* with a simple statement: "A davener should intend in his heart the meaning of the words that he releases from his lips."[3] (Today, of course, we would extend this statement to women as well.) This in itself is hard enough to attain. The story goes that when Rabbi Shlomo Zalman Auerbach, perhaps the greatest halakhic authority of recent times, was in his final years, his prayers would take him even longer than before. When one of his followers asked about this, the rabbi replied, "Today I no longer have the strength I once had to concentrate. I have to stop before every blessing now, to gather strength to have enough focus and *kavanah* for the blessing before me. That is why my prayer takes so long."[4] As anyone who has ever davened knows, saying the words with meaning is challenge enough.

But Chabad tried to reach higher. The acronym Chaba"d, as we have said, denotes three dimensions of divine knowledge: intuition

(*CHokhmah*), understanding (*Binah*), and integrated knowledge (*Da'at*). The first, *Chokhmah,* refers to the intuitive spark of God-knowledge that lies within each of us. Bang! One day, out of the blue, we intuit the God dimension of reality. The second, *Binah,* describes a detailed exploration of that fleeting realization, an unfolding understanding of God's work in the world and in the human soul. The third sphere, *Da'at,* is a fusing of the first two ways of knowing into a single all-encompassing "grokking" of godly creation—a creation in which I am inseparably immersed. *Chokhmah* without *Binah* disappears; it's like a flash of lightning, there and gone. *Binah* analyzes what the lightening illuminates—but without that flash of realization, *Binah* is just intellectualizing, spinning its wheels. But if *Da'at* concludes that what *Chokhmah* and *Binah* are talking about is real, then we can live our lives with a new level of true awareness. These things are foundational to the Chabad philosophy.

I wasn't interested in Chabad because of its wonderful ideas. In the world of ideas, everybody has their own system. The possibility of *actualizing* God-knowledge in my life—that, to me, was the crucial thing. Eyes closed, my tallis over my head, I learned what it means to truly place myself before God. I felt the wordless *niggunim* that we sang together give wings to my soul. I learned that attaining a state of higher *devekut* lay within my reach—that cleaving to God was a real possibility. I was always looking beyond, beyond!

As soon as I settled in Borough Park, I had started going to Rabbi Eliyahu Simpson's shul. Reb Elye, as some called him, was the *gabbai* of Reb Yosef Yitzchak, the sixth Lubavitcher Rebbe, serving him with great humility. He also lived not too far from my parents and held a Shabbos minyan in his home shul. Since there were no other Chabad shuls in Borough Park in those days, I would often go from my parents to daven there. After a while I noticed that several people—Rav Simpson himself, of course, but also other Hasidim, Reb Shmuel Zalmanov and Reb Avrohom Pariz—would stay afterward, after the other daveners had gone home, for further prayer and contemplation. I was curious, so I began to stay a little longer and watch them. I had a friend at that time, Avraham Weingarten, of blessed memory, whom

I knew from my childhood in Vienna. Avraham lived on Fifty-Fifth Street, and I lived on Fifty-Third, so we'd walk home from Simpson together and compare notes: What were they doing? And why were they *davenen be-yechidus*—praying by themselves, after the minyan was over?

I watched other Hasidim, too. The yeshiva was not only a place to take classes, after all. It was a place where we watched the older Hasidim and learned from them. Reb Shmuel Levitan, who was the yeshiva's top *mashpiya*, would pray at considerable length even during the week. He was getting old, so he would walk back and forth as he davened to make sure he wouldn't fall asleep.

As we got a little older, the *mashpiya* who worked with us, Reb Jacobson, began to talk to us about the longer, deeper form of davening that we had seen our teachers doing. We didn't know the word *meditation* at that time; in the Chabad yeshiva, we practiced *hitbonenut*, contemplation of godly things. We studied the section on *hitbonenut* in the *Tanya*, where Reb Schneur Zalman talks about what true knowledge of God requires. We must not only bend our physical bodies to the effort, he says, so that they not obscure the light of our souls. We must exert the soul itself as well, so that we might, without weariness, "*le-ha'amik ve-le-hitbonen bi-gedulat ha-Shem sha'ah gedolah retzufah*, reflect deeply upon the greatness of God for a lengthy and uninterrupted hour" (*Tanya*, chapter 2). Rabbi Jacobson urged us to take on this practice ourselves.

Rav Jacobson's influence on me was very strong. When you learn soul things from somebody, you fall in love with them! I used to go to his house on Friday evening, walking along Eastern Parkway to East New York, with a friend of mine, Sholom Ber Popack, so that we could learn some of the teachings that Rav Jacobson had yet learned from the Rebbe Rashab (Rabbi Sholom DovBer Schneerson), the fifth Lubavitcher Rebbe, back in the rural village of Lyubavichi (Lubawicze) itself, in the early 1900s. I don't remember ever seeing Rabbi Jacobson daven, because he led his own shul and rarely prayed at 770, the Lubavitch headquarters on Eastern Parkway. But every time he set up a *fabrengen*, we would sneak out of the lesson and go to sit with them. The *rosh yeshiva* (head of the yeshiva) would always threaten that we mustn't leave, we had no permission, but I think there was a collusion between them. So we'd bring a bottle of shoe-shine schnapps and sit with our *mashpiya*.

WINDOW: *Learning from Daveners*

How does spiritual insight get passed down to us? How do Jews learn the methods and techniques that put us in touch with our God?

When you read Hasidic literature, you always find the *mefursam*—the famous one, the spiritual master. You had the *nistarim* as well, the hidden ones: the grocery man around the corner whom you thought was an ignoramus, the tzaddik you never found out about. But a *mefursam* was someone who had come out of the closet. He attracted people to him. A person who had davened in his presence would tell a few friends, quietly, "You should daven with so-and-so. You'll find out what davening is." So others came. The master did his best to attune people to where he was, they did their best to make themselves present, and a davening transmission would start to happen.

Today? Same thing. The best way to become a davener is to get with people who are daveners. None of the paths I have taken in adulthood would have been possible if I hadn't been in the presence of my Rebbe when he was davening. Reb Yosef Yitzchak, the sixth Lubavitcher Rebbe, was always talking about the *chush ha-tziyur*, the "drawing sense" or sensory imagination. You can *always* place yourself in a place of light and holiness, he said. You can always make it present. The contemplative imagination has that power, to bring you to a place where you're fully alight and where everything is good and holy and real.

But until we really know for sure, we live in doubt about spiritual things. Most of the time it feels like I'm jazzing myself up to be in the presence of God. I'm doing every mental trick I know to keep myself in *shiviti*, in that sense of "I stand before You always." But being present when the Rebbe was in *shiviti*, I saw that there, before the Rebbe, was an aspect of the living God that he spoke to *be-emet*, in reality and in truth. He wasn't jazzing himself up; he was *there*. He was addressing that Presence directly. He gave my intuition of God's presence a confirmation outside of myself, allowing me, too, to do the same, to speak directly to God's presence in my own way.

The other day I was speaking with Reb Yudel Krinsky, who directs Chabad today. I asked him, who are the real daveners with whom I could have a conversation? He told me a wonderful remark by Reb Yoel Kahn, who for many years served as repeater and transcriber to Reb Menachem Mendel Schneerson, the seventh and last Lubavitcher Rebbe, transmitting the Rebbe's talks to his Hasidim. You can imagine how much Hassidic teaching this guy has in his memory! Reb Yoel, said Reb Krinsky, was once sitting for hours, reviewing a teaching in his mind and doing *hitbonenut*. Finally he shook himself and said, "And now we have to do it in words." It was a wonderful way to describe the davening that makes such a meditation real! Alas, Reb Krinsky told me, Reb Yoel is the exception; most Chabad people today put a lot of energy into outreach, but they don't know much about *hitbonenut* and the prolonged form of prayer we called davening *be-arikhut*.

Look how Reb Shlomo Carlebach would sing a *niggun* or tell a story. He said, "Open your heart—this is the deepest." You loved him, so you said, "Sure. I can trust him, I can open up my soul." People became soft inside, looking for the shape that was the Shlomo shape. It came to them in song, in a sigh, in Shlomo's sense that—*mamesh*, these things were real and true. Shlomo would talk about a holy Rebbe, the *heilege* so-and-so. You, too, opened yourself to that Rebbe. You felt that holy aspiration. If you were serious, you could take something of that attunement home and align your deeds and your davening with it.

This is how such a person can serve as a doorway and a beacon for others. Throughout history, in addition to intellectual geniuses and artistic geniuses, we had spiritual geniuses as well.

Such a person might have learned to pray like everybody else growing up—but then one day he broke through to a different place. After a while he turned to some friends: "I want to share this with you. There is more, whole realms of spiritual experience, well beyond the simple recitation of the words. We could be talking to God on a much higher level than we are."

This is what the giants of my lineage did for me.

Prayer Meditation

Davening *be-arikhut* really begins with two things. The first is taking the time before davening to do a *hitbonenut*, a focused meditation. I would often spend two hours, usually from 7:00 to 9:00 on a Shabbos morning, studying a teaching by one of the Lubavitcher Rebbes with Reb Avrohom Pariz. Then I would close the book and go over the teaching in my mind, reviewing everything that was said: the beginning, the middle, the conclusion. The teachings by these Rebbes were not straightforward. They had many layers; they needed unpacking in class and contemplation afterwards. For a long time, I would do a kind of verbal repeating, making sure that I had it straight. I would go from concept to concept to concept, just as we used to do in studying Talmud, getting the structure and the stepping stones straight in my mind. Then, from there, I gradually went into contemplation, trying to make these spiritual concepts real. What would such a realization look like? What would it feel like?

Here a second important ingredient comes in, which is that your *hitbonenut* has to be *a-da'ata de-nafshei*. This Aramaic expression, used several times in Talmud, often means with one's own good or interest in mind. The Jewish contemplative tradition reframed it to mean the intention and realization that we ourselves are personally involved in the thing we are contemplating.

Let me spell that out. Imagine a person who asks her friend, "Tell me, Esther. What would you do if you won ten million dollars in the lottery?" No doubt she would come up with all kinds of nice ideas. Now the woman says, "Well, Esther, I came to tell you—we won! We bought the winning ticket together the other day!" Suddenly Esther is involved in a completely different way. Before that the conversation was only theoretical. Now she is immersed in all the many ramifications of winning the lottery; she's experiencing it from the inside, *al gufah*, on her own self and body. On the other end of the scale, imagine a person is speaking to a friend who's a radiologist. They're looking at films together, and Joe is saying, "Oh, I understand: this is a cancerous one, this is a normal one. Fascinating!" Then his radiologist friend puts his hand on his shoulder and says, "But Joe, this cancerous one is from the biopsy I took from you." Immediately a shift takes place. This information is no longer outside of you: it *is* you.

That's what Hasidism calls *a-da'ata de-nafshei*: the realization that we have "skin in the game," as the expression goes. Often, our discussions about cosmology, about the universe and nature, treat these things as objective phenomena, outside of ourselves. In fact, every epistemology is *participatory* epistemology: it's only through our participation that any real meaning or truth can emerge. I'm talking about nature—but I'm also *part* of nature. So if I'm meditating on God sustaining the universe by an act of creation that is renewed each and every minute of every day, I need to include myself! I, too, am part of that universe. I, too, am being sustained at every instant by God's life-giving force. How does this affect me? How will this realization change me? I can go and daydream about galaxies, and play in my mind some science fiction story. But that's not *hitbonenut*. I want my meditation to have purpose, to be more than just vague mental meanderings. I want the object of my *hitbonenut* to become a living reality.

When the Maggid of Mezeritch first went to see the Baal Shem Tov, all he heard from the supposed miracle worker and healer were stories about everyday things. Unimpressed, he was about to return home when the Baal Shem opened a copy of the *Etz Chayim*, Reb Chayim Vital's massive work on the complex kabbalah of the Ari ha-Kodesh, Rabbi Isaac Luria of Safed. "Tell me," the Baal Shem asked, "have you studied this portion here?"

"Yes," the Maggid replies. He lays out his understanding of it, but the Baal Shem shakes his head. The Maggid checks the passage again. "My interpretation is correct," he says. But the Baal Shem shakes his head again. Finally the Maggid says, "*Nu*, so tell me how *you* do it." Then the Baal Shem Tov stands up. He recites the text, and suddenly all the spiritual realities that are discussed in the text came alive. "Your understanding was correct," the Baal Shem explains, "but it had no soul." That is what we mean by the need for *hitbonenut* and *ada'ata de-nafshei*.

How does this work in practice? Let's start with a simple example. Imagine I'm meditating on "*Kadosh, kadosh, kadosh*—Holy, holy, holy." Usually we sing this in call-and-response with the *chazan*, without thinking too much about what we are saying. But if I'm davening *be-arikhut*, I want to say and mean these words as the *meshartim*, the ministering angels, are davening them in the higher worlds.

I bring to mind the midrash that says that each utterance of "*Kadosh*" takes two thousand years. Achieving that state of "*Kadosh, kadosh, kadosh*," the words we run through in a few seconds—six thousand years! We can barely begin to comprehend that kind of holiness. These are not things that make sense to our usual ways of understanding words on a page. It's imaginal stuff. It's whisper language. I need to spend some time and go deep into the realm of my imagination if I am to have any hope of making it real.

Years later a verse in Psalms brought this mental unfolding home to me. Psalm 24:7 is usually translated as "Lift up your heads, O gates [*she'arim*] … that the King of glory may enter in." Suddenly, I heard the word *she'arim* as meaning not only gates; I heard a resonance also with another Hebrew word from the same root—*hash'arah*, which means something imagined or conjectured. I recognized something that we do in more prolonged davening. "Raise the gates of your imagination!"

Another example. Let's say I'm looking at *yesh me-ayin*, the belief that God created the world *ex nihilo*—out of nothing.[5] We nod—*yes, yes, of course; that's the theology*. But what does this mean? What does it say about the nature of reality? Our minds are so used to cause and effect, in which the effect is already encoded in the cause. Creation *yesh me-ayin* is not like that. In that primordial *ayin* (No-Thingness), there wasn't any *yesh* (substance): the act of creation was an abrupt break. So I start making that *hitbonenut*. The medieval commentators compared this to the difference between the fire in an ember and the fire in a flint. The fire in an ember is there, even if it's just a tiny spark; you can blow on it, and eventually it will flare up. The fire in a flint, on the other hand, isn't really there yet. Something in the flint's chemical composition is capable of producing fire, but the flint is only fire *in potentia*. This brings me one step closer to getting fire *ex nihilo*—but only a step. Pondering that whole complex of ideas, delving into how *gashmiyus*, corporeality, could not possibly result as cause and effect from *ruchniyus*, from spirit, I'm deepening my sense of the miracle of God's creation.

Now I bring it closer to home. I go to the place where my own body is constantly being created by the direct will of *ha-Shem*. As I continue meditating on the contingency of my own life, I feel how beautiful and miraculous and yet how frighteningly fragile my own existence really is. I start praying, "Please, *Ribboyno sh'l oylom*, give me another moment; give me another moment; give me another moment." So my meditation has started by contemplating big, rich, abstract ideas—and comes down now to the point that I'm asking, from the heart, for just one more breath. I realize now that the whole world, everything I know, is hanging in the balance like that. I say, "Oy, Life of the World, in Your great mercy, take pity on us." Now my *hitbonenut* has become *ada'ata de-nafshei*. I'm invested in it; it has become my issue. That's what has to happen for my *hitbonenut* to be real: my meditation is not merely in the abstract. It has everything to do with my life, with my next breath, with my need to breathe in order to live. It's not a luxury. That's what I mean by *ada'ata de-nafshei*.

The key *kavanah* with which you start fructifies your prayer. It puts juice in there. Your prayer becomes richer, because of that first *kavanah* with which you lay your prayer foundation. Imagine I choose, as the focus for my meditation, the sentence we say in the *Ashrei* prayer, "You open Your hand and Your Will nourishes all living things" (Psalm 145:16). I spend some time meditating, deepening my appreciation of how everything, everything, everything is constantly being nourished by *ha-Shem*, by the Shekhinah, by Mother Earth. Every verse that I then say in my davening will have an echo of that.

So we begin by asking ourselves: what is it that I especially want to concentrate on in my *hitbonenut?* When you study Hasidism, after a while, you find some ideas that you feel drawn to, that you want to spend time with. In the *Tanya*, his greatest work, Reb Schneur Zalman, the Alter Rebbe, frequently came back to the saying "You were before the world was created, You will be after the world passes." He lived there! I found my home more in the question of, what can I do to help the Shekhinah out of exile? In which way can I make myself Her groomsman?

WINDOW: *Dealing with Distractions*

In 1945, I had just arrived in New Haven, Connecticut, sent by the Rebbe to start a little Jewish day school. I knew I needed to learn more about child development, so I went to the public library to look for books by Arnold Gesell, a Yale professor who was the cat's meow in developmental psychology. The library is on the town green, near the three chapels (Battell Chapel, United Church, and Trinity Church), a beautiful place. It had a table at the entrance that said "Recent Acquisitions." So I looked on the table, and I found *The Portable World Bible*, by Robert O. Balou. I opened it up and I saw that he had Jewish and Christian and Muslim texts, but he had Hindu texts as well: the Rig Veda, the Upanishads. He had the Zoroastrian Avesta. He had Confucians, Taoists—*fun aleh gute zachen*, all good things. I discovered that, more than a century after Reb Schneur Zalman studied the way of the Baal Shem Tov with the Maggid of Mezeritch, there was this person by the name of Ramakrishna in India. The Hindus had Rebbes, too! I grabbed the book and turned to Ramakrishna.

> Hast thou got, O preacher, the badge of authority? As the humblest servant of the king authorized by him is heard with respect and awe, and can quell the riot by showing his badge; so must thou, O preacher, obtain first the order and inspiration from God. So long as thou hast not this badge of divine inspiration, thou mayest preach all thy life, but only in vain.

You can imagine how I felt, a young and inexperienced teacher and emissary of Chabad, when I read that.

A second book there was called *Difficulties in Mental Prayer*, by Father Eugene Boylan, the Irish Cistercian monk. Difficulties in mental prayer? I thought only Chabad knew from mental prayer! Even the other Hasidic lineages didn't do *hitbonenut* the way we did. Our *mashpiya* would talk to us about these challenges: profane thoughts, staying focused, and so on. I picked up Father Boylan's book and began to read, and he was talking about the same stuff! I thought, here is somebody with whom I would want to have a conversation. So I took this book, too, which later led me to other Christian contemplatives: Thomas Merton, the Trappist monk; Tikhon of Zadonsk, the Orthodox Christian saint. I began to see that there was a psychology and a literature of prayer and of devotion outside of Judaism as well.

Difficulty in mental prayer was not an abstract topic for me: I knew about it from my own experience. The daughters of Rav Simpson were very nice; I had a crush on one of them, even though there was no realistic possibility of sitting and talking with her. But here I am in the middle of the davening, trying to say that "if my legs were light as gazelles, dear God, I could not do enough to thank you"—and suddenly a thought comes in,

Oy, her legs are beautiful, and I find myself lingering on that line more than I should.

But that would bring me back to my desire to be the Shekhinah's groomsman. I would think: What is the Shekhinah trying to remind me? That She is more beautiful even than Rav Simpson's daughter. She is sustaining the whole world, and nobody even pays attention to Her! On the way home, sometimes, I would pass a store window where undressed mannequins stood. Oy! A yeshiva *bocher*, full of hormones, seeing those imitation breasts! But then I would say, "Go away, Zalman, that's not what you want to do. This is also the Shekhinah in *golus*, in exile." I would walk in the street and sort of wink up at Her. *Sh'khineh, Sh'khineh!*

What Does Deep Prayer Feel Like?

A typical Shabbos in the early 1940s: I am in my late teens. Sometimes I daven at 770 Eastern Parkway, the Lubavitch headquarters in Crown Heights, Brooklyn, where I study during the week. I have a job there, locking the doors of the building at 10:30 at night and opening them again at 6:30 in the morning. In return they give me a little room there to sleep. Other times I wake up at my parents' house in Borough Park, about five miles away, and go to the shul of Rabbi Simpson, where my best davening *be-arikhut* happens. Most of the men who spend the day there with me are much older: Rav Simpson could be my *zaida*, but my connection to him and the other rabbis who davened there—Shmuel Zalmanov, Avrohom Pariz—is strong. We don't talk about it; nobody says, "This is what we're going to do." After the morning davening we just linger, this one here, that one there, and begin our meditations. The room is mostly silent, but I have a very beautiful sense that we are all working at it together.

On Shabbos morning at 770 I get up and say the morning blessings. (Sometimes I would walk from 770 to East New York and back to go to the *mikveh*, for there was no nearer *mikveh* for men in those days.) Then I eat the breakfast that I bought for myself on Friday. I eat a lot: a pound of marble cake, a quarter pound of butter, a pint of whole milk. If you take in enough fat, people told me, you can keep the hunger away and daven as long as you want. After breakfast I attend the Shabbos morning davening. I don't daven myself, because I'm saving that for later, but I listen and say "*Amen*" and other responses. Finally, I begin my own davening.

I start by studying a teaching by one of the Lubavitcher Rebbes. Then I close the book and go over it in my mind, my review slowly becoming a deeper meditation. I sit quietly, immersing myself more and more profoundly in the idea, the vision, the longing. Then, after a long, quiet hour in the presence of God, I turn to my prayer.

What does davening *be-arikhut* feel like? Let's say I begin with *Adon Olam*: "Master of the Universe, who reigned before the first creation … and after all is done, then one and alone will You reign." I look up from my siddur and begin to go there in my mind. Before creation … after creation … from the big bang to the last black hole—all space, all time, filled with God's presence! I sit in that Presence; I *am* that Presence. Already my mind has opened up so wide. I have gotten away from the Old Man in the Sky; I am communicating with a Being of wisdom and beneficence and infinite existence. If I find an image that speaks to me, I don't rush past it. I stay with it awhile, meditating on each word, each phrase.

Then I daven for a while with the words, allowing them to flow around and through me, letting them carry me forward. They do not so much pass by as weave themselves around me, joining together in the matrix of my meditation, filling the spaces around them with meaning, white fire to their black fire. I move on through *P'sukei de-Zimrah*, all the tuneful *Halleluyah*s. The love poetry with which the psalmist takes joy and refuge in God gives me so many opportunities to lose myself in verse! So I spend some time immersed in psalms. Then, like a swimmer who has lost himself a while, delighting in the ocean, I find myself washing up on the shores of the special Shabbos section that comes now, beginning with *Nishmat Kol Chai*, one of my favorite prayers. Now my body, heart, mind, and spirit really start to come together.

"*Nishmat kol chai,* every living breath will bless Your name, O Lord our God." I think of what the Talmud says about this: The Holy One sits and sustains all life, "*mi-beitzei kinim ad karnei re'eimim,*" from the nits of lice to the horns of the great wild ox" (Shabbos 107b; Avodah Zarah 3b). That was the greatest range of life the Rabbis knew! Today we know how much vaster a biosphere we inhabit, from monocellular beings to the total ecology. I think how God, soul of the universe, energizes all that. It's alive, it's alive, all of it, *every* living thing breathing in and breathing out in praise of the Source! My heart wells up and overflows. "*Yay!* I'm so glad to be alive. Thank You for making me. Thank You."

"*Ve-ruach kol basar,*" I continue. "The spirit of all flesh will glorify and elevate your every mention, always." Every time I think of You, *Ribbono shel olam*—oh, wow. All of life: it's not only Zalman who is doing this; a whole universe is praising You. "*Min ha-olam ve-ad olam,* From this world to that world, Thou art God." Wow, wow, wow. If I look in the world of physics, You are there. If I look in the world of chemistry, You are there. If I look in the world of biology, You are there. Psychology, art, history—*From one world to the other, You are God.* All this is You, You, You, You, You. "*Eloha kol beriyot, adon kol toladot,* God of all birthings, Lord of all generations." How many incarnations have I been here already? How many are yet to come?

And I go deeper and deeper into feeling the "You," until it doesn't matter if anybody is around me, it doesn't matter if anybody can hear me or not; I don't care even about my own thoughts and interpretations, I just want You, You, You, You, *Atoh, Atoh, Atoh, Atoh, Ahhhhh-tohhhhhh.* Until finally *Nishmat* ends with a verse of King David's: "*Barkhi nafshi et ha-Shem,* Bless God, O my soul, and may all my innards bless God's holy name" (Psalm 103:1). I know what David meant now. I feel it as he did, soul and *kishkes.* So you see, all the words of my prayer *wake up.* Nothing about it is just rote any more.

Immediately after the *Barekhu* summons the congregation to the heart
of the Shabbos prayer service, many congregations recite a paragraph
that begins, "*Ha-kol yodukha,* All will thank You, all will praise You."
We have moved into *Beriyah* now, and the language here is cosmic.
"*Ein arokh lekha,* There is no comparison to You, *ba-olam ha-zeh,* in
this world." Space, galaxies, all the vastest and mightiest things of
olam ha-zeh have neither proportion nor relation in comparison with
You. You are so far beyond that! And yet, "*ein zulatekha,* nothing
exists without You." This is a verse that the heart might cling to. "O
God! I can't live without You. I need You in my life." I was sometimes brought to tears in this way. "Please. I need You in my life. *Ein
zulatekha, ein zulatekha.* There is nothing without You. How can I
be without You?" And then "*Efes biltekha go'aleinu,* Nothing exists
but You, our Redeemer." Who am I? I don't even exist myself! I'm
God thinking to be Zalman at this point, a tiny expression of God in
a world that is Godding infinitely—infinitely, infinitely, infinitely.

I could go on and on. One song that many congregations sing
at this point is *El Adon,* "God, the Master." Many tunes exist for
El Adon; sometimes a cantor will borrow a holiday mode, like using
the tune for *Ma'oz Tzur* on Chanukah. Some of these upbeat *niggunim* are more appropriate for *P'sukei de-Zimrah;* I prefer tunes after
Barekhu to be more contemplative, in keeping with the content. (I
often like to sing *El Adon* to "Morning Has Broken," by Cat Stevens.)

Because here we are davening more slowly and deeply. I could
focus on almost any verse: "*Tovim me'orot she-bara Eloheinu,* How
good are the luminaries that our God has created, with knowledge,
with insight, and with enlightenment...." To me this suggests that
even God's heavens have their own inner wisdom and knowledge. I
think, "Wow. What is the consciousness of Mars? What is the consciousness of Mercury? What do the galaxies know in their way, a
knowing more abstract than ours but age-old and deep?"

I continue davening, and now I stand one paragraph before the
Shema. "*Ahavat olam ahavtanu,* You have loved us with an eternal
love. Your pity and mercy toward us is exceedingly great." Because
look—after all these years of crushing diaspora, we are still alive. Why?

"*Ba-avur avoteinu*, Because of our ancestors, who trusted in You, and you taught them laws for living and to do Your will wholeheartedly." Oh, please, please, God, "*kein techaneinu u-t'lamedeinu*, give us the same teaching and grace. And give our hearts, too, the wisdom and understanding to fulfill all the words of your teachings with love."

And now I go into a daydream: *What* would it be like, if I lived that holy life? I picture myself, how I would wake up in the morning; how I would go outside and see God's creation. How I would deal with my family. How I would do kindness everywhere. And every time, I would wink up and say, "*Ribboyno sh'l oylom*, You see? I love You so much. Am I doing it right?"

I am trying here to take you into an inner world, a world many people never experience. Jewish prayer offers so many opportunities to feel, to celebrate, to contemplate, to plead. Here I have focused on the blessings that precede *keri'at Shema*, where heart, mind, and soul merge. But the same is true going forward into the awesome territory of the *Shema* itself and then into the *Amidah*.

The weekday *Amidah* is the prayer where we ask for those things that are closest to our hearts. I often prefer to take more time during the afternoon *Amidah*, to pray about all the things that come up in the middle of the day. When these things occur, I often can't do more than put out a quick prayer. But to offer prayers for myself or others with real *kavanah*, I need more time, including my own related prayers in each paragraph. So for the ninth blessing of the *Amidah*, for example, I might say, "Dear God, '*barekh aleinu*, bless this year for us, and all its many different kinds of harvest'—and please, *Ribboyno sh'l oylom*, the person who just lost her job, and the person who needs that grant, and please, please help that family to keep their home. And help me, too, with the projects I'm working on, because my strength is waning, and I'll never have the strength to finish them without Your help."

Davening *be-arikhut* was something we generally did on Shabbat. The Shabbat *Amidah*, as I said in "Following the Map," starts off with the same three blessings that we begin with during the week. In the central section, we take a rest (for ourselves and for God) from all the weekday blessings that ask for things we need. Instead we say just a single blessing, "who sanctifies the Sabbath," then conclude with the same final three blessings that we say during the week.

The *Amidah* of Shabbos still leaves us room for requests, however. "*Tein chelkeinu be-toratekha*, Give us a part in your Torah.' Please let me get something meaningful out of Torah reading this morning. '*Sabe'einu mi-tuvekha*, Satisfy us with Your goodness.' I'm so hungry for something, and I haven't found it yet. '*Ve-samach nafsheinu*, Gladden us with Your help.' I'm in such despair that anything good is going to happen in my life, please help me." This kind of prayer I can still do on Shabbos.

Pacing Yourself

The tuneful verses, the *Shema* and its blessings—you could be there all day. But you have to pee, and you get hungry. So you don't want to exhaust all your davening energy on any one part of your prayers. Pacing yourself is important. If you look at the *Tzava'at ha-Riva"sh*, the Baal Shem Tov's ethical will, he reminds us not to expend all our psychic and spiritual energy in these early sections. Rein yourself in a little; save some davening energy for later. Don't invest so much at the beginning that by the time you come to the *Shema*, you have no strength left. Husband your resources.

On the other hand, I want to say: Don't be a fool. If the *Ribboyno sh'l oylom* gives you a grace in *Pesukei de-Zimrah*, don't say no! Who knows whether you will have a better insight later on. It's coming down; it is so rich. Take hold of it. Love it. Plug into it as much as you can. If you've had a particularly deep and rich encounter with a verse, go forward, and let that high carry you with it. Sometimes the rest of your davening will be closer to business as usual. But you can offer up your davening as your way of saying, "Thank You for that wonderful insight that I had before!"

On the Way Down

Sometimes I might feel, "My prayers aren't being answered. Why doesn't my prayer last? Why don't I feel transformed?" The answer is: Because I'm hanging up too soon. I have said the *Shema* and the *Amidah*, but I still didn't finish. I need to remember the other side of the mountain, the winding down that kabbalists call *yeridat ha-shefa*, the "descent of the plenitude."

The psalmist says, "*Yeshvu yesharim et panekha*, The righteous ones sit in Your presence" (Psalm 140:14). The Talmud (Berakhot 32b) interprets this to mean that we should sit for a while after we've finished davening, to absorb what the davening is telling us. I want to remember all those places that I reached in my prayers. But it's so easy to forget! So I need to sit down and figure out what I am going to take away from my davening this morning.

> Where did I go today?
>
> What did I touch?
>
> What do I want to stay with me?
>
> What can I make up my mind to do?
>
> What is going to give me trouble?

I need to ask myself these things. Sometimes, no matter how blinding an insight can be in the moment, I'm not really *there* in my life. I'm not really at the level where I can truly integrate what I saw. So I try to remember, but I forget. I might say, with love and full *kavanah*, the line from *Ashrei*, "*Pote'ach et yadekha u-masbia le-chol chai ratzon*, You open Your hand and nourish all of life." I might meditate on that: "Oy, how often I come to things with the feeling of scarcity. How often I forget that God's hand is always open! Let me try and remember it during the day." Sometimes, if I'm blessed, I *will* remember. But all too often, looking back over my day before I go to bed at night, I say, "How many times did I forget?"

So looking back is important, and review is important. Remember that in the full framework of prayers laid out by the Rabbis, the morning davening is only part of our review. The other part is *keri'at Shema al ha-mitah*, the bedtime *Shema*. So in contemplating these things after my morning davening, I'm also looking forward, knowing that in my final thoughts and prayers, at the end of the day, I will have to account for myself. Sometimes my soul makes a promise but my mind or body rebels: If I really mean this, it means such-and-such. That feels like too much to commit to right now. I'm not there yet. I don't align myself with this completely. All too often, then, I will say, "Well, Zalman. Look where you were flying in the davening, and then look how you behaved later on."

So I need to sit a little bit more after *yeridat ha-shefa*, after I've said *Aleinu* and the other prayers I wind down with, and to ask: What are my action directives, based on the insights I brought down? What are my marching orders for the day?

Your meditation matrix can help you here. In Chabad, for example, we used to meditate on a phrase from the *Zohar* that describes God as "filling all worlds and encompassing all worlds."[6] Filling all worlds (*memaleh kol almin*) refers to God's immanent presence. Encompassing all worlds (*sovev kol almin*) refers to God's transcendence, the vaster dimension in which all of God's immanence is anchored. So I look inside my body and feel: *Memaleh kol almin* is breathing in me. *Memaleh kol almin* is beating my heartbeat. *Memaleh kol almin* is doing my digestion. And I know that the matrix in which all this takes place is *sovev kol almin*.

I'm not talking here about thinking objective thoughts, producing some intellectual idea about how to go forward. I'm talking about making myself a vehicle for God's will. I mean to go inside and say, "*Ribboyno sh'l oylom*, please, think in me. I am offering my mind as an instrument. Dear God, act in me. Please accept my body as Your vehicle." If my davening is truly to have the transformative effect it's meant to have, then spending the time to do this is vital.

Aftermath

After a while I got to the point where, if I didn't linger this way, davening until deep into Shabbos afternoon, *nisht gewein ubgedavvened,* I hadn't undavened myself, as it were: I hadn't unburdened myself. So I would daven until about 3 or 4 o'clock in the afternoon. Then I made *Kiddush* over the two rolls—I didn't have wine—and ate them with a can of sardines. (In those days I was so *frum* that I opened the can before Shabbos and left it open.) If I had davened at Rabbi Simpson's shul, I would go home to my parents. By now it was late in the afternoon, but they knew that I needed the time and freedom to be able to daven as much as I wanted.

On the same street as Rabbi Simpson's shul there was a Reform temple, where people would drive up with their cars, something I considered a grave violation of Shabbos. With my heart full from davening, though, all I could do was say, "Oy, dear God, you see? Those people are so far away from true Yiddishkeit. Yet still they come, and they want to daven! Please give them blessings."

Once I had been meditating and praying on the Hasidic teaching about the *ko'ach ha-mafli la'asot,* the "wondrous force." This comes from the *Shulchan Arukh* discussion of *Asher Yatzar,* the paragraph we say after going to the bathroom. The paragraph ends by blessing the God who "heals all flesh and acts wondrously." Reb Moshe Isserles comments there[7] that *ha-mafli la'asot,* the wondrous force, is that which sustains our soul within our bodies. To bind a spiritual entity to a corporeal one you need a miracle! If God did not inhabit us, we couldn't exist; but if God were to manifest fully, we couldn't exist either. So God has to be there within us, but in hiding.

Finally I emerged from my davening, and my eyes fell upon a great maple tree. In the spiritual state that I was in, all my pores open, the miracle of that tree's very existence struck me with full force. I must have stood at least an hour there, marveling at its intricate structure and the many scales on which it functioned. To the casual bystander, perhaps, it was just another maple tree. To me, at that moment, it was a breathtaking expression of God's creative power, the mysterious life force that was hidden and yet obvious and available to any onlooker.

This touches upon an important question. You might say, "*Nu*, so you spent all that time davening. What good did it do you?" My answer is that transformation doesn't always show itself in *Asiyah*. The shift is not so much what others will see on the outside. Yes, it will show itself afterward in better behavior and so on. How could I not be more caring to my partner and my children after spending such quality time in the presence of God? But most of the shift that takes place in a person is not something that another would necessarily be able to observe. The tree stopped me in my tracks that day. Yet how many times did I come out and just looked at the sky, had a moment of "*Mah rabu ma'asekha*, How wondrous are Thy works," and moved off down the street? An onlooker may not have noted any difference—but *inside* of me was a deep connection, an intuiting of the divinity of creation and a love of the world.

The Rabbis believed that only a limited portion of our souls can be packed into our physical bodies. "Not all the soul enrobes itself in the human body," said the Tzemach Tzedek, commenting on the *Tanya*.[8] He pointed to a Rabbinic saying that "only a third of an angel stands in the physical world.[9] Since the human soul was seen as more elevated even than an angel, how then could that soul dress itself completely in the human form here below? Abraham Joshua Heschel once quoted his grandfather, Rabbi Abraham Joshua Heschel of Apt, known as the Ohev Yisrael (lover of Israel). The Apter was comparing the two most solemn fasts of the Jewish year: Tisha be-Av, the day both Temples were destroyed, and Yom Kippur, the Day of Atonement, when we reach for the highest level of purity and holiness. "On Tisha be-Av," he said, "*ver ken essen* [who can eat]? And on Yom Kippur, *ver darf essen* [who needs to eat]?"[10] At times we can feel so exalted in our spiritual selves that our physical needs temporarily drop away. But most of the time we exist, as we must, in *Asiyah*. The davener is like the Zen master who was asked what difference all his years of meditation had made. "The same," he said. "Just feet a little bit above the ground."

Taste and See

"The pious ones of old," the Talmud tells us, "would spend an hour before the prayer, an hour at their prayers, then another hour after their prayers" (Berakhot 32b). Most of us don't live in conditions of such monastic serenity. For many who read this, the prolonged personal prayer (davening *be-arikhut*) that I have described here may lie in another lifetime. But if you have ever experienced a real davening moment, a moment of true connection, you might wonder: What would it be like if I could take as long as I needed on every sentence, every word? What would it be like if I could really say things with *kavanah*, if I didn't have to shush my kids or keep up with the congregation? Would I catch glimpses of God that I've never had before?

Even if you can't spend all day, you can do things that will help give you such glimpses. My first suggestion is to connect with a quick *hirhur teshuvah*, an aspiration to turn again to God. The Seer of Lublin had a wonderful but difficult custom. Every day, before he sat down to learn, he would murmur a verse from Psalms: "To the wicked, God has said, 'What business do you have to converse in My law, and to bear My covenant in your mouth?'" (Psalm 50:16). He would meditate on that, and he would sigh, *Oy. I want to be a righteous one. I don't want to be a wicked one. Please, dear God, help me ...* I do this as well: before I sit down and do my studying, I do a moment of *teshuvah*, turning and re-turning to God. I've also done it with groups that I teach. You don't have to go with the verse the Lubliner used; the important thing is to be able to open up to your heart's ever-present desire to return to God. For those who use the Orthodox liturgy, it is appropriate before you say the *Birkhat ha-Torah* in the morning, where daveners set aside a few moments for Torah study, or before you do *Tachanun*, the prayer for forgiveness.

My next suggestion is simply to pick just one prayer and to say it very slowly. This is important. Don't sing it, just say it, one word or small phrase at a time. Leave enough space between the words to allow your mind and heart to align with what your lips are saying. Allow your soul to really soak in the words, as I described earlier. Do just one prayer in this way, and then go back to your normal davening. Many of the verses in the davening are thoughts you can really spend time with; they will be good company on your journey.

Take It with You

I don't want to give the impression that I have always been able to do the kind of davening I talk about here. There are some days, especially now, when it takes me much longer just to get into my body, and I'm happy if I can finish my davening and quota of study without any fancy stuff. Come Shabbos, I do a little bit more. But I can also call upon all the good memories of the places I have been before. I can access it still.

I have a hope and a goal that at some point you will find the time to *go* to these inner places, not just to imagine it in your mind. As long as you just say, "Oh, let me think about that," then you're still in the mental realm, still only with the left brain. You're not experiencing it empirically; you're not touching it. On the other hand, if you do it with both your left brain *and* your right brain, and your heart says, *Yes, I feel that,* and your intuition says, *That's the way it really is,* then you're like the Maggid in that story we started out with: you have been there. You have actually traveled to these places yourself. After that, even just a quick remembrance will awaken what you felt in your heart when you were able to spend more time.

It is really possible to get there once you have been there the other way. Reb Nachman says: You have to teach your body all the things that the soul knows. That way, when you feel rushed, when your soul falters and forgets, your body can repeat the same actions and remind you. Even just singing a *niggun* with *kavanah* can bring you back! But it's important to know that you have been there.

The theologian Franz Rosenzweig, a close friend and collaborator of Martin Buber, ends his great work *The Star of Redemption* with the image of a gate that opens up. "Wither, then, do the wings of the gate open? Thou knowest it not? INTO LIFE."[11] These are the book's final words. Similarly, I want to say: Where does all this davening lead to? Into *devekut,* into a loving closeness with God. When you come to the end of your sit, you'll be able to say, I am now going home. You'll have that wonderful memory. It is written in your body now—*al luach libekha,* on the tablet of your heart.[12] You'll be able to take this with you, back out into the world. And, if it speaks to you, to carry on the work.

Notes

Introduction

1. Will Herberg, "The God-Idea and the Living God," *Judaism and Modern Man* (New York: Jewish Publication Society, 1951; Atheneum, 1983).
2. See Ezekiel 1:1.
3. See Rashi on Exodus 15:2.
4. See *Iggeret ha-Kodesh*, epistle 13.
5. See, for example, *Tzava'at ha-Riva"sh*, 65.

Intention: Davening with *Kavanah*

1. The phrase is from the final paragraph of the *Amidah*.
2. Ibid., Sephardic *nusach*.
3. Bachya ibn Pakuda, an eleventh-century philosopher, wrote a book called *Guide to the Duties of the Heart*, which set out the first Jewish system of ethics.
4. Seth Kadish, *Kavvana: Directing the Heart in Jewish Prayer* (Northvale, NJ: Jason Aronson, 1997).
5. Originally *libo do'eg be-kirbo*, in the third person singular, suggested in Babylonian Talmud, Chagigah 13a as characterizing a person to whom it is permitted to reveal a certain level of esotericism.
6. Author of *Divrei Chayim*, a work on *halakhah*.
7. "*Adonal* is God" are the words that the people of Israel spoke when Elijah performed the miracle on Mount Carmel before hundreds of priests of Ba'al and Asherah (1 Kings 18:39). The words are the closing declaration of *Ne'ilah*, the fifth and final service of Yom Kippur, the highest moment of awareness that we reach, at the very end of our fast. We sing them together seven times.
8. See Farid al-Din Attar, *Muslim Saints and Mystics: Episodes from the Tadhkirat al-Auliya' ('Memorial of the Saints')*, trans. A. J. Arberry (London: Arkana, 1990), p. 210.

9. Excerpted from "Prayer Song," from the play *David Dances*, by Stephen Mo Hanan. Used with permission.

10. See Rabbi Yosef Wineberg, ed., *Lessons in Tanya* (Brooklyn: Kehot, 1982), vol. 1, p. 264.

11. Reb Zalman derives the word takhlitic from *takhlit* (Hebrew) or *takhlis* (Yiddish), meaning the purpose, end point, or bottom-line substance.

Niggun! A Soul in Song

1. Mishnah Shabbos 5:1. See also Babylonian Talmud, Shabbos 51b.

2. Rabbi Zallman Schachter Shalomi with Joel Segel, *Jewish with Feeling: A Guide to Meaningful Jewish Practice* (New York: Riverhead Books, 2005).

3. For the Hebrew words, see www.zemereshet.co.il/song.asp?id=394. To listen to the poem set to music by David Zahavi, see www.zemereshet.co.il/song. asp?id=394#versions.

4. For another biblical source relating the use of instruments by "the children of the prophets," a group that lived a life conducive to prophecy, see 1 Samuel 10:5.

5. David ben Yehudah ha-Chasid, *Livnat ha-Sapir, Parashat Noach.* Quoted by Rabbi Meir ben Gabbai, *Avodat HaKodesh*, 3:10, and by the modern teacher Rabbi DovBer Pinson; see iyyun.com/teachings/kabbalah/kabbalah-music-an-interview-with-rav-dovber-pinson.

6. The blessing before the haftarah, which is said with its own *trope* in many communities, is a rare exception. One source reports Max Helfman (see Reb Zalman's *At the Rebbe's Table: Rabbi Zalman Schachter-Shalomi's Legacy of Songs and Melodies, Volume II, ed.* Eyal Rinlin, with Netanel Miles-Yepez [Boulder, CO: The Reb Zalman Legacy Project, 2007], p. 4n) as saying that "haftarah blessing melody [is used] in Bernstein's 'Jeremiah Symphony.'"

7. This phrase is used in the Talmud to support the idea that service to God is best done in a multitude—the more the better.

8. See Reb Zalman's *Into My Garden: Reb Zalman Schachter-Shalomi's Legacy of Songs and Meoldies, Volume I*, ed. Eyal Rinlin, with Netanel Miles-Yepez (Boulder, CO: The Reb Zalman Legacy Project, 2007), p. 56.

9. The fourth Belzer Rebbe, Rabbi Aharon Rokeach.

10. See video at video.google.com/videoplay?docid=5447725737858098635&q=belzer&time=20000#, at approx 2:45.

11. See, for example, Reb Zalman's *At the Rebbe's Table*, pp. 28, 37, 45.

12. Pirkei Avot 6:6 singles this out from among forty-eight different qualities necessary to acquire Torah. See also Talmud, Megillah 15a. It is

traced to the behavior of Queen Esther in the book of Esther 2:22: "And the thing [Bigtan and Teresh's plan to harm King Ahasuerus] became known to Mordechai, and he told Esther, and Esther told the king in Mordechai's name."

13. See www.sichosinenglish.org/books/letters-Rebbe-2/20.htm for a letter from "Rabbi Menachem Schneerson, then executive director, *Merkos L'Inyonei Chinuch and Machne Yisrael*," addressed to Rabbi Moshe Yehudah Chechoval, "a distinguished Rabbi who had just arrived from war-torn Europe to a camp for refugees established by the American government in upstate New York." The letter is dated 21 Menachem Av, 5704, which implies that he arrived in the United States circa summer 1944.

14. See Reb Zalman's *At the Rebbe's Table*, p. 27.

15. Ibid., p. 57.

16. For the complete words, see ibid., pp. 72–74.

17. For the complete words, see ibid., pp. 82–84.

18. See Song of Songs 5:1.

19. Velvel Pasternak, *The Jewish Music Companion* (Hal Leonard, 2003), p. 198.

20. See *Likutei Moharan*, part 2, paragraph 63.

21. Naomi Shemer wrote a beautiful song based on this teaching by the Breslover, called "The Song of the Grasses (*Shirat ha-Asavim*)."

22. The phrase is originally condensed from Jeremiah 33:10–11.

23. This haftarah, from Isaiah, chapter 40, is recited on the first Shabbos after the Ninth of Av, the first of seven consolation haftarot.

24. See *Into My Garden: Reb Zalman Schachter-Shalomi's Legacy of Songs and Meoldies, Volume I*, ed. Eyal Rinlin, with Netanel Miles-Yepez (Boulder, CO: The Reb Zalman Legacy Project, 2007), pp. 32–33.

25. See p. 16.

Davening in the Four Worlds: A Deep Structure of Prayer

1. See, for example, Berakhot 62a and Megillah 28a; also *Mishneh Torah*, Sefer Ha-Mada, Hilchot Talmud Torah 4:6.

2. Used by the Ashkenazi communities in the evening prayer, and by Sephardi and Chabad communities in the morning prayers as well.

3. Thanks to Cantor Shoshana Brown for the substance of this question. See *Journal of Synagogue Music* 34 (Fall 2009): 142, www.cantors.org/JSM/2009.pdf.

4. From the eighth blessing of the Amidah.

5. From the final blessing of the Amidah.

6. From the eighth blessing of the Amidah.

7. Gikatilla was a Spanish kabbalist and a pupil of Abraham Abulafia who lived in the second half of the thirteenth century. Isaac of Akko was a contemporary of Gikatilla who fled the city of Akko (Acre) when it was captured by the Turks and went to Spain as well.

8. See Rabbi Schneur Zalman of Liadi, *Likutei Amarim (Tanya)*, chap. 4.

9. See, for example, Maurice Freedman, *Martin Buber: The Life of Dialogue* (New York: HarperTorchbook, 1960); and Paul Arthur Schlipp and Maurice Freedman, eds., *The Philosophy of Martin Buber* (La Salle, IL: Open Court, 1967).

Following the Map: A Traveler's Guide

1. Sephardic communities say a section from the *Zohar* here instead.

2. Thanks to Susie Dym of Rehovot, Israel, who heard this story from the old man's other son and passed it on to us.

3. The Hebrew here, *merachem*, means "has mercy on" but comes from the root *resh-chet-mem*, which is also at the heart of *rechem*, "womb."

4. Rabbi Daniel Siegel and I wrote extensively about *Ashrei* at the beginning of *Credo of a Modern Kabbalist* (Bloomington, IN: Trafford Publishing, 2006), but I will summarize it here.

5. The only letter missing is *nun*, the fourteenth letter of the alphabet. It is alluded to in the following verse, the one that begins with *samech*, the fifteenth letter, which says that God will support those who have fallen (*noflim*, which begins with *nun*). Not wishing to speak explicitly of such unpleasant topics, the psalmist let the *nun* of *noflim* stand as quiet representation of the letter.

6. Today Rabbi Yitzchak Husbands-Hankin is senior rabbi at Temple Beth Israel of Eugene, Oregon.

7. Reb Zalman adds, "Friday night is also a good time to sing this, or *shaleshudes*, the third meal on Shabbos, as the light is fading. You can find it in a good collection of *z'miros*, Shabbos songs."

8. Reb Zalman says, "This comes from a little old-time siddur that I saw called *Kavanot* that has *kavanot peshutot* [simple *kavanot*]. It's only in the Sephardic siddur."

9. Ashkenazi siddurim have "*Ahavah rabbah ahavtanu*" in the morning prayers and "*Ahavat olam beit Yisrael amkha ahavtah*" in the evening prayer. Chabad and some of the Sepharad siddurim, however, follow the Ari, who saw an important *kavanah* in the first letters of *ahavat olam ahavtanu*: *aleph* (1) + *ayin* (70) + *aleph* (1) add up to 72, a number the

kabbalists saw as a permutation of *YHVH*: *yud* = 10; *yud hey* = 15; *yud hey vav* = 21; *yud hey vav hey* = 26. And 10 + 15 + 21 + 26 = 72.

10. See www.yivoencyclopedia.org/article.aspx/Brivnshtelers.

11. From *The Making of Chassidim: A Letter Written by the Previous Lubavitcher Rebbe, Rabbi Yosef Yitzchak Schneersohn.* Chapter 4: "Davening: The Avodah of a Chossid." Translated from the Yiddish by Shimon Neubort. Published and copyright © by Sichos In English. See www.sichosinenglish.org/books/making-chassidim/08.htm.

12. Torah's first use of the verb *sha'ah* is from the Cain and Abel story: God turns (*va-yisha*) to Abel and his offering, but to Cain and his offering God doesn't turn (*lo sha'ah*) (Genesis 4:4–5).

13. "*Ein keli machazik berakhah elah shalom,*" quoted in the name of Rabbi Shimon ben Chalifta in Genesis Rabbah on *Parashat Pinchas,* 21:1.

14. Zalman Schachter-Shalomi, *All Breathing Life Adores Your Name,* ed. Michael L. Kagan (Santa Fe, NM: Gaon, 2011).

15. Reb Zalman adds, "The connection between elevators and prayer is not as far-fetched as it seems. In Europe, they used to have what was called a *paternoster*, a passenger elevator made of a chain of compartments that moved in a loop without stopping. If you wanted to go up or down in a building, you'd watch for the next car and step in, quick. Then you'd get off at the floor you wanted. They called it a *paternoster* ("our father") because the loop of cars reminded people of rosary beads."

Who Am I to Give Blessings?

1. *Iggeret ha-Kodesh*, Epistle 27. The *Iggeret ha-Kodesh* or "Letter of Holiness" is actually a series of letters written by the first Lubavitcher Rebbe, Schneur Zalman of Liadi, to his followers and Jews in other communities. It comprises the fourth part of the *Tanya*, foundational work of Chabad Chasidism.

Advanced Practice

1. See, for example, *Tanya* 4:1.

2. In *Parashat va-Yishlach,* Jacob instructs his men to deliver a very large gift to Esau his brother, "and leave space between one flock and the next" (Genesis 32:17). Such surprising borrowings have been part of Hasidic thinking and exegesis since the Baal Shem Tov.

3. *Shulchan Arukh* 98: "*Ha-mitpallel tzarikh she-yekhaven be-libo perush ha-milot she-motzi mi-piv.*"

4. See www.yeshiva.org.il/midrash/shiur.asp?id=4919.

5. Reb Schneur Zalman focuses on this idea in *Shaar ha-Yichud ve-ha-Emunah*, the second volume of the *Tanya*.

6. See, for example, *Zohar* 3:225a, Raya Mehemna, *Parashat Pinchas*.

7. See Isserles on the *Shulchan Arukh*, Orach Chayim 6:1.

8. *Sefer ha-Ken: Kovetz Ma'amarim al ADMo"R ha-Zaken, Rabbi Schneur Zalman me-Liadi le-Mil'ot K"N [150] Shana le-Histalkuto* (Jerusalem: Kiryat Sefer, 1963), p. 23.

9. See, for example, Genesis Rabbah 68:12; and Maimonides, *Guide to the Perplexed* 2:10.

10. From Abraham Joshua Heschel "No Time for Neutrality," *Moral Grandeur and Spiritual Audacity*, (New York: Macmillan, 1997), p. 147.

11. Franz Rosenzweig, *The Star of Redemption*, trans. Barbara E. Galli (Madison, WI: University of Wisconsin Press, 2005), p. 447.

12. Proverbs 3:3, 7:3.

Acknowledgments

When I review my life, the one thread that runs through it is davenology. From the time that I was a child reciting my good-night prayer through my life in the yeshiva and the years afterwards, what happens in prayer was always in the landscape of my mind. When I see what has happened to congregational prayer I feel that even in the places where people observe the liturgy meticulously there is a lack of soul. I wanted to have one more book out that would help the average davener to enter into the sacred realm of prayer and to feel the reality of the encounter with God.

I asked Joel Segel, with whom I wrote *Jewish with Feeling*, to take the most telling material from my many talks and articles and create the present volume. Joel is both an enabler of my thoughts and a representative of the reader, making sure my teachings will reach the reader in a way that he/she can absorb it. He is an extraordinary wordsmith. His background makes it possible for me to use a Jewishly learned shorthand, which he in turn transmits in a way that conveys the core, preserves the inspiration, and touches the heart. I have the sense that in *Jewish with Feeling* and in this book, Reb Joel has become one of the outstanding transmitters of my teaching, and I trust that people wanting to learn more will invite him to teach.

Many people provided financial support to help me in getting this material to you, the reader. I ask you to add your blessings and prayers to mine for their generosity. Some gave to commemorate a loved one, some to honor people present in their life. All donated generously. May they all be blessed:

Alon Nashman, in memory of Harold Nashman

Beth Hirschfield, in memory of my beloved husband, Rabbi Aryeh Hirschfield, *zatz"l*

Dr. Daniel Pewsner

Rabbis Diane Elliot and Burt Jacobson, in memory of Diane's mother, Florence Asher Elliot, Tziporah bat Shmuel v'Hannah Dreisl

Rabbi Elie Kaplan Spitz

Estelle Frankel

Gary Davis

Gloria Krasno

Helena Rachel Foster

Rabbi Irwin Kula

Rabbi J. Rolando Matalon

Rabbi Jeff Roth, in honor of the gates opened for me by Reb Zalman

Jeffrey G. Shapiro, in honor of the learning I and others have done with you

Jessica Zeller

Joel and Fern Levin

Jonathan and Diana Rose

Jonathan David Stoler, in memory of my beloved mother, Rose Fishlyn Stoler

Rabbi Judith HaLevy

Klaus and Ute Teschemacher

Lucinda Kurtz and Oran Hesterman

Rabbi Malka Drucker, in memory of my father, William Treiber, Velvel ben Leib

Rabbi Marcelo Bronstein

Rabbi Michael Paley

Congregation P'nai Or, Long Beach, California

Rabbi Richard Simon

Dr. Roger Dreyfus

Rabbi Schachar Orenstein

Rabbi Shohama Harris Wiener

Rabbi Shoshanah Devorah

Rabbi Stan Levy

Susan Raskin Abrams

Rabbi T'mimah Ickovitz, in loving and grateful memory of Ava Grosz-Ickovits and Andre "Bundy" Ickovits of blessed memory. You survived and flourished after the Shoah. You are loved and missed.

Rabbi Yitzhak Husbands-Hankin, in memory of our beloved Reb Aryeh Hirschfield *zatz"l.*

Rabbi Yocheved Mintz

Rabbi David Zaslow

Rabbi Elliot Ginsburg and Linda Jo Doctor

Rabbi Arthur Gross-Schaefer

—Z. S. S.

Thanks to Reb Zalman, for his love, his trust, and his wisdom; for his open-sky, open-heart Judaism; and for his tireless work for our people, for the planet, and for God. You are and always will be my Rebbe.

To my mother, Ruth Segel, who taught me my first prayers, and my father, Lee Segel, *z"l,* for whom work was prayer.

To Zaida, Myer Galinksi, who davened for an hour every morning without haste, putting his world in order one *b'rokhah* at a time.

To my siblings, Susie Dym, Daniel Segel, and Michael Segel; *z'mirot* still don't feel quite right unless we're singing them together.

To Cantor Lorel Zar-Kessler and Rabbi David Thomas, for encouraging and nurturing my own expression of prayer.

To Rabbi Larry Kushner, who introduced me to Jewish Lights, wrote the foreword, and imagined our beloved community of Beth El Sudbury.

To Stuart M. Matlins, who gets what Reb Zalman is all about and may be the last great Jewish publisher still standing; to our editor, Emily Wichland, and to all the dedicated folks at Jewish Lights.

To my beloved wife, Laura, and our wonderful children, Eve Margalit and Jesse Akiva, who give my heart something to pray for every single day.

And finally, to the One who loves and listens. Were every letter here a song, it would not be enough.

—J. J. S.

GLOSSARY

R eb Zalman, as a native Yiddish speaker, tends to prefer Yiddish terms and pronunciations for sacred subjects over their Hebrew or English equivalents: *Shabbos* versus Shabbat or Sabbath, *tallis* versus *tallit, Ch'siddus* versus Hasidism. Because some readers are more familiar with the Hebrew versions and others more comfortable with the English equivalents, we have interspersed these other variations throughout the text.

Pronunciation

A word can be pronounced one way in Hebrew, another way in Yiddish, and yet a third way in English-speaking countries. The word *kabbalah,* for instance, is pronounced *kah-ba-LAH, ka-BAH-lah,* and *ka-BOLL-leh.* And what of words that should be pronounced one way but in fact are pronounced otherwise? It is a rare Israeli indeed, for instance, who doesn't elide the initial *schwa* on many words, preferring *p'sukei* to *pesukei* and *k'riyat* to *keriyat.* Here, too, we have split the difference, preferring widespread usage over correctness for more common forms but retaining the correct form in other cases.

> "kh" *(khaf)* and "ch" *(chet)* represent a guttural sound, similar to the German "sprach" or the Scots "loch." While the *chet* is more guttural among Jews descended from Arab countries, Jews of Ashkenazi descent do not generally distinguish between the two.

> "a" is pronounced as in "father" and appears in the pronunciation guides here as "ah."

"e" is pronounced as in "get" and appears in the pronunciation guides as either "e" (when it is in the middle of a syllable) or "eh" (when it ends a syllable).

"ei" is pronounced as in "neighbor" and appears in the pronunciation guides as "ai" (when it is in the middle of a syllable) or "ay" (when it ends a syllable).

"i" is pronounced as in "tin" and appears in the pronunciation guides as either "i" (when it is in the middle of a syllable) or "ih" (when it ends a syllable).

"o" is commonly pronounced as a long "o" (as in Moses) in the English-speaking diaspora. Among Israelis, however, its pronunciation lies between the long and short "o" in English, being closer to the German *Bonn* or the French *Sorbonne*. It appears here in the pronunciation guides simply as "o" (when it is in the middle of a syllable) or "oh" (when it ends a syllable).

"u" is pronounced with a long "oo," as in "soon," in Hebrew, and often with a short "oo" as in "look," in the diaspora.

A-da'ata de-nafshei (Aramaic: a-DAH-a-tah de-NAF-shay): Literally, with [one's own] soul or self in mind. An expression used in Talmud to designate something done with the intention of benefiting oneself. The Jewish contemplative tradition reframed it to mean the intention and realization that we ourselves are personally involved in the thing we are contemplating.

Aggadah (Hebrew: ah-gah-DAH): Storytelling. More broadly, any form of Rabbinic discussion that is outside the realm of halakhah, Jewish law.

Ahavah (Hebrew: ah-hah-VAH): Love. With *yir'ah*, one of the two pillars of human relationship to God.

A hin un a her (Yiddish: ah HIN oon ah HEHR): Literally, "to there and to here," going and coming. All over the place, mixed up.

Aleph beys, *Aleph bet* (Yiddish: AH-lef BAIS; Hebrew: AH-lef BET): The Hebrew alphabet.

Aliyah, *aliyot* (pl.) (Hebrew: ah-lee-YAH, ah-lee-YOT): Literally, ascending. In modern times, the act of immigration to Israel. Also, the honor of reciting the blessings before and after the reading of a portion of Torah in synagogue; or the portion itself.

Alter (Yiddish: AHL-ter): Also *elter* in the Yiddish of Galicia. Elder. *Alter Rebbe* often refers to the first, founding rebbe in a Hasidic line. *Alter Zaida* means great-grandfather.

Amidah (Hebrew: ah-mee-DAH or, in the diaspora, ah-MEE-dah): Literally, the act of standing: the *Amidah* is traditionally recited standing, with one's feet together, and in silence. The *Amidah* is a central piece of the worship service, together with the *Shema* (which appears in the morning and evening but not afternoon prayers). Often simply called the *T'fillah* (prayer) in halakhic literature, the *Amidah* is also known as the *Sh'moneh Esreh*, meaning eighteen, for the number of blessings contained in the everyday version, though later Rabbinic authorities added a nineteenth. The Sabbath and holiday *Amidah* contains only seven blessings.

Aron, aron kodesh (Hebrew: ah-RON, ah-RON KOH-desh): The ark or holy ark, in which the scrolls of the Torah are kept in a synagogue. Typically, though not always, placed toward the East, the direction traditionally faced when praying the *Amidah.*

Ashkenazi, Ashkenazim (pl.) (Hebrew: ahsh-keh-nah-ZEE or, in the diaspora, ahsh-keh-NAH-zee; ahsh-keh-nah-ZEEM or, in the diaspora, ahsh-keh-NAH-zim): Pertaining to Ashkenaz, meaning the geographic area of northern and eastern Europe. Used to designate an individual, community, ritual, or custom of Ashkenaz, as opposed to people or rituals from Sepharad, Spain).

Asiyah (Hebrew: ah-see-YAH or, in the diaspora, ah-SEE-yah): Literally, doing or action. The physical, apprehensible world of action and sensation, lowest of the four worlds of *Asiyah, Yetzirah, Beriyah,* and *Atzilut* in the kabbalistic Four Worlds system. Associated with the morning blessings especially, which pertain to the physical body, and also with any aspect of prayer that involves the physical body.

Atzilut (Hebrew: ah-tzee-LOOT or, in the diaspora, ah-TZEE-loot): Literally, exaltedness or nobility. The world of transcendence or emanation, highest of the four worlds of *Asiyah, Yetzirah, Beriyah,* and *Atzilut* in the kabbalistic Four World system. Associated with the *Amidah* especially, and with any aspect of prayer that transcends our individual awareness.

Avodah (Hebrew: ah-voh-DAH or, in the diaspora, ah-VOH-dah): Work or, especially in sacred contexts, service. Used, for example, in *avodah she-ba-lev*, service of the heart or prayer, and *avodat ha-shem*, God's work or prayer.

Ba'al (Hebrew: BAH-ahl): Owner or master of. Also husband.

Ba'al Shem Tov (Hebrew: BAH-ahl SHEM TOV): Literally, "master good name," meaning either someone of good reputation or someone adept at using the Divine Name for shamanic healing. A mystic from a small village in an area now belonging to Ukraine, considered to be the founder of Hasidism in the mid-1700s.

Beis medrash, **bet midrash** (Yiddish: BAIS MED-resh; Hebrew: BAIT meed-RASH): House of study. See **midrash**.

Berakhah, **b'rokhah** (Hebrew: b'-rah-KHAH; Yiddish: B'ROH-khah): Blessing.

Beriyah (Hebrew: b'-ree-AH or, in the diaspora, B'REE-ah): Literally, creation. The world of higher intellect, second highest of the four worlds of *Asiyah, Yetzirah, Beriyah,* and *Atzilut* in the kabbalistic Four World system. Associated with the *Shema* and the blessings that surround it, and with any contemplative aspect of prayer.

Besh"t (Hebrew: BESHT): An acronym for the Baal Shem Tov, founder of Hasidism.

Bimah (Hebrew: bee-MAH or, in the diaspora, BIH-mah): Podium or stage. In a synagogue, platform from which prayers are led or the Torah read out.

Binah (Hebrew: bee-NAH or, in the diaspora, BEE-nah): A discerning understanding or intelligence. In kabbalistic circles, it is one of the uppermost *sefirot*, representing a stage of divine thought prior to creation. The *sefirah* of *Binah* is often associated with the maternal, the womb from which the seven lower spheres are born. In the Chabad system (named for *Chokhmah, Binah,* and *Da'at*), *Binah* is the counterpart of *Chokhmah*: whereas *Chokhmah* denotes the flash of intuition, *Binah* represents the careful investigation and study, the two coming together in *Da'at*.

Birkhot ha-Shachar (Hebrew: beer-KHOT hah-SHAH-char): Literally, the dawn blessings. The first part of the morning prayers, containing blessings and prayers pertaining to physical things.

Blatt (Yiddish: BLAHT): Page(s), commonly used of Talmud.

Bocher (Yiddish: BOCH-'r): From Hebrew *bachur*, lad. A youth. Often, a student at a yeshiva.

Brokhah: See **Berakhah**.

Chabad (Hebrew: chah-BAHD): Acronym of *Chokhmah, Binah,* and *Da'at*: an intellectual brand of Hasidism founded by Schneur Zalman of Liadi. Today the name Chabad is virtually interchangeable with the Lubavitch Hasidim, Chabad's chief remaining lineage.

Chazan (Hebrew: chah-ZAHN; Yiddish: CHAH-z'n): Cantor.

Chesed (Hebrew: CHEH-sehd): Literally, grace or kindness. Also the name of the fourth *sefirah*.

Cheder (Yiddish: CHAY-der): Literally, a room. School to teach young children basic religious studies.

Chokhmah (Hebrew: chokh-MAH or, in the diaspora, CHOKH-mah): Wisdom. In kabbalistic circles, one of the uppermost *sefirot*, representing a stage of divine thought prior to creation. *Chokhmah* is the counterpart of *Binah* in Chabad philosophy: *Chokhmah* denotes the flash of intuition, *Binah* investigation and study. The two come together in *Da'at*.

Chumash (Hebrew: choo-MAHSH; Yiddish: CHOO-m'sh): A book containing the Five Books of Moses, typically used in synagogue to follow the Torah reading.

Da'at (Hebrew: DAH-aht): Knowledge, awareness. In the sefirotic system, *Da'at* represents the synthesis of the other intellectual *sefirot* of *Chokhmah* and *Binah*, completing the highest triad of the *sefirot*.

Daven (Yiddish: DAH-v'n): To pray, especially to chant liturgical prayers in the style of traditionally pious Jews. Can also be used to mean leading prayers. Of uncertain derivation.

Daven be-arikhut (Yiddish: DAH-v'n beh-ah-REE-khut): From the Hebrew *arokh*, long. To daven at length and with heightened awareness and involvement.

De-oraita (Aramaic: deh-oh-RY-tah): Literally, of the Torah. Used most commonly to distinguish a commandment that comes from Torah rather than being a later Rabbinical addition (*de-rabbanan*).

De-rabbanan (Aramaic: deh-rah-bah-NAHN): Literally, of the rabbis. A mitzvah that represents a later addition to, or interpretation of, the mitzvot of Torah by the Rabbis.

Devekus, **devekut** (Yiddish: deh-VAY-kus; Hebrew: deh-vay-KUT): Adherence, cleaving, or deep devotion to God.

Droshah, **drashah**, (Yiddish: DROH-shoh; Hebrew: d'rah-SHAH): Sermon, homiletical interpretation.

Echad (Hebrew: eh-CHAD): One. *Echad* is the final word in the opening *Shema* statement, indicating the oneness of God.

Ein Sof (Hebrew: eyn-SOF): Literally, no end, no limitation. "Infinite," a kabbalistic name of God, denoting God in God's most abstract form, prior to any manifestation whatsoever.

Erev (Hebrew: EH-rehv): Evening. Often used to designate the evening or start of a Hebrew holy day, like *erev Shabbat* or *erev Pesach.* Sometimes used to denote part or all of the day before the Shabbat (i.e., Friday) or festival.

Fabrengen (Yiddish: fah-BRENG'n): Get-together. A Chabad term for what other Hasidic groups call a *tisch,* a Hasidic gathering, with the Rebbe or by themselves, for teaching, singing, and stories, often with some drinks and light refreshments.

Frum (Yiddish: FROOM): Religious, Orthodox. A person who keeps the commandments.

Ga'agu'im (Hebrew: gah-ah-goo-im; Yiddish: gah-ah-GOO-im): Yearnings.

Gabbai, **gabbayim** (pl.) (Hebrew: gah-BY, gah-by-EEM or, in the diaspora, GAH-by, ga-BOH-yim): Official in a synagogue, often responsible for calling people to the Torah and handing out other honors; often also the treasurer.

Gemara, **Gemorah** See **Talmud**.

Gematria (Hebrew: geh-MAHT-ree-yah): The practice of assigning a numerical value to each letter of the Hebrew alphabet, thereby finding equivalences between words or phrases and, often, hidden meanings or correspondences encoded therein.

Gemilut chasadim (Hebrew: geh-mee-LOOT chah-sah-DEEM): Literally, a gift or mutual exchange of kindness, or simply a kindness. Singular: *Gemilat chesed.*

Geschrei (Yiddish: geh-SH'RY): A shout or cry, from the Yiddish *schreien,* to shout.

Gesheft (Yiddish: geh-SHEFT): Business, to-do.

Gesunterheit (Yiddish: geh-ZUN-ter-hait): Good health, a benediction.

Halakhah (Hebrew: hah-lah-KHAH or, in the diaspora, hah-LAH-khah): Literally, the walking or going, denoting the proper and godly way to walk through life. Normative or Rabbinic Jewish law. Also used as an Anglicized adjective, halakhic, meaning pertaining to Jewish law.

Hallel (Hebrew: hah-LEL or, in the diaspora, HAH-lel): Literally, praise. A set of psalms recited in praise of God. The best known *Hallel* is recited on holidays and comprises Psalms 113–118.

Ha-Shem (Hebrew: hah-SHEM): Literally, the name. A common term for God, used in order to avoid saying the Tetragrammaton or other biblical names for God.

Hasid, **Hasidim** (pl.) (Hebrew: khah-SEED, khah-sih-DIM; Yiddish: KHAH-sihd, khah-SIH-dim): An adherent of Hasidism. See **Hasidism**.

Hasidism (English: KHAH-sih-diz'm): A movement traced to the Baal Shem Tov that seeks a direct connection to God, emphasizing singing, prayer, and contemplation over learning and pedantry.

Heimisch (Yiddish: HAY-mish): Homey.

Hisbonenus, ***hitbonenut***, (Yiddish: hiss-BOH-neh-noos; Hebrew: hit-boh-neh-NOOT): Literally, contemplation or examination. A general term for Chabad meditation.

Ish chesed (Hebrew: EESH CHEH-sed): Person (m.) of kindness, a kindly or charitable man. *Eshet chesed* (AY-shet CHEH-sed) is a woman of kindness.

Kabbalah (Hebrew: kah-bah-LAH or, in the diaspora, kah-BAH-lah; Yiddish: kah-BOH-leh): Literally, a receiving, or that which is received. The teachings of Jewish mysticism, including especially the Zohar and surrounding Zoharic literature and the kabbalah of Rabbi Isaac Luria of Safed, known as the Ari.

Kappotte (Yiddish: kah-POT-teh): Caftan, usually black, worn by Ultra-Orthodox men.

Kavanah, kavanot (pl.) (Hebrew: kah-vah-NAH or, in the diaspora, kah-VAHN-ah; Yiddish: kah-VOH-neh): Literally, direction or intention. To pray with *kavanah* is to pray with focus and to direct one's words and thoughts sincerely to God, as opposed to merely rote recitation.

Kedushah (Hebrew: keh-doo-SHAH or, in the diaspora, k'-DOO-shah): Literally, holiness. Also denotes one of several prayers from the first or second century, all of which include Isaiah 6:3: "Holy, holy, holy *[kadosh, kadosh, kadosh]* is the Lord of hosts; the whole earth is full of his glory."

Khap (Yiddish: KHAHP): Catch, hold.

Kiddush (Hebrew: kee-DOOSH or, in the diaspora, KIH-d'sh): Literally, sanctification, the act of making holy. A prayer said to sanctify the day at the Friday night and Shabbat meals (or the corresponding meals on certain festivals), accompanied by the blessing over wine.

Kinderlach (Yiddish: KIN-der-lakh): Little children.

Kippah, kippot (pl.) (Hebrew: kee-PAH or in the diaspora, KEE-pah): Yarmulke or skull cap: a head covering that serves to remind us of God's presence, worn by men in Orthodox circles and increasingly by both men and women in more liberal communities.

Kishkes (Yiddish: KISH-kuz): Innards, viscera. To feel something in one's *kishkes* is to feel it viscerally.

K'lal Yisrael (Hebrew: K'LAL yis-rah-EL or, in the diaspora, k'lal yis-ROH-el): The body of the people Israel.

Keri'at Shema (Hebrew: kree-YAHT sheh-MAH or, in the diaspora, KREE-yaht sh'MAH): See **Shema**.

Krechts (Yiddish: KRECHTS): A moan or groan, signifying complaint or inner pain.

Le-chayim (Hebrew: Leh-chah-YIM or, most commonly, leh-CHAH-yim): Literally, to life! An expression used as a toast before drinking together, as in the *kiddush.*

Litvaks (Yiddish: LIT-vaks): Jews of Lithuanian origin, often assumed to refer specifically to *Mitnagdim,* the opposers of Hasidism, who were particularly vocal in Lithuania, where the tradition of intellectual Rabbinic learning was strong.

Lubavitch (Loo-BAH-vich, Loo-BAH-vih-cher): Today synonymous with Chabad, of which the Lubavitch are the major surviving lineage. From the Russian village of Lyubavichi (Lubawicze), where the Rebbes of Chabad were based until the October Revolution. An adherent of Chabad is often known as a Lubavitcher.

Ma'ariv (Hebrew: mah-ah-REEV or, in the diaspora, MAH'-riv): The evening prayer, from the Hebrew word *erev*, meaning evening. The service is also known in Hebrew as *Arvit.*

Maggid (Yiddish: MAH-gid; Hebrew: mah-GEED): A storyteller, a popular and often itinerant preacher. Sometimes used to refer specifically to the Maggid of Mezeritch, heir to the Baal Shem Tov and the principal architect of the Hasidic movement.

Malkhut (Hebrew: mahl-KHOOT or, in the diaspora: MAHL-khoot): Majesty, kingliness, from the Hebrew *melekh*, king. A central theme in the Rosh ha-Shanah prayers (often rendered in plural, *malkhuyot*). Also refers to the lowest *sefirah.*

Mama loshen (Yiddish: MAH-mah LOSH-'n): Mother tongue.

Mamesh (Yiddish: MAH-m'sh; Hebrew: ma-MAHSH): Really, actually, tangibly, in truth.

Mashpiya (Hebrew: mahsh-PEE-yah): Literally, influencer. A guide in matters of prayer and the soul; a teacher of Hasidic texts.

Mechayeh (Yiddish: meh-CHAH-yeh): Literally, "life-giving." Used to describe a very pleasurable or life-giving thing.

Megillah (Hebrew: meh-gee-LAH or, in the diaspora, meh-GILL-ah): Scroll.

Midrash (Hebrew: meed-RAHSH or, in the diaspora, MID-rahsh): From a Hebrew root *dalet-resh-shin,* meaning to ask or seek insistently. A Rabbinic or homiletic interpretation of a biblical word or verse. By extension, a classic body of Rabbinic literature that offers homiletic interpretations of the Bible.

Mikveh (Hebrew: meek-VEH or, more commonly, MIK-veh or MIK-vah): Literally, gathering, as waters do. An immersion pool for purification.

Minchah (Hebrew: meen-KHAH or, in the diaspora, MIN-khah): Literally, gift or offering. Originally a sacrifice, currently meaning the afternoon prayer.

Minyan (Hebrew: meen-YAHN or, in the diaspora, MIN-y'n): Literally, a counting. Quorum or minimum number required for prayer, traditionally a group of ten Jewish males older than thirteen years; today, outside of Orthodox and some Conservative congregations, including women of post–bat mitzvah age as well. By extension, a group, usually informal and lay led, that meets regularly to pray.

Mi she-beirakh (Hebrew: MEE sheh-bay-RAKH or, more commonly, MEE sheh-BAY-rakh): Literally, "The one who blessed." A standard blessing beginning, "May the One who blessed our ancestors [names of patriarchs and/or matriarchs]...." Most commonly recited to request God's blessing on those who receive an *aliyah* or as a prayer for those in need of healing.

Mishkan (Hebrew: meesh-KAHN or, in the diaspora, MISH-kahn): From the Hebrew root *shin-khaf-nun*, to dwell. The tabernacle, seen as the temporary "dwelling place" of God among the Israelites in the desert before the Temple.

Mishnah (Hebrew: meesh-NAH or, in the diaspora, MISH-nah): Literally, that which is repeated or taught. The first recorded layer of canonical "oral law"; the basic text on which the Talmud comments. Compiled in the Land of Israel about the year 200 CE.

Misnagged, *Mitnagged* (Yiddish: mihs-NAH-gehd; Hebrew: meet-nah-GEHD): Opposer of Hasidism.

Mitzvah, mitzvot (pl.) (Hebrew: meetz-VAH, meetz-VOT or, in the diaspora, MITZ-vah, MITZ-v's): Commandment. Sometimes used in the narrower sense to mean a good deed.

Moshiach, *mashiach* (Hebrew: mah-SHEE-ahkh or, in the diaspora, moh-SHEE-och): Literally, anointed one, whence: Messiah. Originally a term for those anointed (often with oil) to be a king, prophet, or High Priest.

Myseh (Yiddish: MY-seh): Literally, an action or creation. A story, usually short and informal. Abraham Joshua Heschel defined a *myseh* as a story in which the soul surprises the mind.

Nebech (Yiddish: NEH-bech): From Hebrew *navoch,* meaning confused or bewildered. An expression of compassion for an unfortunate person. In modern times this has further evolved to mean a hapless or spineless person, a *nebbish,* but that is not how it is used here.

Nefesh (Hebrew: NEH-fesh): In biblical Hebrew, individual. By extension, the soul, or, in kabbalistic circles, a layer or dimension of soul.

Neshomeh, Neshamah (Yiddish: neh-SHOH-meh; Hebrew: neh-shah-MAH): Soul; a person's spiritual essence. Derived from *neshimah,* breath.

Niggun, niggunim (pl.) (Hebrew: nee-GOON, nee-goo-NEEM or, in the diaspora, NIG-g'n, ni-GOO-nim): An often wordless melody, derived from the Hebrew for "to play [music]." In Hasidic circles, a usually wordless melody sung to get closer to God. Abraham Joshua Heschel defined a *niggun* as "a tune flowing in search of its own unattainable end."

Nusach (Hebrew: NOO-sakh): Literally, formulation or version. Used to denote the prayer rite of a given congregation, as in *nusach* Ashkenaz, *nusach* Sepharad; also the tunes or modes that characterize prayer of a given occasion or place.

Payyetanim See **Piyyut.**

Pardes (Hebrew: pahr-DESS or, in the diaspora, PAHR-dess): Literally, orchard or grove of fruit trees. Also used in mystical circles as the acronym for *Peshat, Remez, Derash, Sod,* denoting four levels of textual exegesis and meaning: plain, hinted at, homiletical, secret. By extension, the realm of holy mysteries.

Peshat (p'SHAHT): The simple meaning of a text.

Pesach (PEH-sakh): Passover, from the Hebrew *peh-samekh-chet,* passed over. The festival falling on the fourteenth day of the Hebrew month of Nissan and commemorating God's deliverance of the Israelites from slavery in Egypt, as related in the book of Exodus. One of three annual festivals (including also Sukkot and Shavuot) in which Israelites made a pilgrimage to the Temple in Jerusalem.

Piyyut, piyyutim (pl.) (Hebrew: pee-YOOT; pee-yoo-TEEM): Devotional or liturgical poem, often referring specifically to a liturgical poem composed in classical and medieval times and used to augment the proscribed prayers, often on the Sabbath and holidays. Poets who wrote such *piyyutim* were known as *payyetanim.*

P'sukei de-Zimrah (Hebrew: p'-soo-KAY deh-zeem-RAH or, in the diaspora, p'-SOO-kay deh-ZIM-rah): Literally, verses of song or tuneful verses. A set of psalms and other prayers recited after the morning blessings and before *Barekhu*, the formal call to worship.

Purim (Hebrew: poo-REEM or, more commonly, POO-rim): A festival falling on the fourteenth day of the Hebrew month of Adar and celebrating the deliverance of the Jews from the plot of Haman and the edict of the Persian king Ahasuerus, as related in the biblical book of Esther. Literally, *purim* means lots, because the date on which the Jews were to have been killed was chosen by drawing lots.

Rashi (RAH-shee): The acronym of Rabbi Solomon ben Isaac (1040–1105), the most widely published and consulted Jewish biblical and Talmudic commentator.

Reb (REHB): Honorific, used in place of Rabbi, especially in Hasidic circles, or simply as "Mister."

Rebbe (REH-beh): From *Rabbi*. The head of a Hasidic community or lineage. Master teacher.

Ribboyno sh'l oylom, Ribbono shel olam (Yiddish: ree-BOY-noy sh'l OY-lom; Hebrew: ree-boh-NOH shel oh-LAHM): Literally, master of the universe. A common name of God, often used for direct address.

Rosh Chodesh (Hebrew: rohsh KHOH-desh): Literally, the head of the month. The one- or two-day period of the new moon, with which lunar months begin, and which is marked by special prayers and insertions in prayer.

Rosh ha-Shanah (Hebrew: ROHSH hah-shah-NAH or, in the diaspora, ROSH hah-SHOH-noh): Literally, the head of the year. The two-day festival marking the beginning of the Jewish calendar and the "Ten Days of Repentance" that culminate on Yom Kippur, the Day of Atonement.

Ruchniyus, ruchaniyut (Yiddish: ROOKH-nih-yus; Hebrew: roo-khah-nee-YOOT): Spirituality, spiritual matters. The spiritual dimension.

Sefer, **sefarim** (pl.) (Hebrew: SAY-fer, s'fah-REEM; Yiddish; SAY-f'r, S'FOH-rim): A book, especially a sacred text or book on sacred topics.

Sefirah, **sefirot** (pl.) (Hebrew: s'-fee-RAH, s'fee-ROT; Yiddish: s'FEE-reh, s'FEE-r's): Literally, number or counting. In kabbalistic literature, a "sphere" or emanation of God, each having its own character and together constituting the "Tree of Life," a kabbalistic rendering of the process by which the utter abstraction of God becomes tangible and revealed.

Sephardi, **Sephardim** (pl.) (Hebrew: s'-fah-rah-DEE, s'fah-rah-DEEM or, in the diaspora, s'-FAHR-dee, s'FAHR-dim): From the Hebrew word for Spain or the Iberian peninsula. Used to designate an individual, community, ritual, or custom of the descendants of the Iberian community, as opposed to people or rituals from Ashkenaz or northern Europe. In modern times the word is often used to include the Jews of North Africa and Arab lands, who pray with the Sephardic rite, and their descendants, customs, rites, etc.

Se'udah shelishit, **shaleshudes** (Hebrew: seh-oo-DAH sh'lee-SHEET; Yiddish: SHAH-leh-SHOO-dis): Literally, the third meal. A third meal, one that includes saying the *motzi* or blessing over bread, is regarded as obligatory on Shabbat. In practice, especially in winter, when the afternoons are short, *se'udah shelishit* was often more an occasion for singing and storytelling, particularly in Hasidic circles, than for eating another large meal.

Shabbos, **Shabbat** (Yiddish: SHAH-b's; Hebrew: shah-BAHT): The Sabbath, the Jewish day of rest. From the Hebrew root *shin-vet-tav*, meaning to cease or rest.

Shacharit (Hebrew: shah-khah-REET or, in the diaspora, SHAHKH-reet): The morning prayer service. From the Hebrew word *shachar*, meaning dawn or the darkness before the dawn.

Shaleshudes See **Se'udah shelishit**.

Shaliach tzibur (Hebrew: shah-LEE-yahkh tzee-BOOR): A leader of prayers, referring to either a layperson so designated or to a professional cantor or *chazan*. Literally, messenger of the congregation.

Shavuot, **Shavuos** (Hebrew: shah-voo-OHT or, in the diaspora, sh'VOO-es): Literally, weeks. The Feast of Weeks, a Jewish holiday that falls on the sixth day of the Hebrew month of Sivan. In

Torah, Shavuot marks the end of the counting of the Omer, seven weeks from the second day of Passover. In Rabbinic times, Shavuot was also decreed as the anniversary of the giving of the Torah on Sinai. It was one of three annual festivals (including also Passover and Sukkot) in which Israelites made a pilgrimage to the Temple in Jerusalem.

Shefa (Hebrew: SHEH-fah): Literally, abundance; hence, the constant outpouring of divine grace and plentitude that makes our very existence possible. In kabbalistic and Hasidic circles, the plenitude of divine blessing that descends through the *sefirot* to the world we inhabit.

Shekhinah, **Shekhineh** (Hebrew: sh'khee-NAH; Yiddish: sh'KHEE-neh): Literally: dwelling or temporary abiding, from the Hebrew root *shin-khaf-nun*, to dwell or abide. The divine presence in the world. A more revealed aspect of the highest conception of God. The Shekhinah is commonly associated with the feminine and with exile.

Shema (Hebrew, sheh-MAH): The quintessential declaration of the Jewish faith, "Hear (*Shema*) O Israel, YHVH is our God, YHVH is One" (Deuteronomy 6:4), expressing Jews' absolute commitment to a single and unique God who pervades all time and space. In the larger sense, *keri'at Shema* (the reading of the *Shema*) comprises three paragraphs from the Bible and is one of the two central prayers in the morning and evening worship services, the second being the *Amidah*. The morning *Shema* and the surrounding blessings are referred to as *keri'at Shema u-virkhotehah,* the *Shema* and its blessings.

Shiviti (Hebrew: shee-VEE-tee): Literally, I have set, put, or placed before me. The constant awareness of God, taken from the first word of a sentence embroidered on arks throughout the Jewish world, "*Shiviti ha-shem le-negdi tamid,* I have placed God before me always" (Psalms 16:8).

Shmatteh (Yiddish: SH'MAH-teh): Rag.

Shmegeg (Yiddish: sh'meh-GEG): A clueless fool.

Shteibel, shteiblach (pl.) (Yiddish: SH'TEE-b'l, SH'TEEB-lach): Literally, little room. An informal, often small, and generally lay-led synagogue, often for Hasidim.

Shtickl, shtickeleh (Yiddish: SHTICK'l, SHTICK-eh-leh): A little bit, a morsel.

Shul (Yiddish: SHOOL): Literally, school. Today, more often, a synagogue.

Shulchan Arukh (Hebrew: shool-KHAN ah-ROOKH or, in the diaspora, SHOOL-khan OH-rookh): Literally, "set table." The best-known compendium of Jewish law, compiled in four volumes by Joseph Caro in the Land of Israel and published in 1565. "The Set Table" refers to the ease with which the various laws are set forth—like a table prepared with food ready for consumption.

Siddur, siddurim (pl.) (Hebrew: see-DOOR, see-doo-REEM or, in the diaspora, SIH-d'r, sih-DOO-rim): Literally, order or sequence. By extension, the name given to the "order of prayers," or prayer book.

Sukkot, Sukkos (Hebrew: soo-KOT or, in the diaspora, SOOK's): Literally, booths or shacks. The Festival of Booths or Tabernacles, falling on the fourteenth day of the Hebrew month of Tishrei to commemorate the booths in which the Israelites lived in the desert after their deliverance from Egypt. Also an agricultural festival, one of three annual festivals (along with Passover and Shavuot) in which Israelites made a pilgrimage to the Temple in Jerusalem.

Tachanun (Hebrew: tah-khah-NOON or, more commonly, TAH-khah-noon): Literally, pleading, supplication. By extension, a set of largely confessional and penitential prayers that follows the *Amidah*, recited on weekdays, except those days (normally Monday and Thursday) on which the Torah is read.

Tachlis (Yiddish: TAKH-lis): Literally, the end or end result. By extension, an expression indicating the bottom line or practical implications of a matter.

Tallis, tallit (Yiddish: TAH-liss; Hebrew: tah-LEET): The rectangular prayer shawl equipped with tassels (*tzitzit*) on each corner and generally worn during the morning (*Shacharit*) and additional (*Musaf*) synagogue services. Plural: *tallitot* (Hebrew, tah-lee-TOT) or *talleisim* (Yiddish, tah-LAY-sim).

Talmid (Hebrew: tahl-MEED): Student or disciple.

Talmud (Hebrew: tahl-MOOD or, in the diaspora, TAHL-mood): Literally, learning. The name given to each of two great compendia of Jewish law and lore compiled over several centuries and, ever since, the literary core of the Rabbinic heritage. The better-known *Talmud Bavli* or Babylonian Talmud took shape in Babylonia (present-day Iraq) and is traditionally dated about 550 CE. The *Talmud Yerushalmi* or Jerusalem Talmud is earlier, a product of the Land of Israel generally dated about 400 CE. (When no version is specified, the reference is to the more authoritative and far more commonly studied Babylonian Talmud.) The Talmuds were comprised of Mishnaic texts and later Rabbinic commentary, called the *Gemara* (Hebrew) or *Gemora* (Yiddish).

Tanya (Aramaic: TAHN-yah): Informal name of the foundational, multivolume opus of Chabad Hasidism, written by that movement's founder, Reb Schneur Zalman of Liadi. Literally, "it is taught," after the first word of that work. Also known as *Likkutei Amarim*, meaning a collection of articles or sayings.

Tefillah (Hebrew: t'-fee-LAH): Prayer. Also used in Rabbinic literature to mean the *Amidah*.

Tefillin (Hebrew: t'-fee-LEEN or, in the diaspora, t'-FIH-lin): Phylacteries, traditionally worn by men (and today sometimes by women) to fulfill the instruction to "let them be a sign on your arm and a diadem above your eyes" (Deuteronomy 6:8). Two cube-shaped black boxes containing scrolls with hand-scribed biblical quotations (Exod. 13:1–10 and 13:11–16; Deut. 6:4–9 and 11:13–21) and affixed by means of attached leather straps to the forehead and left arm (right arm for left-handed people).

Tetragrammaton See *YHVH*.

Teshuvah (Hebrew: t'shoo-VAH or, in the diaspora, T'SHOO-vah): Literally, return. Repentance or penitence. Jews are commanded to "return one day before your death" (Wisdom of the Fathers 2:10). Since no person knows the day they will die, it follows that Jewish life should constitute a constant turning and re-turning to God.

Tikkun (Hebrew: tee-KOON or, in the diaspora, TEE-koon): Literally, correction or fixing. Refers to the belief that Jews should engage as much as possible in *tikkun olam,* the repairing of the world, by means of fulfilling the commandments, a central concept in Lurianic kabbalah.

Tisch (Yiddish: TISH): Literally, table. A Hasidic gathering, with the Rebbe or another leader, for teaching, singing, and stories, often with some drinks and light refreshments. Known in Chabad as a *fabrengen*.

Torah (Hebrew: toh-RAH or, in the diaspora, TOH-rah): Literally, instruction or teaching. Torah can have a number of meanings, depending on the context: (1) The first five books of the Bible, also called the Pentateuch, Five Books of Moses, or the *Chumash*. (2) The parchment scroll on which these books are written for public reading in the synagogue. (3) Later, during Rabbinic times (approximately the first to the sixth centuries C.E), the Five Books of Moses are referred to as the Written Torah (*toh-RAH she-bikh-TAHV*), in contrast to the Oral Torah (*toh-RAH she-beh-al PEH*), ongoing interpretations and expansions of the meaning of the Written Torah as well as the customs that evolved over time, as ultimately recorded in the Mishnaic, midrashic, and Talmudic compendia. (4) By extension, all of Jewish sacred literature, including the Bible, Mishnah, Talmud, midrash: that is, teachings written or redacted in the ancient times, through the Middle Ages, and even down to the modern period. Study of these texts thus constitutes "studying Torah" in the expanded sense.

Trope (TROHP): Cantillation marks for reading Torah, or the melody they indicate.

Tsuris (Yiddish: TSU-ris or TSOH-res): Troubles. From Hebrew *tzarot*, troubles.

Tzaddik (Hebrew: tsah-DEEK or, in the diaspora, TSAH-dik): A righteous person, often said in Hasidic circles to refer to a Rebbe, sometimes in the belief that the *tzaddik* has certain magical or mystical powers through a closer relationship to God and familiarity with (or even ability to travel to) the supernal realms.

Tzedakah (Hebrew: ts'dah-KAH or, in the diaspora, tzeh-DAH-kah): Money given to help the disadvantaged, or the practice of such giving. The derivation from *tzedek*, the Hebrew word for justice, emphasizes the Jewish view that such giving is not to be regarded as a charitable (i.e., optional) gift but as doing justice and so, by implication, required.

Tzitzis, tzitzit (Yiddish: TSI-tsis; Hebrew: tsee-TSEET): Literally, tassels or fringes, used to refer to the tassels affixed to the four corners of the *tallit* or prayer shawl, as Numbers 15:38 instructs. By extension, a four-cornered garment containing such tassels.

Yah A name of God, often construed as feminine or relating to the breath.

Yahrzeit (Yiddish: YAHR-tseit or YOHR-tseit): Literally, year's time. The anniversary of a loved one's death. By extension, the practice of marking that anniversary by lighting a memorial candle and saying Kaddish. People speak of "having yahrzeit" on a given day, at which time the name of the person being memorialized may be mentioned aloud at services prior to the Mourner's Kaddish.

Yasher koach or **koyach** (YAH-sher KOH-ahkh, yash' KOH-ahkh or KOY-ahkh): From the Aramaic *y-sh-r*, strengthen, and the Hebrew *ko'akh*, power. An expression meaning "more power to you," recognizing a person's contribution to a service as a Torah reader, prayer leader, receiver of an *aliyah* or other honor, etc., or for other such contributions to sacred aims, and wishing them the strength to do likewise in future. Deriving from a midrashic passage in Talmud (Shabbat 87a) in which God says to Moses *"yishar kokhakha she-shibarta,"* praising Moses's breaking of the tablets and wishing him such strength in future.

Yeridat ha-shefa (Hebrew: yeh-ree-DAHT hah-SHEH-fah): The "descent of the plenitude," a kabbalistic term for the "descent" of God's grace and plenitude from the higher, supernal realms to our world, the revealed world of creation. Also refers to the portion of morning prayers that follows, which constitutes a descent from the peak of the *Amidah*.

Yeshiva (Hebrew: yeh-shee-VAH or, in the diaspora, y'-SHEE-vah): Literally, sitting. A school where Jewish law, lore, texts, etc., are studied.

Yetzirah (Hebrew: yeh-tsee-RAH or, in the diaspora, yeh-TSEE-rah): Literally, creation or formation. The world of emotion, second of the four worlds of *Asiyah, Yetzirah, Beriyah,* and *Atzilut* in the kabbalistic Four World system. Associated with the morning section of *P'sukei de-Zimrah* or "tuneful verses" especially, which awaken the emotions to God's service.

YHVH English rendition of the Hebrew letters of the Tetragrammaton, *yud-heh-vav-heh* (often pronounced *yud kay vav kay* by people wishing to avoid even the explicit spelling out of God's name). The actual pronunciation has been lost and replaced in speech (though often only in sacred or educational contexts) by the alternative name of God, Adonai.

Yichud (Hebrew yee-KHOOD or, in the diaspora, YEE-khood):
Literally, unification. A centralizing *kavanah* or one-on-one
encounter. In kabbalistic worship, where prayers have esoteric
significance, *yichud* denotes the unification of the letters that make
up God's name; the conjoining of God's masculine and feminine
aspects; and, deeper still, the coming together of the shattered
universe in which we live.

Yiddishkeit (Yiddish: YIHD-ish-kite): Colloquial expression for
Jewish practice and culture.

Yir'ah (Hebrew: yir-AH or, in the diaspora, YEER-ah): Fear and awe,
in the sense of "he was a god-fearing man." With *ahavah* (love),
one of the two main pillars of human relationship to God.

Yom Kippur (Hebrew: YOHM kee-POOR or, in the diaspora, yom
KIH-p'r): The Day of Atonement, falling on the tenth day of the
Hebrew month of Tishrei, in which Jews pray for forgiveness and
to be inscribed in the book of life for the coming year.

Yom tov (Hebrew: YOM tov): Literally, good day. A Jewish holiday.

Z'miros, **zemirot** (Yiddish: z'-MEE-ros; Hebrew: z'mee-ROHT):
Literally, songs. Usually, table songs sung during meals on Shabbat.

Zaida (Yiddish: ZAY-duh): Grandfather.

Zohar (Hebrew: ZOE-hahr): Shorthand title for *Sefer ha-Zohar* (SAY-
fer hah-ZOE-hahr), literally, "The Book of Splendor," central
work of Jewish Kabbalah and mysticism. The *Zohar* is traditionally
attributed to Rabbi Shimon bar Yochai, the Mishnaic sage.
Modern scholarship attributes its writing to Moses de Leon in
Spain near the end of the thirteenth century.

CPSIA information can be obtained
at www.ICGtesting.com
Printed in the USA
JSHW012004310820
7497JS00001BA/21